Modern Classics in Entrepreneurship Studies

Banu Ozkazanc-Pan · Arturo E. Osorio ·
Dev K. Dutta · Vishal K. Gupta ·
Golshan Javadian · Grace Chun Guo
Editors

Modern Classics in Entrepreneurship Studies

Building the Future of the Field

palgrave
macmillan

Editors
Banu Ozkazanc-Pan
School of Engineering
Brown University
Providence, CT, USA

Dev K. Dutta
Peter T Paul College of Business and Economics
Univerity of New Hampshire
Durham, NH, USA

Golshan Javadian
Business Administration
Morgan State University
Baltimore, MD, USA

Arturo E. Osorio
Rutgers Business School
Rutgers, The State University of New Jersey
Newark, NJ, USA

Vishal K. Gupta
Culverhouse College of Business
The University of Alabama
Tuscaloosa, AL, USA

Grace Chun Guo
Jack Welch College of Business & Technology
Sacred Heart University
Fairfield, CT, USA

ISBN 978-3-030-61028-9 ISBN 978-3-030-61029-6 (eBook)
https://doi.org/10.1007/978-3-030-61029-6

This Palgrave Macmillan imprint is published by the registered company Springer Nature Switzerland AG
The registered company address is: Gewerbestrasse 11, 6330 Cham, Switzerland

Contents

List of Contributors

Ba Anh Khoa Dao Université du Québec à Montréal, Montreal, QC, Canada

Dev K. Dutta Peter T Paul College of Business and Economics, Univerity of New Hampshire, Durham, NH, USA

Mary K. Foster Morgan State University, Baltimore, MD, USA

Connie Marie Gaglio San Francisco State University, San Francisco, CA, USA

Grace Chun Guo Jack Welch College of Business & Technology, Sacred Heart University, Fairfield, CT, USA

Vishal K. Gupta Department of Management, Culverhouse College of Business, The University of Alabama, Tuscaloosa, AL, USA

Rick Hunt Department of Management, Pamplin College of Business, Virginia Tech, Blacksburg, VA, USA

Golshan Javadian Business Administration, Morgan State University, Baltimore, MD, USA

Jerome A. Katz Saint Louis University, St. Louis, MO, USA

Parul Manocha Department of Management, Pamplin College of Business, Virginia Tech, Blacksburg, VA, USA

Arturo E. Osorio Rutgers Business School & New Brunswick, Rutgers, The State University of New Jersey, Newark, NJ, USA

Banu Ozkazanc-Pan School of Engineering, Brown University, Providence, CT, USA

Swapnil Saurav Department of Management, Culverhouse College of Business, The University of Alabama, Tuscaloosa, AL, USA

Alexander Settles Warrington College of Business, University of Florida, Gainesville, FL, USA

David Townsend Department of Management, Pamplin College of Business, Virginia Tech, Blacksburg, VA, USA

Joshua V. White Department of Management, Culverhouse College of Business, The University of Alabama, Tuscaloosa, AL, USA

Susan J. Winter University of Maryland, College Park, MD, USA

Qin Yang Robert Morris University, Moon Township, PA, USA

List of Figures

List of Tables

CHAPTER 1

Introduction

Arturo E. Osorio, Banu Ozkazanc-Pan, Dev K. Dutta, Golshan Javadian, Vishal K. Gupta, and Grace Chun Guo

A. E. Osorio (✉)
Rutgers Business School, Rutgers, The State University of New Jersey, Newark, NJ, USA
e-mail: osorio@business.rutgers.edu

B. Ozkazanc-Pan
School of Engineering, Brown University, Providence, CT, USA

D. K. Dutta
Peter T Paul College of Business and Economics, Univerity of New Hampshire, Durham, NH, USA

G. Javadian
Business Administration, Morgan State University, Baltimore, MD, USA

V. K. Gupta
Culverhouse College of Business, The University of Alabama, Tuscaloosa, AL, USA

G. C. Guo
Jack Welch College of Business & Technology, Sacred Heart University, Fairfield, CT, USA

A. E. Osorio et al. (eds.), *Modern Classics in Entrepreneurship Studies*,
https://doi.org/10.1007/978-3-030-61029-6_1

Why This Book on "Modern Classics"? Why Now?

The history of entrepreneurship is as old as human civilization (Gartner & Carter, 2003; Herbert & Link, 1982). There is likely no civilization that flourished without entrepreneurs, enterprising men and women, who created new products or services, or at the very least bought at a low price to sell at a higher price in a different time or place. Indeed, entrepreneurship has been central to the functioning of human society. Yet, entrepreneurial activities have generally been taken-for-granted. Little attention has been paid to the role of entrepreneurs in the rise and fall of civilizations, the spread of ideas and trends across societies, and the advancement of economic prosperity and well-being of communities. As was the case with many other aspects of life, entrepreneurship became a subject of intellectual curiosity only during the latter part of the renaissance in Europe. The interest in entrepreneurship as a rigorous intellectual discipline is more recent, beginning in the second half of the twentieth century (Landström & Lindhe, 2016). As such, the field is still quite young, with some of the most trailblazing research to expand the field's boundaries appearing in the first decade of the new millennium. This last topic is the subject matter of this book.

Inquiring into Entrepreneurship

The French merchant banker Richard Cantillon is believed to be the "first significant writer to make frequent and obtrusive use of the term entrepreneurship in a semblance of its modern form" (Hébert & Link, 2006, p. 589) and particularly as a concept suitable for formal theoretical purposes (Filion, 2011; Long, 1983).[1] Cantillon's economic system recognizes three types of agents: (a) landowners (capitalists), (b) entrepreneurs (arbitrageurs), and (c) hirelings (wage workers). In this system, the entrepreneur is responsible "for all the exchange and circulation in the economy," thus playing a central role in the market (van Praag, 1999, p. 313). Jean-Baptiste Say extended the entrepreneurial function defined by Cantillon, which subsequently served as a foundation

[1] An early form of the word *entrepreneur* appears as early as the fourteenth century (Hoselitz, 1960) and over the next few hundred years it was used to refer to a sort of government contractor who built large structures and fortifications for the government or provided supplies to the military for a fee (Herbert & Link, 1982) until Cantillon tried to redefine its meaning to bring more analytical precision and focus (Thornton, 2019).

for economists like Alfred Marshall (1842–1924) and Carl Menger (1840–1921) on entrepreneurship.

Beginning in the 1970s, entrepreneurship began to emerge as a field of study in its own right. At the 1974 annual meeting of the *Academy of Management* (AoM) in Seattle, an organizational meeting was held for those interested in forming an interest group on entrepreneurship as part of the Division of Business Policy and Planning. In 1976, the entrepreneurship interest group established the Heizer Doctoral Dissertation Award with funding from the Heizer Corporation (and its founder, Edgar F. Heizer Jr) to recognize and honor outstanding doctoral research in the area of new enterprise development. The first Babson Entrepreneurship Research Conference was organized in 1981. At the 1984 AoM meeting, targeted efforts were initiated with the goal of gaining full division status. Despite some opposition from entrenched divisions (e.g., Business Policy), the entrepreneurship interest group was approved for full division status at the 1986 AoM meeting.[2] The attainment of division status brought credibility and legitimacy for entrepreneurship as a research field, promoting tremendous growth in scholarship around entrepreneurial phenomena.

Identifying Classics

It is widely understood that knowledge of the past is essential to society's progress in the future. The ideas and events of the past have shaped what happens in the present while influencing how things will turn out in the future. Attending to this concatenated causality, a common analytical tool that historians use to understand the past is *periodization*; the dividing of the past into eras or periods. While the periods we use to understand the past (e.g., the common practice of dating events as B.C.E. ("before common era") and A.C.E. ("after common era") have no a priori existence, periodization can still have a profound influence on how we organize our knowledge of the past. Periodization is also, by its very nature, culturally construed and subjective. Yet, periodization offers the benefit of imposing order on the messiness of history, organizing the past in a way that makes it easier for us to understand what has transpired before our time.

[2] The history of AoM's entrepreneurship division presented here is based on Landström and Lindhe (2016).

When looking at the evolution of entrepreneurship research, we can discern two distinct phases. The first phase, spanning the 1980s and 1990s, is considered the early years of entrepreneurship research, which Landström (2020) considers as the formative and growth period of the field. The second phase is the post-2000 years, particularly the first decade of the new millennia (2000–2010). This second phase is what Landström (2020) calls this second phase the "*golden era*" for entrepreneurship research.

The first phase, encompassing the 1980s and 1990s, was the birth period of several foundational articles considered classics within the discipline (Gupta et al., 2018). These early articles have left an enduring impression on the discipline. They have become a must-read for new researchers coming into entrepreneurship, as they are cited for their "continual relevance" (Dutta & Javadian, 2018, p. 265). Readers interested in delving deeper into these classical entrepreneurship articles from the first phase may like to browse the 2018 book "*Foundational Research in Entrepreneurship Studies: Insightful Contributions and Future Pathways*" by the editorial team behind the current publication.

The second phase, presented as the post-2000 period, specifically the first decade of the twenty-first century, gave us the modern classics. These modern classics are influential articles that are expected to, in due time, impact the field in the same way as the foundational articles have done before them. These modern classics, being of less than 20 years of age, might be considered as still young. Yet, we believe they contain insights and ideas that will pave the way for the next several decades of entrepreneurship research.

The identification of these modern classics proved to be interesting and challenging. We began by asking the following two broad questions:

1. What novel and emerging research topics, questions, and approaches have been engaging the attention of entrepreneurship scholars in the post-2000 period?
2. What have been some of the emerging topics (phenomena, theoretical frameworks, methodological innovations, and interesting research settings, among others) that are continuing to push the boundaries of entrepreneurship as a scholarly field of study?

Framed by these two core questions, we drafted a call for papers. We reached out to the broad community of entrepreneurship researchers through several channels. We contacted authors who had contributed to the previous well-received volume on foundational articles in entrepreneurship (Javadian et al., 2018). We encouraged scholars within our networks to submit their proposals. We also used the formidable list-serve of the AoM entrepreneurship division to solicit submissions. Following prior efforts (e.g., Gupta et al., 2016; Guo et al., 2016), the call for proposals asked researchers to identify articles that they considered "modern classics"—akin to key informant survey methodology in management research. We encouraged, but did not require, our respondents to pay attention to works that have already achieved a noticeable academic footprint (understood as the number of academic citations received).

To help us evaluate the incoming proposals, we established two ground rules to identify the articles considered deserving of the recognition as a *modern classic*. The first rule required that any article under consideration must have been published in a peer-review academic journal. This rule ensured the article had already been through a stringent review process (e.g., double-blind peer review). The journal article is a *sine qua non* of scientific information exchange (Shepherd, 2016; Shepherd et al., 2019), though we do recognize that alternative forms, such as books, have also come to occupy an important venue for knowledge creation in the social sciences. The second rule presented that any article to be considered for this project had to be published between the 2000 to 2010 time period (i.e., "*golden era*" for entrepreneurship research). The temporal boundaries helped to mitigate "recency bias" in the recollection of influential articles. The time frame rule also served to ensure articles under consideration have had enough time to make a rightful impact on the field of entrepreneurship. From our perspective, these two ground rules provided some structure to our ambitious quest for the modern equivalents of seminal articles in entrepreneurship.

The Crowd's Wisdom

Leaving the choice of studies and the criteria by which authors considered the studies to be modern classics largely open-ended (except the two ground rules discussed above) served us well by engaging with the "wisdom of the crowds" (Hosseini et al., 2015) (the research community in entrepreneurship) for guidance. The proposal asked scholars to recommend the articles that they considered modern classics, based on their own academic expertise and experience. As part of the evaluation process, scholars were asked to submit written proposals addressing three key points. First, the proposal was to discuss the reasons that made the suggested article a modern classic. Second, the proposal needed to explain why this article could appeal to the larger audience of entrepreneurship researchers. Finally, the proposal needed to present the argument to explain why the suggested article could remain an enduring work in the years to come. This third point forced us to consider the future research possibilities emerging from the proposed article, thus assessing its lasting impact as a modern classic. If needed, we contacted the authors to ask for further clarification and evidence supporting their proposals. All proposals were collectively evaluated based on the strength of their arguments and the academic merits of the submission. After the proposals were accepted and the chapters were submitted, a two-step peer-review process took place. As a first step, the editors reviewed each one of the manuscripts and provided developmental feedback to the authors. In the second step, an anonymous (double-blind) peer-review process took place. The purpose of this step-wise review process was to enable authors to refine their submissions to ensure the clarity and strength of their arguments.

Featured Articles

The editors of this volume carefully vetted each submitted proposal and selected eight articles for publication in this volume. Table 1.1 summarizes these eight chapters of the book, with each chapter focusing on a specific article that the authors deemed to have an enduring influence on entrepreneurship research. We now discuss each of these articles in turn.

Javadian's (2021) interest in Bird and Brush (2002) focuses on its gendered perspective on organizational creation. In her chapter, Javadian provides an overview of Bird and Brush's (2002) work, and also reviews the studies that have used their arguments to advance other theoretical developments. Concerned about threats to the "legitimacy of entrepreneurship as an academic discipline," White et al. (2021) present Chiles et al.'s (2007) conceptual framework to integrate the fragmented literature in entrepreneurship. By revisiting this framework, White et al. (2021) renew the calls for entrepreneurship scholars to reconceive the

Table 1.1 Chapters at a glance

Ch	*Author*	*Classic discussed*	*Core theme of classic*	*Core theme of book chapter*
2	Javadian	Bird and Brush (2002)	Focuses on its gendered perspective on organizational creation	Provides an overview of Bird and Brush's (2002) work. Also reviews the studies that have used their arguments to advance other theoretical developments
3	White, Saurav, & Gupta	Chiles et al. (2007)	Conceptual framework to integrate the fragmented literature in entrepreneurship	Renew the calls to theoretically reconceive entrepreneurship by treating it as a perpetually disequilibrating process and retool it methodologically by pursuing a historical analysis to explain sequences of events and activities in time and space
4	Yang & Guo	Dess et al. (2003)	Discuss ideas of corporate entrepreneurship (CE) research	Explores knowledge creation and types of CE, the importance of social exchanges and CE processes, the interplay between CE an d internationalization, and lastly, outcome variables in CE research
5	Gaglio, Winter, & Katz	Gaglio and Katz (2001)	Operationalization of Kirzner's theory of entrepreneurial discovery	Revisit one of the most rigorously developed and respected conceptual models of entrepreneurship

(continued)

Table 1.1 (continued)

Ch	*Author*	*Classic discussed*	*Core theme of classic*	*Core theme of book chapter*
6	Foster	Kuratko (2005)	Tipping point in the literature regarding the recognition of the legitimacy and professionalization of entrepreneurship education	Kuratko's insights are discussed in the context of entrepreneurship training in today's educational framework, including the traditional business plan approach, the Lean Startup/Lean Launchpad approach, the Disciplined Entrepreneurship approach, and the Practice-Based approach
7	Townsend & Hunt	McMullen and Shepherd (2006)	Examines entrepreneurial action and judgment in the face of an uncertain and unknowable future	Discusses how the advent and emergence of intelligent machine learning systems present both opportunities and challenges for the uncertainty-bearing thesis of entrepreneurial action
8	Osorio & Settles	Steyaert and Katz (2004)	Acknowledges entrepreneurship as a social construction to present it as a socially embedded event taking place at a particular location	Seek to change entrepreneurship's focus from the exceptional individual performing exceptional actions into the everyday developments enacted by ordinary people orchestrating entrepreneurship as a local process

(continued)

Table 1.1 (continued)

Ch	*Author*	*Classic discussed*	*Core theme of classic*	*Core theme of book chapter*
9	Dao	Sarasvathy (2001)	Explores the differences between causation and effectuation	Argue that causal and effectual processes are interwoven and should be considered a continuum

field theoretically by treating entrepreneurship as a perpetually disequilibrating process and retool methodologically by pursuing historical analysis to explain sequences of events and activities in time and space.

Yang and Guo (2021) reflect on Dess et al. (2003), discussing the latter's original ideas in corporate entrepreneurship (CE) research. These ideas include knowledge creation and types of CE, the importance of social exchanges and CE processes, the interplay between CE and internationalization, and lastly, outcome variables in CE research.

Gaglio et al. (2021) delve deeper into the theory of entrepreneurial discovery (e.g., Kirzner, 1973). As such, Gaglio et al. (2021) revisit one of the most rigorously developed and respected conceptual models of entrepreneurship.

Focusing on entrepreneurship education, Foster (2021) points a critical eye towards Kuratko (2005), which is seen as a tipping point in the literature regarding the recognition of the legitimacy and professionalization of entrepreneurship education. Kuratko's insights are discussed in the context of entrepreneurship training in today's educational framework, including the traditional business plan approach, the Lean Startup/Lean Launchpad approach, the Disciplined Entrepreneurship approach, and the Practice-Based approach. Townsend and Hunt (2021) revisit McMullen and Shepherd (2006) to examine entrepreneurial action and judgment in the face of an uncertain and unknowable future. For Townsend and Hunt (2021), the advent and emergence of intelligent machine learning systems present both opportunities and challenges for the uncertainty-bearing thesis of entrepreneurial action.

Osorio and Settle (2021) seek to change entrepreneurship's focus from the exceptional individual performing exceptional actions into the everyday developments enacted by ordinary people orchestrating entrepreneurship as a local process by calling attention to the work of Steyaert and Katz (2004). Dao (2021) analyzes Sarasvathy's (2001) work to explore the differences between causation and effectuation, to argue that causal and effectual processes are interwoven and should be considered a continuum.

We hope the review of works included and their wide dissemination through this book accomplishes two major objectives. First, we aim to inspire younger generation of scholars by providing a better understanding of the contributions that have come before their time. Second, we attempt to stimulate and advance conversations that bring new insights into entrepreneurship research. We trust the chapters in this book will help fill some gaps in what we know about these contemporary classics and provoke further thought and action in the field. We understand that there might be other modern classics that were not included in this effort and that their absence provides us with an opportunity to explore them in future works. Scientific and social progress results from educated conversations, and we encourage other entrepreneurship scholars to join us in this conversation. *Welcome, aboard*!

References

Bird, B., & Brush, C. (2002). A gendered perspective on organizational creation. *Entrepreneurship Theory and Practice, 26*(3), 41–65.

Chiles, T. H., Bluedorn, A. C., & Gupta, V. K. (2007). Beyond creative destruction and entrepreneurial discovery: A radical Austrian approach to entrepreneurship. *Organization Studies, 28*(4), 467–493.

Dao, K. (2021). Causation and effectuation. In B. Ozkazanc-Pan, A. E. Osorio, D. Dutta, V. K. Gupta, G. Javadian, & C. Guo. (Eds.), *Modern classics in entrepreneurship studies: Building the future of the field*. Palgrave Macmillan.

Dess, G. G., Ireland, R. D., Zahra, S. A., Floyd, S. W., Janney, J. J., & Lane, P. J. (2003). Emerging issues in corporate entrepreneurship. *Journal of Management, 29*(3), 351–378.

Dutta, D. K., & Javadian, G. (2018). Conclusion. In G. Javadian, V. K. Gupta, C. Guo, A. E. Osorio, B. Ozkazanc-Pan, & D. Dutta (Eds.), *Foundational research in entrepreneurship studies—Insightful contributions and future pathways* (pp. 265–270). Palgrave Macmillan.

Filion, L. J. (2011). Defining the entrepreneur. In *World encyclopedia of entrepreneurship* (p. 41).

Foster, M. (2021). The Emergence of entrepreneurship education. In B. Ozkazanc-Pan, A. E. Osorio, D. Dutta, V. K. Gupta, G. Javadian, & C. Guo.

(Eds.), *Modern classics in entrepreneurship studies: Building the future of the field*. Palgrave Macmillan.

Gaglio, C. M., & Katz, J. A. (2001). The psychological basis of opportunity identification: Entrepreneurial alertness. *Small Business Economics, 16*, 95–111.

Gaglio, C., Winter, S. J., & Katz, J. (2021). Entrepreneurial alertness and opportunity identification: Suggestions for the new generation. In B. Ozkazanc-Pan, A. E. Osorio, D. Dutta, V. K. Gupta, G. Javadian, & C. Guo. (Eds.), *Modern classics in entrepreneurship studies: Building the future of the field*. Palgrave Macmillan.

Gartner, W. B., & Carter, N. M. (2003). Entrepreneurial behavior and firm organizing processes. *Handbook of entrepreneurship research* (pp. 195–221). Springer.

Guo, C., Jiang, C. X., Dutta, D., Osorio, A., Javadian, G., & Gupta, V. (2016). *Caucus on "classics in entrepreneurship research and their impact on scholarship today"*. Academy of Management Annual Meeting.

Gupta, V., Dutta, D., Guo, G. C., Javadian, G., Jiang, C., Osorio, A., & Ozkazanc-Pan, B. (2016). Classics in entrepreneurship research: Enduring insights, future promises. *New England Journal of Entrepreneurship, 19*(1), 7–16.

Gupta, V. K., Guo, G. C., & Ozkazanc-Pan, B. (2018). Introduction. In G. Javadian, V. K. Gupta, C. Guo, A. E. Osorio, B. Ozkazanc-Pan, & D. Dutta (Eds.), *Foundational research in entrepreneurship studies—Insightful contributions and future pathways* (pp. 1–12). Palgrave Macmillan.

Herbert, R. F., & Link, A. N. (1982). *The entrepreneur*. Preager.

Hébert, R. F., & Link, A. N. (2006). The entrepreneur as innovator. *Journal of Technology Transfer, 31*(5), 589–597.

Hoselitz, B. F. (1960). *Entrepreneurship and economic growth*. Available at https://ssrn.com/abstract=1497771

Hosseini, M., Moore, J., Almaliki, M., Shahri, A., Phalp, K., & Ali, R. (2015). Wisdom of the crowd within enterprises: Practices and challenges. *Computer Networks, 90*, 121–132.

Javadian, G., Gupta, V. K., Dutta, D. K., Guo, G. C., Osorio, A. E., & Ozkazanc-Pan, B. (2018). *Foundational research in entrepreneurship studies: Insightful contributions and future pathways*. Palgrave Macmillan. https://doi.org/10.1007/978-3-319-73528-3

Javadian, G. (2021). Gendered perspectives on organizational creation: Lessons from the past and insights for the future. In B. Ozkazanc-Pan, A. E. Osorio, D. Dutta, V. K. Gupta, G. Javadian, & C. Guo. (Eds.), *Modern classics in entrepreneurship studies: Building the future of the field*. Palgrave Macmillan.

Kirzner, I. M. (1973). *Competition and entrepreneurship*. University of Chicago Press.
Kuratko, D. F. (2005). The emergence of entrepreneurship education: Development, trends, and challenges. *Entrepreneurship: Theory & Practice, 29*(5), 577–597. https://doi.org/10.1111/j.1540-6520.2005.00099.x
Landstrom, H. (2020). The evolution of entrepreneurship as a scholarly field. *Foundations and Trends in Entrepreneurship Research, 16*(2), 65–243.
Landström, H., & Lindhe, J. (2016). *A history of the entrepreneurship division of the academy of management*. ENT Division of the Academy of Management.
Long, W. (1983). The meaning of entrepreneurship. *American Journal of Small Business, 8*(2), 47–59.
McMullen, J. S., & Shepherd, D. A. (2006). Entrepreneurial action and the role of uncertainty in the theory of the entrepreneur. *Academy of Management Review, 31*(1), 132–152.
Osorio, A. E. & Settes, A. (2021). Entrepreneurship is so much more than just money making: Reclaiming the space of entrepreneurship in society. In B. Ozkazanc-Pan, A. E. Osorio, D. Dutta, V. K. Gupta, G. Javadian, & C. Guo. (Eds.), *Modern classics in entrepreneurship studies: Building the future of the field*. Palgrave Macmillan.
Sarasvathy, S. D. (2001). Causation and effectuation: Toward a theoretical shift from economic inevitability to entrepreneurial contingency. *Academy of Management Review, 26*(2), 243–263.
Shepherd, D. A. (2016). An emotions perspective for advancing the fields of family business and entrepreneurship: Stocks, flows, reactions, and responses. *Family Business Review, 29*(2), 151–158.
Shepherd, D. A., Wennberg, K., Suddaby, R., & Wiklund, J. (2019). What are we explaining? A review and agenda on initiating, engaging, performing, and contextualizing entrepreneurship. *Journal of Management, 45*(1), 159–196.
Steyaert, C., & Katz, J. (2004). Reclaiming the space of entrepreneurship in society: Geographical, discursive and social dimensions. *Entrepreneurship & Regional Development, 16*(3), 179–196.
Thornton, M. (2019). Turning the word upside down: How Cantillon changed the meaning of entrepreneurship. *Quarterly Journal of Austrian Economics, 22*(2), 307–307.
Townsend, D. & Hunt, R. (2021). The path beyond the opportunity wars: Exploring the continued relevance of McMullen and Shepperd (2006) for the future of entrepreneurial action theory. In B. Ozkazanc-Pan, A. E. Osorio, D. Dutta, V. K. Gupta, G. Javadian, & C. Guo. (Eds.), *Modern classics in entrepreneurship studies: Building the future of the field*. Palgrave Macmillan.
Van Praag, C. M. (1999). Some classic views on entrepreneurship. *De Economist, 147*(3), 311–335.

White, J., Saurav, S., & Gupta, V. K. (2021). Entrepreneurship research after Chiles, Bluedorn, and Gupta (2007): Has the field delivered on the promise of good scholarship? In B. Ozkazanc-Pan, A. E. Osorio, D. Dutta, V. K. Gupta, G. Javadian, & C. Guo. (Eds.), *Modern classics in entrepreneurship studies: Building the future of the field*. Palgrave Macmillan.

Yang, A. Q., & Guo, C. (2021). A reflection on "emerging issues in corporate entrepreneurship" by Dess, Ireland, Zahra, Floyd, Janney and Lane (2003, JOM). In B. Ozkazanc-Pan, A. E. Osorio, D. Dutta, V. K. Gupta, G. Javadian, & C. Guo. (Eds.), *Modern classics in entrepreneurship studies: Building the future of the field*. Palgrave Macmillan.

CHAPTER 2

Gendered Perspectives on Organizational Creation: Lessons from the Past and Insights for the Future

Golshan Javadian

Introduction

Every so often, a research study has a profound impact on a field by calling into question previously held assumptions and by generating new avenues of understanding that form the foundation for subsequent studies. In their seminal piece, *A Gendered Perspective on Organizational Creation*, Barbra Bird and Candida Brush (2002) draw from three theoretical frameworks (Jungian psychology, cognitive and moral development, and feminist theory) to develop a new and more balanced perspective on organizational creation that reflects both feminine and masculine perspectives in the venture creation process and new venture attributes. Prior to their work, the study of venture creation relied almost exclusively on masculine gender frameworks. By highlighting both the feminine and masculine

G. Javadian (✉)
Morgan State University, Baltimore, MD, USA
e-mail: golshan.javadian@morgan.edu

A. E. Osorio et al. (eds.), *Modern Classics in Entrepreneurship Studies*,
https://doi.org/10.1007/978-3-030-61029-6_2

aspects of venture creation, Bird and Brush introduced novel concepts such as gender maturity (an individual difference) and gender balance (an organization quality) into the venture creation process.

Bird and Brush explain that entrepreneurial behavior is shaped through masculine and feminine attributes and demonstrate that the venture creation process is impacted by the gender maturity of the entrepreneurs. More specifically, they argue that gender awareness and gender integration form gender maturity, which influences the gendered processes in venture creation. These gendered processes include several dimensions, such as the concept of reality, time, power, and ethics, which eventually lead to gendered-balanced organizations that entail the use of resources, structuring, controlling, integration through systems, policy, and culture. Throughout their discussion, the authors distinguish between sex in terms of biology, and gender in terms of socialized perspective in an effort to help us better understand how social processes impact entrepreneurial behavior and venture creation.

The purpose of this chapter is to reflect upon this pivotal study, which has become the foundation for many future studies on women's entrepreneurship. The following section begins with a review of Bird and Brush's work and identifies the most salient and influential features of their discussion. Next, I provide a review of the research articles that build on Bird and Brush's arguments in their theoretical development, which are categorized according to theme. An exploration of the studies within each category traces how Bird and Brush's argument is taken up and extended by subsequent researchers. Finally, I discuss why and how the ideas first proposed by Bird and Brush continue to be relevant to the field today and how future research can build on their original insights.

Bird and Brush's work stands out from prior research because it drew attention to the less visible feminine perspective of venture creation and compared it to the traditional masculine perspective in an effort to tease out how gender impacts the various dimensions of an organization. To this day, many studies persist in defining entrepreneurship as a masculine activity. Despite Bird and Brush's broad influence, there is still room for their message to reach a wider audience. In this chapter I will highlight their most compelling arguments and propose how future studies can continue to expand on the important foundation they laid for a new, more gender-inclusive understanding of the venture creation process.

Summary of Bird and Brush (2002)

Bird and Brush begin their discussion by describing the role of the entrepreneur in the process of venture creation and explaining how historical descriptions of entrepreneurs and their activities typically employed traditionally masculine terms (e.g., entrepreneurship was defined as risk bearing, initiative taking, opportunism, etc.). The authors point out that until recently, entrepreneurship has been a "man's" domain (p. 41) and that the discourse of entrepreneurship, whether it is found in textbooks or in the practitioner literature, refers to entrepreneurship as a masculine task and frequently portrays successful entrepreneurs as successful men. The authors draw attention to the way in which the process of entrepreneurship is defined as a chain of hierarchy or demand in which the entrepreneur is motivated by power and achievement, is willing to take risks, needs instrumental feedback, and assumes that the new venture's primary purpose is to make a profit. Bird and Brush argue, however, that this sequential, economically driven process does not necessarily reflect the organizational process of women entrepreneurs. The authors explain that women may not follow a similar path or sequence in venture creation due to interrupted careers, responsibility for family and children, and/or due to their preferences for more nurturing and relational policies. Moreover, Bird and Brush argue that the venture creation process is gendered because it omits the feminine aspects of organizing, and that it is less visible because there are fewer examples of women-led organizations in the literature that might clarify the distinctions between women and men entrepreneurs. To address these shortcomings, Bird and Brush borrow from Jungian psychology, cognitive and moral development, and feminist theory in an effort to submit an alternative organizing process that attempts to combine masculine and feminine perspectives and is applicable to both men and women.

Bird and Brush begin by categorizing the steps in the process of starting a new organization into five broad activities. These steps include: identifying an opportunity and forming the intention to start a new venture, obtaining resources to pursue the opportunity, deploying resources and establishing procedures for their use in producing and marketing products and services, building an organization and developing structure, and forming strategies to survive, and grow and harvest values created. Traditionally, this was viewed as a linear process as seen from the masculine perspective. However, Bird and Brush propose an alternative gendered process of venture creation by (1) emphasizing the importance of caring and information sharing, (2) comparing future versus present time orientation, (3) deliberating on the positive outcomes of emotional actions and interaction, (4) highlighting the negative consequences of the power motive, and (5) discussing the importance of feminine ethic. They reveal the importance of recognizing gendered maturity (gender awareness and gender integration) as the antecedent of this gendered process and also identify gendered-balanced organizations as the consequence of this process.

According to Bird and Brush, there are four aspects of gendered-balanced organization: the use of resources, structuring, controlling, and integration. In each case, the authors highlight the masculine and feminine dimensions of each aspect. For example, a masculine dimension of the use of resources is "leasing people" whereas the feminine aspect could be framed as "commitment to people." Similarly, "personal control" is the masculine aspect of controlling, whereas "sharing control" is the feminine aspect. Bird and Brush also attempt to unpack the concept of gendered maturity as the antecedent of the gendered process, but point out that it is not the purpose of their paper to fully operationalize gendered maturity. They end their discussion by offering three insightful propositions on the impact of gendered maturity on the venture creation process of male and female entrepreneurs.

Based on Google Scholar, the Bird and Brush article has been cited 825 times as of July 2020. Citations are considered to be a reliable and effective measure for assessing the influence of a publication on the field of research (Culnan et al., 1990; Hota et al., 2019). Bird and Brush's work is considered influential both because of its high number of citations and because of its groundbreaking perspective of the feminine aspects of venture creation.

To trace the impact of their seminal work on the field, I present a review of the research articles that cite Bird and Brush's arguments in their theoretical development. These research articles are categorized according to different themes. I look at studies within each category to explore how they incorporated or expanded on Bird and Brush's argument. Finally, I discuss how future research can build on the original insights of their study.

Theme 1: Developing Frameworks or an Agenda for Women Entrepreneurship Research

Several studies that cite Bird and Brush developed a framework or agenda for women entrepreneurship research. Table 2.1 lists a number of articles that include this theme. Among them is Ahl (2006), who made use of Bird and Brush's argument to explain how the terms entrepreneur and entrepreneurship are male-gendered concepts. Through a discourse analysis of selected texts, Ahl revealed that the words used to describe entrepreneurs are predominantly masculine. In fact, this analysis revealed that feminine words were often used to describe the very opposite of the words associated with entrepreneurs. In this way, Ahl's discourse analysis became the evidence for Bird and Brush's argument that entrepreneurship is mainly defined as a masculine activity. For this reason, Ahl (2006) made several suggestions for future research on women's entrepreneurship and encouraged researchers to study woman entrepreneurs without "reproducing their secondary position" (p. 611). Similarly, De Bruin et al. (2007) reinforced Bird and Brush's argument that the venture creation process includes feminine perspectives and encouraged future researchers to broaden their views of entrepreneurship by paying closer attention to the underexplored feminine processes and behaviors that influence new venture creation.

In the same vein, Brush et al. (2009) developed a gender-aware framework for women's entrepreneurship. They expanded on Bird and Brush's argument of the impact of gender on the venture creation process by suggesting that in order to understand women entrepreneurship, we must go beyond the models used to study entrepreneurs in general, and include factors such as motherhood and culture, which have historically had a greater impact on women than men.

A recent study in the same thematic category is Foss et al. (2019), which focuses on women's entrepreneurship policy as a core component of the entrepreneurial ecosystem. By means of a systematic literature review, they assess the policy implication of women's entrepreneurship research and examine the link between the nature of policy implications, the theoretical perspectives, and subsequent changes to women's entrepreneurship research. Based on their findings, they offer recommendations to improve the entrepreneurial ecosystems for women from a policy perspective. They include Bird and Brush's study among a number

Table 2.1 Articles in theme 1 (developing frameworks or an agenda for women entrepreneurship research)

Article	*Main argument*	*Perspective utilized from Bird and Brush (2002)*
Ahl (2006)	Research articles on women's entrepreneurship reveal a tendency to recreate the idea of women as being secondary to men and of women's businesses being of less significance or, at best, as being a complement	Entrepreneur and entrepreneurship are male-gendered concepts
De Bruin et al. (2007)	Offered a framework for coherent research on women's entrepreneurship	There is an underexplored and unarticulated feminine set of processes and behaviors that influence new venture creation
Brush et al. (2009)	Offered a gender-aware framework to provide a springboard for furthering a holistic understanding of women's entrepreneurship	Women are less likely to approach tasks with a rational and deliberate approach
Calás et al. (2009)	Attempted to reframe entrepreneurship as positive economic activity to entrepreneurship as social change	New venture creation is a gendered process incorporating both masculine and feminine aspects
Jennings and Brush (2013)	Reviewed the literature on women's entrepreneurship and explored whether and how women's entrepreneurship research offers extensions to—and can be extended by—general research on entrepreneurs and their ventures	Bringing feminine perspectives into venture creation process
Brush et al. (2014)	Gender moderates the relationship aspects of embeddedness, desirability, and feasibility, and venture creation	Current frameworks of venture creation do not consider the influence of social settings, such as family and household, culture and context
Poggesi et al. (2016)	Reviews the literature of woman entrepreneurship and offers future research insights	Research needs to look for and measure the feminine and masculine dimensions of venture creation in order to identify ways that men and women behave similarly and differently

(continued)

Table 2.1 (continued)

Article	*Main argument*	*Perspective utilized from Bird and Brush (2002)*
Foss et al. (2019)	Links women entrepreneurship research and policy	There are feminine perspectives on new venture creation

of examples of research that has utilized feminist theories to cast light on feminine perspectives on organizational creation.

Theme 2: Gender Stereotypes in the Entrepreneurship Context

The second theme used to categorize articles that cite Bird and Brush is that of gender stereotypes in the entrepreneurship context. Gender stereotypes are the shared beliefs about the attitudes and characteristics associated with each sex (Powell & Graves, 2003) that result from the distribution of men and women into social roles (Eagly & Steffen, 1984). Gender stereotypes both describe and prescribe how men and women actually are, as well as how they "should be" (Heilman, 2004). Gender stereotypes, which are predominant in many societies (Heilman & Okimoto, 2007), influence individuals' cognitions, attitudes, and behaviors (Wegener et al., 2006).

Although Bird and Brush did not specifically focus on the topic of gender stereotypes, their insights into the traditionally masculine nature of entrepreneurship and the lack of attention to feminine aspects have paved the way for several studies to identify the impact of negative gender stereotypes on women's entrepreneurial intention and behavior. Table 2.2 lists several articles with this theme. For example, Gupta et al. (2009) expand Bird and Brush's argument that most role models in entrepreneurship tend to be men by arguing that the existence of primarily male role models creates a gender stereotypical context in which entrepreneurs are perceived to have predominately masculine characteristics. Gupta et al. (2009) also maintain that gender stereotypes impact women's perceptions of their own entrepreneurial capabilities. These researchers found that women who perceive themselves as similar to males have higher entrepreneurial intentions than those who see themselves as similar to

Table 2.2 Articles in theme 2 (Gender stereotypes in the entrepreneurship context)

Article	*Main argument*	*Perspective utilized from Bird and Brush (2002)*
Gupta and Bhawe (2007), Gupta et al. (2008, 2009, 2013, 2014)	Negative gender stereotypes impact women entrepreneurs negatively	Most role models in entrepreneurship tend to be men
Eddleston and Powell (2008)	Gender identity explains what male and female business owners look for from their careers	Little attention has been devoted to a feminine perspective of businessownership
Edelman et al. (2018)	Within an angel group that is composed of predominantly men, role stereotypes of entrepreneurs as masculine will be expected, therefore creating gender biases againstwomen	Engaging in entrepreneurship is viewed as a masculine endeavor
Balachandra et al. (2019)	Investors prefer ventures pitched by men to those pitched by women, and the display of feminine-stereotyped behaviors by entrepreneurs while they pitch to investors is viewed negatively by the investors	Men are believed to be more entrepreneurial and growth oriented than women, and femininity has not been associated with successful entrepreneurs
Malmström et al. (2017)	Female entrepreneurs risk receiving significantly less venture capital, which is caused by the language and rhetoric used that relates to gender differences when funding decisions are made	New venture creations align to a great extent with the masculine character
van Ewijk and Belghiti-Mahut (2019)	Gender differences in entrepreneurial intentions change when entrepreneurship education is added to the force field	Entrepreneurship is viewed as a masculine process

females. Similarly, in later studies Gupta and colleagues discuss how stereotypes affect women's evaluations of business opportunities and their assessment of business ideas (Gupta et al., 2013; Gupta & Turban, 2012).

They also explain that women have lower levels of opportunity evaluation and that they evaluate masculine business ideas more favorably in the presence of masculine stereotypical information.

Another article within this category is Balachandra et al. (2019), which builds on Bird and Brush's argument that men are believed to be more entrepreneurial and growth oriented than women. This study hypothesizes that investors prefer ventures pitched by men to those pitched by women. The authors of this study also extend Bird and Brush's argument that femininity was historically not associated with successful entrepreneurs and propose that the display of feminine behaviors by entrepreneurs while they pitch to investors is viewed negatively by investors.

Theme 3: Gender Differences in Entrepreneurial Activities

The majority of research citing Bird and Brush examines the gendered differences in entrepreneurial activities. This is not surprising given that much of the literature on women's entrepreneurship has focused on documenting the differences between male and female entrepreneurs and their ventures, and on explaining why such differences exist (James, 2012; Jennings & Brush, 2013). Early studies on women entrepreneurs viewed women's ways of doing business, such as their approach to networking, which prioritizes maintaining relationships over focusing on business matters (e.g., Olm et al., 1988), or their desire to balance work and family life, as a disadvantage (e.g., Allen & Truman, 1993; Buttner, 1993). The majority of these early studies identified "men's way of doing business" as the standard and attributed the differences in entrepreneurial activities of men and women to women's nonconformity to this standard (Mirchandani, 1999).

More recent studies have changed tack. Instead of viewing women's approaches to doing business as a disadvantage, they seek to explain the difficulties facing women entrepreneurs and explore potential reasons for why their approach to doing business is so different. Various studies have suggested that one reason is that women entrepreneurs have limited access to resources (Boden & Nucci, 2000; Carter & Williams, 2003; Coleman & Robb, 2012; García & Carter, 2009). Compared to businesses headed by men, businesses with women at the helm are financed at lower rates, are less likely to be funded by venture and angel capital, and tend to operate with lower degrees of equity and debt, especially in the early stages (Boden & Nucci, 2000; Coleman & Robb, 2012; Verheul & Thurik, 2001). Moreover, women business owners tend to have less work experience and education in managerial, technical, and executive areas, but more experience in retail, teaching, office administration, and secretarial areas, which could be considered disadvantageousin their entrepreneurial activities (Hisrich & Brush, 1983).

In addition to practical limitations such as a lack of access to capital, it has been suggested that female entrepreneurs face conflicting demands between their professional and personal lives (Allen & Truman, 1993; Stoner et al., 1990). Unlike their male counterparts, women entrepreneurs are not usually free of their domestic responsibilities when they start a business (Belcourt et al., 1991). Furthermore, this conflict may be related to the adoption of reduced growth intentions (Cliff, 1998).

A lower entrepreneurial activity rate of women has also been attributed to cognitive factors. Women tend to perceive themselves and their entrepreneurial environment less favorably as compared to men (Langowitz & Minniti, 2007). Women tend to have lower levels of entrepreneurial self-efficacy as compared to men, which can negatively impact their entrepreneurial intentions (Bandura et al., 2001; Gatewood et al., 2002).

More recent studies have proposed that women's different approaches to doing business are caused by gendered differences in the process of socialization (e.g., Eddleston & Powell, 2008). It has also been argued that firms headed by women are more likely to pursue social as well as economic goals, which have been shown to contribute to slower growth for woman-owned ventures (Hechavarria et al., 2012; Meyskens et al. 2011). Whereas both female and male entrepreneurs are likely to use a mix of feminine and masculine approaches in running their firms (Jennings & Brush, 2013), differences have been observed in terms of the performance of female- and male-led firms based on standard economic indicators. Whether size is measured by gross revenue, the number of employees, or profit level, businesses headed by women tend to be smaller than those headed by men (Fischer et al., 1993; Kalleberg & Leicht, 1991). In addition, businesses headed by women grow less quickly than those owned by men (Cooper et al., 1994). Although some view the slower growth rate of woman-owned business as a problem (Cliff, 1998), others argue that female business owners often prefer to keep their businesses smaller for various reasons (Belcourt et al., 1991).

A number of studies that have been influenced by Bird and Brush's argument to document gender differences in entrepreneurial activities are listed in Table 2.3. For example, Alsos et al. (2006) consider Bird and Brush's discussion of the tendency of women entrepreneurs to be more likely to take a feminine approach in their ventures than men. In addition, they point out that men and women differ in regard to how they perceive funding options because woman-owned ventures are more likely to be self or family funded.

Kalnins and Williams (2014) take a slightly different approach when they explore the circumstances in which woman-owned ventures out survive those owned by men. In an expansion of Bird and Brush's discussion of the differences between female-owned businesses and male-owned businesses, which vary from setting to setting, they argue that female-owned businesses out survive male-owned businesses in certain industries and geographic areas.

Discussion and Future Research Directions

Bird and Brush's seminal work on gendered perspectives in the creation of organizations was the first study to examine venture creation through an explicitly feminist lens. They identified feminine perspectives on the venture creation process, including women's tendency to employ less focused and more diffuse concepts of venturing and organizing, more emotional and cooperative interaction, shared power, focus on relationships and caring, as well as a different orientation toward time, which implies more concentration on the present than on the future. Although Bird and Brush called for future studies to investigate the feminine perspectives of business creation they had identified, not much progress has been made in this regard. The majority of studies influenced by Bird and Brush tend to limit themselves to the discussion of how entrepreneurship has historically been viewed and defined as a masculine activity. Studies that offer insights into the future of woman entrepreneurship research have noted Bird and Brush's emphasis on the presence and importance of feminine aspects of venture creation and have suggested that this is an area that should be explored in the future. Nevertheless, only a handful of studies have either theoretically or empirically examined the feminine aspects of new venture creation.

Table 2.3 Articles in theme 3 (Gender differences in entrepreneurial activities)

Article	*Main argument*	*Perspective utilized from Bird and Brush (2002)*
Alsos et al. (2006)	While there are few detected gender differences with respect tofunding perceptions and behavior, women obtain significantly less financial capital to develop their new businesses	Women entrepreneurs more thanmen take a feminine approach to venture creation
Carter et al. (2007)	Explores the role of gender in bank-lending decisions, focusing on the criteria and processes used by male and female loan officers	Women's experience ofbusiness ownership differs substantially from that of men
Manolova et al. (2007)	Looks at the differential effects of men and women entrepreneurs' human capital and networking on their growth expectancies in the context of a transitional economy	The female entrepreneur is morethan "other than male"
Eddleston and Powell (2008)	Examines how gender identity explains what male and female business owners look for from their careers	Feminine perspectives of venture creation need to be examined
Fairlie and Robb (2009)	Female-owned businesses are less successful than male-owned businesses because they have less startup capital, less business human capital, and less prior work experience	Different preferences, discrimination, and risk aversion, may be responsible for low levels of female entrepreneurship
Manolova et al. (2012)	Proposes differences in growth expectancies of nascent men and women entrepreneurs	Woman business owners frequently pursue both economic and social goals, which may detract from economic performance or growth

Article	*Main argument*	*Perspective utilized from Bird and Brush (2002)*
Kalnins and Williams (2014)	Female-owned businesses consistently outsurvive male-owned businesses in many industries and areas	Differences in outcomes between female-owned businesses and male-owned businesses may vary from setting to setting
Santos et al. (2016)	Analyzes the interplay between gender differences and the social environment in the formation of entrepreneurial intentions	Cognitive differences inentrepreneurial behaviors are explained by gender stereotypes and socially conditioned perceptions of what it means to be masculine or feminine
Kanze et al. (2018)	Examines the underlying mechanism for funding disparity between male and female entrepreneurs	Entrepreneurship is viewed as a masculine-typed endeavorthat women are incapable of successfully undertaking
Hmieleski and Sheppard (2019)	Examines the gender differences in the relationships of entrepreneurs' agentic and communal personality characteristics with measures of subjective well-being and new venture performance	Feminine and masculine characteristics are important for achieving entrepreneurial success

One notable exception that examines venture creation from a feminine perspective is Calás et al. (2009), which attempts to reframe entrepreneurship as seen through a feminist lens. The authors offer a new definition of entrepreneurship as social change rather than as a positive economic activity. Another study by Eddleston and Powell (2008) argues that femininity mediates the relationship between sex and preferences for employee relationship satisfiers and contribution to society satisfiers. More recently, Hmieleski and Sheppard (2019) published a study on gender differences in the importance of communal and agentic characteristics for entrepreneurs' subjective well-being and performance that showed how a feminine characteristic (team work) is beneficial for male entrepreneurs. In their work, they point to Bird and Brush's discussion of the importance of feminine and masculine characteristics in achieving entrepreneurial success and attempt to develop a balanced perspective of entrepreneurship that considers the importance of both masculine *and* feminine characteristics for entrepreneurs.

Although these few studies rely on Bird and Brush's pioneering work to offer some understanding of the feminine perspective of venture creation, it is important for future research to go even further by considering how feminine characteristics and behaviors, such as building customer and supplier relationships or motivating employees, could offer advantages for certain entrepreneurship activities. It is also imperative for future research to identify the feminine and masculine dimensions of the venture creation process and examine whether men and women behave similarly or differently with regard to those dimensions.

In addition to highlighting the feminine aspects of the venture creation process, Bird and Brush's identification of gendered maturity (gender awareness and gender integration) as the antecedent of gendered processes merits additional study, given that recent research has not led to a better understanding of gender maturity or offered any empirical tests. Bird and Brush proposed that the greater the gendered maturity of an entrepreneur, the greater the likelihood that the venture creation process and outcome would result in a balance of traditional and personal qualities. Future research is essential to examine this assumption and to investigate what the implications of having a gendered-balance organization might be. Bird and Brush's suggestion that the gendered maturity of female and male entrepreneurs results in different outcomes should also be considered in future studies to analyze any such differences.

Bird and Brush's novel perspective on entrepreneurship research in general and research on women's entrepreneurship specifically laid the groundwork for additional questions and studies. Their work revealed a previously invisible side of the venture creation process and identified the antecedents and outcomes of this process. Although many studies have expanded on their discussion in order to enhance the understanding of gendered perspectives of venture creation, much remains to be done. Indeed, entrepreneurship continues to be understood as a predominantly masculine activity, which suggests that the feminine perspectives Bird and Brush identified have not been fully explored or accepted as an important element of the venture creation process. In addition, several of the research questions raised by their work have yet to be answered. For example, we do not know how the gendered perspectives identified by Bird and Brush impact venture growth, success, and survival. We also do not know how gendered ventures respond during economic downturns. If longstanding gender stereotypes are to be dismantled, additional research on these important topics is essential in order to form a more accurate picture of the venture creation process and how it is impacted by both male and female entrepreneurs.

References

Ahl, H. (2006). Why research on women entrepreneurs needs new directions. *Entrepreneurship Theory and Practice, 30*(5), 595–621.

Allen, S., & Truman, C. (1993). *Women in business: Perspectives on women entrepreneurs*. Routledge.

Alsos, G. A., Isaksen, E. J., & Ljunggren, E. (2006). New venture financing and subsequent business growth in men–and women–led businesses. *Entrepreneurship Theory and Practice, 30*(5), 667–686.

Balachandra, L., Briggs, T., Eddleston, K., & Brush, C. (2019). Don't pitch like a girl! How gender stereotypes influence investor decisions. *Entrepreneurship Theory and Practice, 43*(1), 116–137.

Bandura, A., Barbaranelli, C., Caprara, G., & Pastorelli, C. (2001). Self-efficacy beliefs as shapers of children's aspirations and career trajectories. *Child Development, 72*(1), 187–206.

Belcourt, M., Burke, R., & Lee-Gosselin, H. (1991). *The glass box: Women business owners in Canada*. Canadian Advisory Council on the Status of Women.

Bird, B., & Brush, C. (2002). A gendered perspective on organizational creation. *Entrepreneurship Theory and Practice, 26*(3), 41–65.

Boden, R. J., Jr., & Nucci, A. R. (2000). On the survival prospects of men's and women's new business ventures. *Journal of Business Venturing, 15*, 347–362.

Brush, C. G., De Bruin, A., & Welter, F. (2009). A gender-aware framework for women's entrepreneurship. *International Journal of Gender and Entrepreneurship, 1*(1), 8–24.

Brush, C. G., de Bruin, A., & Welter, F. (2014). Advancing theory development in venture creation: Signposts for understanding gender. In *Women's entrepreneurship in the 21st century*. Edward Elgar.

Buttner, E. (1993). Female entrepreneurs: How far have they come? *Business Horizons, 36*(2), 59–65.

Calás, M. B., Smircich, L., & Bourne, K. A. (2009). Extending the boundaries: Reframing "entrepreneurship as social change" through feminist perspectives. *Academy of Management Review, 34*(3), 552–569.

Carter, N., & Williams, M. (2003). Comparing social feminism and liberal feminism: The case of new firm growth. In J. E. Butler (Eds.), *New perspectives on women entrepreneurs*. Information Age Publishing.

Carter, S., Shaw, E., Lam, W., & Wilson, F. (2007). Gender, entrepreneurship, and bank lending: The criteria and processes used by bank loan officers in assessing applications. *Entrepreneurship Theory and Practice, 31*(3), 427–444.

Cliff, J. E. (1998). Does one size fit all? Exploring the relationship between attitudes towards growth, gender, and business size. *Journal of Business Venturing, 13*(6), 523–542.

Coleman, S., & Robb, A. (2012). *A rising tide: Financing strategies for women-owned firms*. Stanford Press.

Cooper, A. C., Gimeno-Gascon, F. J., & Woo, C. Y. (1994). Initial human and financial capital as predictors of new venture performance. *Journal of Business Venturing, 9*(5), 371–395.

Culnan, M. J., O'Reilly, C. A., & Chatman, J. A. (1990). Intellectual structure of research in organizational behavior, 1972–1984: A cocitation analysis. *Journal of the American Society for Information Science, 41*(6), 453.

De Bruin, A., Brush, C. G., & Welter, F. (2007). Advancing a framework for coherent research on women's entrepreneurship. *Entrepreneurship Theory and Practice, 31*(3), 323–339.

Eagly, A. H., & Steffen, V. J. (1984). Gender stereotypes stem from the distribution of women and men into social roles. *Journal of Personality and Social Psychology, 46*(4), 735.

Eddleston, K. A., & Powell, G. N. (2008). The role of gender identity in explaining sex differences in business owners' career satisfier preferences. *Journal of Business Venturing, 23*(2), 244–256.

Edelman, L. F., Donnelly, R., Manolova, T., & Brush, C. G. (2018). Gender stereotypes in the angel investment process. *International Journal of Gender and Entrepreneurship, 10*(2), 134–157.

Fairlie, R. W., & Robb, A. M. (2009). Gender differences in business performance: Evidence from the characteristics of business owners survey. *Small Business Economics, 33*(4), 375.
Fischer, E., Reuber, R., & Dyke, L. (1993). A theoretical overview and extension of research on sex, gender, and entrepreneurship. *Journal of Business Venturing, 8*, 151–168.
Foss, L., Henry, C., Ahl, H., & Mikalsen, G. H. (2019). Women's entrepreneurship policy research: A 30-year review of the evidence. *Small Business Economics, 53*(2), 409–429.
García, M. C. D., & Carter, S. (2009). Resource mobilization through business owners' networks: Is gender an issue? *International Journal of Gender and Entrepreneurship, 1*(3), 226–252.
Gatewood, E., Shaver, K., Powers, J., & Gartner, W. (2002). Entrepreneurial expectancy, task, effort and performance. *Entrepreneurship Theory and Practice, 27*(Winter), 187–206.
Gupta, V. K., & Bhawe, N. M. (2007). The influence of proactive personality and stereotype threat on women's entrepreneurial intentions. *Journal of Leadership & Organizational Studies, 13*(4), 73–85.
Gupta, V. K., Goktan, A. B., & Gunay, G. (2014). Gender differences in evaluation of new business opportunity: A stereotype threat perspective. *Journal of Business Venturing, 29*(2), 273–288.
Gupta, V. K., & Turban, D. B. (2012). Evaluation of new business ideas: Do gender stereotypes play a role? *Journal of Managerial Issues*, 140–156.
Gupta, V. K., Turban, D. B., & Bhawe, N. M. (2008). The effect of gender stereotype activation on entrepreneurial intentions. *Journal of Applied Psychology, 93*(5), 1053.
Gupta, V. K., Turban, D. B., & Pareek, A. (2013). Differences between men and women in opportunity evaluation as a function of gender stereotypes and stereotype activation. *Entrepreneurship Theory and Practice, 37*(4), 771–788.
Gupta, V. K., Turban, D. B., Wasti, S. A., & Sikdar, A. (2009). The role of gender stereotypes in perceptions of entrepreneurs and intentions to become an entrepreneur. *Entrepreneurship Theory and Practice, 33*(2), 397–417.
Hechavarria, D. M., Ingram, A., Justo, R., & Terjesen, S. (2012). Are women more likely to pursue social and environmental entrepreneurship? In K. D. Hughes & J. E. Jennings (Eds.), *Global women's entrepreneurship research: Diverse settings, questions and approaches*. Edward Elgar.
Heilman, A. (2004). *New woman strategies: Sarah Grand, Olive Schreiner, and Mona Caird*. Manchester University Press.
Heilman, M. E., & Okimoto, T. G. (2007). Why are women penalized for success at male tasks? The implied communality deficit. *Journal of Applied Psychology, 92*(1), 81.

Hisrich, R. D., & Brush, C. G. (1983). The woman entrepreneur: Implications of family, education, and occupation. In J. A. Hornaday, J. A. Timmons, & K. H. Vesper (Eds.), *Frontiers of entrepreneurship research—Proceedings of the Babson College conference on entrepreneurship*. Babson College.

Hmieleski, K. M., & Sheppard, L. D. (2019). The Yin and Yang of entrepreneurship: Gender differences in the importance of communal and agentic characteristics for entrepreneurs' subjective well-being and performance. *Journal of Business Venturing, 34*(4), 709–730.

Hota, P. K., Subramanian, B., & Narayanamurthy, G. (2019). Mapping the intellectual structure of social entrepreneurship research: A citation/co-citation analysis. *Journal of Business Ethics*, 1–26.

James, A. E. (2012). Conceptualizing 'woman' as an entrepreneurial advantage: A reflexive approach. In K. D. Hughes & J. E. Jennings (Eds.), *Global women's entrepreneurship research: Diverse settings, questions and approaches*. Edward Elgar.

Jennings, J. E., & Brush, C. G. (2013). Research on women entrepreneurs: Challenges to (and from) the broader entrepreneurship literature? *Academy of Management Annals, 7*(1), 663–715.

Kalleberg, A., & Leicht, K. (1991). Gender and organizational performance: Determinants of small business survival and success. *Academy of Management Journal, 34*(1), 136–161.

Kalnins, A., & Williams, M. (2014). When do female-owned businesses out-survive male-owned businesses? A disaggregated approach by industry and geography. *Journal of Business Venturing, 29*(6), 822–835.

Kanze, D., Huang, L., Conley, M. A., & Higgins, E. T. (2018). We ask men to win and women not to lose: Closing the gender gap in startup funding. *Academy of Management Journal, 61*(2), 586–614.

Langowitz, N., & Minniti, M. (2007). The entrepreneurial propensity of women. *Entrepreneurship Theory and Practice, 31*(3), 341–364.

Malmström, M., Johansson, J., & Wincent, J. (2017). Gender stereotypes and venture support decisions: How governmental venture capitalists socially construct entrepreneurs' potential. *Entrepreneurship Theory and Practice, 41*(5), 833–860.

Manolova, T. S., Brush, C. G., Edelman, L. F., & Shaver, K. G. (2012). One size does not fit all: Entrepreneurial expectancies and growth intentions of US women and men nascent entrepreneurs. *Entrepreneurship & Regional Development, 24*(1–2), 7–27.

Manolova, T. S., Carter, N. M., Manev, I. M., & Gyoshev, B. S. (2007). The differential effect of men and women entrepreneurs' human capital and networking on growth expectancies in Bulgaria. *Entrepreneurship Theory and Practice, 31*(3), 407–426.

Meyskens, M., Brush, C., & Allen, E. (2011). Human capital and hybrid ventures. In T. Lumpkin & J. Katz (Eds.), *Social and sustainable entrepreneurship: Advances in firm emergence and growth*. Emerald.

Mirchandani, K. (1999). Feminist insight on gendered work: New directions in research on women and entrepreneurship. *Gender, Work & Organization, 6*(4), 224–235.

Olm, K., Carsrud, A., & Alvey, L. (1988). The role of networks in new venture funding for the female entrepreneur: A continuing analysis. In *Frontiers of entrepreneurship research* (pp. 658–659).

Poggesi, S., Mari, M., & De Vita, L. (2016). What's new in female entrepreneurship research? Answers from the literature. *International Entrepreneurship and Management Journal, 12*(3), 735–764.

Powell, G. N., & Graves, L. M. (2003). *Women and men in management* (3rd ed.). Thousand Oaks, CA: Sage.

Santos, F. J., Roomi, M. A., & Liñán, F. (2016). About gender differences and the social environment in the development of entrepreneurial intentions. *Journal of Small Business Management, 54*(1), 49–66.

Stoner, C. R., Hartman, R. I., & Arora, R. (1990). Work-home role conflict in female owners of small businesses: An exploratory study. *Journal of Small Business Management, 28*, 30–38.

van Ewijk, A. R., & Belghiti-Mahut, S. (2019). Context, gender and entrepreneurial intentions. *International Journal of Gender and Entrepreneurship, 11*(1), 75–98.

Verheul, I., & Thurik, R. (2001). Start-up capital: Does gender matter? *Small Business Economics, 16*, 32–345.

Wegener, D. T., Clark, J. K., & Petty, R. E. (2006). Not all stereotyping is created equal: Differential consequences of thoughtful versus non thoughtful stereotyping. *Journal of Personality and Social Psychology, 90*, 42–59.

CHAPTER 3

Entrepreneurship Research After Chiles, Bluedorn, and Gupta (2007): Has the Field Delivered on the Promise of Good Scholarship?

Joshua V. White, Swapnil Saurav, and Vishal K. Gupta

Introduction

Entrepreneurship is attracting ever-greater attention in scholarly journals, college classrooms, and public affairs (Nightingale & Coad, 2014; Wiklund et al., 2019). After several decades of scholarly inquiry (Jennings & Brush, 2013), entrepreneurship "has emerged as one of the most vital, dynamic, and relevant" fields of study in management and the broader social sciences (Wiklund et al., 2011). The academic field of

J. V. White · S. Saurav · V. K. Gupta (✉)
Department of Management, Culverhouse College of Business,
The University of Alabama, Tuscaloosa, AL, USA
e-mail: vkgupta@cba.ua.edu

J. V. White
e-mail: jvwhite@crimson.ua.edu

A. E. Osorio et al. (eds.), *Modern Classics in Entrepreneurship Studies*,
https://doi.org/10.1007/978-3-030-61029-6_3

entrepreneurship today is truly a global community, with researchers from around the world submitting an ever-increasing number of manuscripts for publication in leading general organizational journals (e.g., *Academy of Management Review*) and disciplinary journals (e.g., *Journal of Business Venturing*, *Entrepreneurship Theory & Practice*). Several factors have contributed to the flourishing of entrepreneurship research, including the publication of impactful, high-quality, influential articles that help move the field forward and advance knowledge (Shepherd, 2015). There is likely a large number of articles that can lay claim to steer the field in new directions (Ferreira et al., 2019), but the one that will be the focus of our inquiry here is Chiles et al. (2007; henceforth CBG) as it is considered an "excellent" research paper in the entrepreneurship canon (Sarasvathy & Dew, 2008, p. 239). CBG advanced a novel "foundation for … process-intensive, context-rich, temporally oriented research" (p. 468) in entrepreneurship based on the work of radical subjectivist Austrian economist Ludwig Lachmann. CBG attempted to herald a new era for rigorous scholarship in entrepreneurship, and presently, we reflect on their work to discern and gauge its true impact.

Organizational scholars have long been interested in impactful scholarship (Davis, 1971; Schilling & Green, 2011), as evident from the growing number of published articles that have examined the antecedents and consequences of publishing high-quality research (Aguinis et al., 2020; Podsakoff et al., 2008). Many prestigious journals give out best-paper awards on an annual basis (e.g., *Academy of Management Journal* and *Strategic Management Journal*), and journal editors regularly express their desire to publish more high-impact papers (e.g., Bello & Kostova, 2012; Shepherd, 2016; Tihanyi, 2020). Although there is no agreement among scholars on what makes an article impactful (Clark & Wright, 2007; Conlon et al., 2006), there seems to be considerable convergence around the idea that a research paper has an impact when it informs subsequent scholarship (Bergh et al., 2006). For scientists, including those engaged in organizational research, an article's role in development of subsequent knowledge is a critical consideration, with impact often (but not always) evidenced by subsequent citations (Leung, 2007; Mingers & Lipitakis, 2010).

S. Saurav
e-mail: ssaurav@crimson.ua.edu

Our purpose here is to analyze the influence of CBG on scholarship in entrepreneurial studies, discussing how the article has contributed to knowledge development so far and highlighting possible opportunities for future research. To do so, we take a multi-pronged approach. First, we provide a brief summary of CBG, and an informative synthesis of the growing body of work that elaborates its key ideas and tenets (e.g., Chiles et al., 2010b; Streb & Gupta, 2011). Second, we obtain all articles that cite CBG to conduct a bibliometric analysis and employ word cloud analyses with the goal of better understanding its impact in the subsequent literature. We join the small, but growing, body of literature that takes a deep dive into the role of specific influential articles in advancing the knowledge frontier in organizational studies (e.g., Eckhardt, 2019; Ferreira, 2011). Our analysis of CBG and the articles that cite it should help rejuvenate academic conversation about the usefulness and potential of a radical subjectivist agenda in entrepreneurship research (Phelan, 2016). Our hope is that our critical analysis enriches ongoing conversations about the enduring value and impact of seminal publications in entrepreneurship research (Gupta et al., 2018).

The rest of the paper is structured as follows. In the next section, we provide an overview of CBG, with the goal of conveying its important themes and thrusts to the reader. We then contextualize CBG by discussing some notable articles that sought to explicate and clarify the major issues raised in the original publication. Subsequently, we analyze the journal publications that cite CBG to capture the notable achievements and omissions in the literature accumulating around this seminal article. We conclude with a brief discussion of theoretical and empirical crevices and cul-de-sacs in the disequilibrium-based creativity-focused entrepreneurship literature that CBG pioneered. We cast new light on the extent to which entrepreneurship research over the past decade (2008–2019 time-period) has delivered on the promise of the revolutionary framework proposed by CBG and highlight new avenues for future studies interested in further advancing the radical subjectivist research agenda.

Summarizing the Original Article

CBG "borrowed boldly" from the work of "maverick economist" Ludwig Lachmann (Vaughn, 1998), and by so doing, contributed to entrepreneurship research in three primary ways. First, CBG responded to concerns that entrepreneurship research is plagued with an "absence and inadequacy of theory" (p. 468). As CBG discuss, the field's history almost exclusively embraced neoclassical, equilibrium-based models of entrepreneurial activity (Eckhardt & Shane, 2003), even though favored views such as Schumpeter's "creative destruction" and Kirzner's "entrepreneurial discovery" "lack theoretical frameworks" capable of assessing the totality of entrepreneurial action (p. 476). CBG posit that mis-specified theoretical models based on such assumptions could partially explain the fragmentation within entrepreneurship in general. Second, CBG offered a novel Austrian economic framework based on the work of twentieth century economist of the Austrian school, Ludwig Lachmann. This "radical subjectivist" approach—predicated on disequilibrium—offered explanatory prowess in navigating nuanced entrepreneurial activity that would otherwise remain unachievable through neoclassical frames. For example, the authors illustrate the mechanics and linkages between individual-level creativity and firm-level recombination of resources, while incorporating complex real-world constraints that were unexplainable by prior theory, such as the heterogeneity of time. Finally, CBG recommended an "even more radical approach" by inviting future scholars to embrace their innovative conceptual framework (p. 469). After illustrating the robust flexibility of the radical subjectivist approach through the analysis of multiple issues pertinent to entrepreneurship researchers, CBG outlined future steps that would bring cohesiveness to the fragmented discipline. Thus, CBG identified a critical factor impeding the progress of entrepreneurial scholarship, proposed a remedy, and outlined a practical conceptual framework for future researchers.

CBG were among the first to synthesize critical shortcomings of the prevailing paradigms, as well as illustrate how these fundamental shortcomings result in unforeseen consequences when misapplied to entrepreneurial phenomena. CBG take a critical position toward the two most notable members of the Austrian School, Joseph Schumpeter and Israel Kirzner (Vaughn, 1998). The "two fundamental premises" (Venkataraman, 1997, p. 121) advanced by Schumpeter and Kirzner offer complementary paradigms for assessing entrepreneurial behavior and market creation. Namely, Schumpeterian entrepreneurs creatively disrupt equilibrium-based markets, and Kirznerian entrepreneurs are arbitrageurs who coordinate action to converge back to the desirable state of stability. Thus, equilibrium is the "ultimate reference point" for many scholars, and in the words of CBG, "neither [entrepreneur] has meaning without the other" (pp. 468–469).

Although the equilibrium approach offers a succinct and well-accepted framework for entrepreneurship researchers, CBG brought to light its main shortcomings. Specifically, they explain how Schumpeter rejected subjectivism of the human mind and personal creativity. Kirzner is criticized for emphasizing that entrepreneurs merely discover existing opportunities and do not ever truly create, but rely instead on exogenous change to introduce novelty. Such omissions can be problematic when applying these frameworks to dynamic and complex entrepreneurial phenomena. Further, CBG argue that Schumpeter gave limited explanation for why entrepreneurs disrupt equilibrium in the first place. Moreover, the logical flaws present within traditional paradigms are not limited to the disequilibrium event itself. Indeed, as CBG show, Kirzner argued that entrepreneurs cannot perceive incorrectly and are not subject to "actions based on faulty perception" (Vaughn, 1998, p. 143). Thus, although it may be convenient to theorize that entrepreneurs interpret all information correctly, it is highly unlikely in practice. Similarly, Kirzner also largely ignored the constraint of time. Finally, CBG emphasize that both Schumpeter and Kirzner distinguished capitalists from entrepreneurs, and did so in ways that (1) advanced socialism (in the case of Schumpeter), and (2) ignored capital requirements of starting entrepreneurial ventures in the first place. In summary, while CBG acknowledged a widespread acceptance of traditional models prioritizing equilibrium, they show that such models leave much to be desired.

To redress these theoretical shortcomings, CBG argued that scholars should "slip the shackles of neoclassical economics and the yoke of equilibrium" in order to "bring greater coherence to a fragmented literature" (p. 470). To organize and frame their arguments, CBG leveraged Low and MacMillan (1988)'s key specifications as a rubric for evaluating a new paradigm within entrepreneurship research: Lachmann's radical subjectivist approach. Low and MacMillan (1988) specify purpose, theory, focus, levels, time, and methods as necessary requisites for developing an entrepreneurship research program. Using these six key specifications, CBG systematically illustrate that the Lachmannian slant to Austrian economics overcomes critical constraints of the more traditional theories. For example, Lachmann emphasizes entrepreneurial creation at an individual level, and as CBG claim, this "opens new ways of thinking about entrepreneurial exploitation as a continuous recombinative process" (p. 473). Moreover, Lachmann's incorporation of intermediate goods into the exploitation process gives much needed context to the purpose of sustained entrepreneurial action. From a theoretical standpoint, CBG demonstrate how Lachmann "charts new territory" by incorporating individual subjectivism with respect to anticipated future events (p. 473). This "creative imagination" diverges from prior theory which eschewed individual creativity.

Additionally, incorporating anticipatory ideas alongside actualized experiences facilitates planning that is "incessantly formed and revised" (p. 474). CBG argue that this process of negotiating expectations is critical to understanding realistic market processes. In addition, the authors claim that Lachmann's theory of capital is "essential to understanding the purpose of entrepreneurship, because it addresses opportunity exploitation" (p. 474). Lachmann's approach to capital structure is one that is heterogeneous, complex, and complementary (Lewin, 1997). His work advances capital combinations that are continuous rather than episodic, as entrepreneurs "bundle and re-bundle resources as new ventures grow" (p. 475). Thus, CBG contend that Lachmann's approach is more proximal to the realities faced by practicing entrepreneurs.

Further, CBG also discuss how Lachmann "explicitly rejects the idea of equilibrium as a resting point or as a position toward which the economy naturally trends, emphasizing instead the continuously disequilibrating nature of entrepreneurship" (p. 477). As a "consequence of his imaginative ability" (Gloria-Palermo, 1999, p. 126), entrepreneurs may never fully coordinate action or diffuse these expectations within the market. Thus, the market is never fully resting and there is not a desired state. Rather, Lachmann embraces both equilibrium and disequilibrium as causal forces, arguing that markets trend toward the latter over time. As CBG claim, "disequilibrium is rooted primarily in (divergent) expectations" (p. 478).

Lachmann's work also held promise for entrepreneurial scholars interested in studying the manifestation of phenomena within different institutional environments. That is, Lachmann's theories accounted for coordination of expectations through the establishment and maintenance of institutions. As highlighted by CBG, Lachmann pointed to institutional rules and norms as "common signposts" for coordinating individual expectations, and he advocated for building coherent "institutional order." As CBG note, this institutional theory fully embodied Lachmann's radical subjectivist approach in that it also argued for the incorporation of "flexibility and change."

CBG illustrate the power of applying the subjectivist approach to studies of entrepreneurship within the context of Low and MacMillan (1988)'s six-dimensional framework. They demonstrate how Lachmann's work is "inherently multilevel" and can be useful in studying entrepreneurial phenomena that are rooted in interdependence and reciprocity (p. 480). Additionally, they reveal that the radical subjectivist approach is best suited to account for the heterogeneity of time, and that the "ideal-types" method favored within the Lachmannian slant "are entirely appropriate for answering" fundamental questions in entrepreneurship studies (p. 485).

To summarize, CBG sought to unify the fragmented entrepreneurship literature—what Shane (2012, p. 11) derides as "a hodgepodge of papers"—by illuminating otherwise taken-for-granted theoretical issues that underlie much of entrepreneurial scholarship. As a remedy, the authors proposed a radical subjectivist approach based on the work of Lachmann, a previously under-appreciated Austrian scholar (Vaughn, 1998). As CBG bridged the structural hole between entrepreneurship and Austrian economics, they initiated an intriguing conversation, and challenged their peers within the field to embrace a novel theoretical approach capable of generating powerful and novel insights about entrepreneurial phenomena.

Extending the Original Article

When CBG was published, the entrepreneurship literature was dominated by the discovery perspective (e.g., Shane, 2000), which claimed that opportunities for entrepreneurial endeavors exist objectively waiting to be discovered (Eckhardt & Shane, 2003). CBG introduced a novel "creation" perspective, challenging the hegemony of the discovery view in entrepreneurship research (Alvarez & Barney, 2019). The initial treatment of the creation view—grounded in the rich theoretical tradition of Lachmann's work (Lewin, 2019; Storr, 2019)—was elaborated in several subsequent articles. Chiles et al. (2010b) extended the Austrian approach of radical subjectivism beyond the work of Ludwig Lachmann to include the works of notable theorist George Shackle. An "unusual economist" (Earl & Littleboy, 2014), Shackle conceptualized entrepreneurs' subjective imagination as "a process by which individuals choose among a variety of imagined sequels associated with a particular course of action" (Chiles et al., 2010b, p. 143). In this view, entrepreneurs execute plans only after evaluating possible outcomes based on their perceived likelihood of occurrence and ranking these imagined outcomes from most to least desirable. The subjective expectations of individual entrepreneurs "continually introduce novelty" as individuals negotiate amidst complex and uncertain environments (Chiles et al., 2010b, p. 143). Shackle's (1972) kaleidic metaphor was invoked to explain the "nonlinear, rapid, continuous, and unpredictable change" characteristic of markets in perpetual disequilibrium (Chiles et al., 2010b, p. 148).

As this body of work continued to grow, further academic work clarified that disequilibrium, while mischaracterized by many scholars, was not an inherently negative outcome. Contrary to accepted wisdom in the academic literature, as noted by Chiles et al. (2010a, p. 29), the "tensions between equilibrium, with its imitation, negative feedback, and homogeneity; and disequilibrium, with its innovation, positive feedback, and heterogeneity" produce a "far-from-equilibrium market order." This market order, predicated on a radical subjective paradigm, characterizes entrepreneurship as hypercompetitive, heterogeneous with respect to resources and time, and constrained only by individual's imagination and creativity; thus, it facilitates more holistic evaluation of entrepreneurial behavior.

The "unique multilevel nature of entrepreneurial phenomena" is "consistent with the radical Austrian paradigm's subjectivist ontological and epistemological assumptions" (Streb & Gupta, 2011, p. 264). Indeed, scholars embraced the radical subjectivist approach introduced by CBG to investigate complex and dynamic entrepreneurial processes. For example, Elias et al. (2018) applied a radical subjectivist approach to study the process of co-creation between arts entrepreneurs and their customers, highlighting serendipitous value creation from the continuous negotiations between entrepreneurs' desires and expectations and their clients in real time. For these scholars, some entrepreneurial pursuits are perhaps "non-rational, sensible, and embodied" and occur "*between* phenomena, rather than solely *within* human beings" Elias et al. (2018, p. 347).

More broadly, negotiation with clients or competitors is inherent within many nascent industries that emerge from ambiguity. As Gupta et al. (2015, p. 64) demonstrate, uncertainty is a characteristic feature of new industries, and would-be entrepreneurs are forced to "test new ideas that are retained, discarded, or refined, depending on market responses." Firms operating within emerging or otherwise hypercompetitive industries benefit by embracing such dynamic co-creativity. For example, Xerox invented the now-standard computer interface, which Apple then combined with proprietary technology to "[redefine] the trajectory of the computer industry" as a whole (Gupta et al., 2015, p. 72). This dynamic competition, produced by divergence in entrepreneurs' "subjective imagination," left behind a "trail of fossils—material objects that entrepreneurs had mistakenly invested capital with the intention of realizing their plans" (Chiles et al., 2010b, p. 144). The recombination of these "fossils" is only explainable by radical subjectivism and firms' inclination to creatively recombine existing resources.

In short, entrepreneurial endeavors are imaginative, divergent, and "as long as the kaleidoscope is kept in motion, these novel patterns of colors and shapes continually form and dissolve—often incrementally, sometimes abruptly, but always unpredictably" (Chiles et al., 2013, p. 277). As explained by Streb and Gupta (2011, p. 266), "radical subjectivist methodology is grounded in [the] philosophical assumption that realities (plural) emerge from multiple mental concepts grounded in subjective experience and social context"; thus, entrepreneurship researchers have increasingly embraced these methods to explore dynamic phenomena. Our present goal is to systematically map the influence of this body of work over time.

Methods

We conducted a systematic search of Clarivate Analytics' Web of Science and SCOPUS, which are jointly considered to be among the most comprehensive databases within the social sciences (Short, 2009; Vogel & Güttel, 2013). Our primary inclusion criterion was citation to CBG. We followed prior research (David & Han, 2004) and focused our efforts toward publications subjected to substantive peer review; consequently we eliminated book chapters and conference proceedings from our sample.

We also removed articles that were not published in English. Our final sample includes 134 published journal articles.[1]

We leveraged a mixed-method design to investigate the lasting influence of CBG. We first used bibliometric analysis, which is a methodological approach that originated from the field of library and information science, and is receiving increasing attention by the scientific community (Merigó & Yang, 2017). Bibliometrics involves the conversion of demographic information about an article (e.g., authors, keywords, references) into visual maps comprised of individual nodes and clusters (Waltman et al., 2010). Evaluating the overall network density and strength of links between individual nodes and clusters is effective for interpreting the substantive relationship between published articles (Vogel & Güttel, 2013). Using this technique enabled us to better understand which academic work was most influenced by CBG.

While bibliometric analyses examine the artifacts of an article (e.g., reference list), it does not cast light on the actual contents of the articles. To redress this issue, we employed a second method—word cloud representation—to systematically analyze the abstracts of all work within our sample. Word cloud representation is a data visualization method "in which the more frequently used words are highlighted by occupying greater prominence in the representation" (Ertug et al., 2018, p. 1613). For our purpose here, word cloud analysis provided insight regarding the content of work that was inspired by CBG.

Bibliographic Coupling

Bibliographic coupling occurs when two documents have at least one reference in common, in other words, their bibliographies overlap (Kessler, 1963). Researchers can use the degree of overlap between two documents' bibliographies to evaluate the similarity of the authors' research streams. If two documents have heavily overlapped bibliographies, they are presumed to be sourced from the same literature base and to be written for similar audiences. Cited work provides the foundation for future research. Consequently, bibliographic coupling can evaluate the current state of the literature, isolate pockets of productive research,

[1] As one may expect, the number of Google Scholar citations to CBG is much higher. While WOS and GS citation counts tend to be highly correlated (Javadian et al., 2020), GS usually overstates the academic impact of a published article (Gupta & Dutta, 2018).

and in some cases identify future research thrusts (Boyack & Klavans, 2010; Meyer et al., 2014). We employed a coupling technique on the reference lists of all articles within our sample to better understand the conversations to which CBG has contributed.

Word Cloud

Word Cloud is a popular data visualization approach used to highlight textual information by presenting the most frequently used words in the form of a cloud (Dietz, 2016; McNaught & Lam, 2010). These words are emphasized on the basis of their count of appearance such that words appearing more frequently are depicted in growingly larger fonts (Ertug et al., 2018). Several scholars in management (Colquitt, 2013; Evanschitzky & Goergen, 2018; Zhou & Mi, 2017) have used word clouds to illustrate their research findings. Data visualization can help researchers identify commonly appearing themes in the text (Mariano & Awazu, 2016; Zhou & Mi, 2017) or discover thematic similarity and differences across texts by comparing word clouds (Ertug et al., 2018). Thus, to gain insights into the underlying themes and trends in the citing works, we employed word cloud analysis to their titles and abstracts.

There are multiple software options for conducting a word cloud analysis such as programming tools like Python/R (Ertug et al., 2018) or using software like Wordle, NVivo (Zhou & Mi, 2017). To conduct our word cloud analysis, we selected NVivo, an extensively used data analysis and visualization tool for qualitative and mixed-methods assessments. Two separate excel workbooks, one each for titles and abstracts, were compiled. Of the 134 articles, six did not have an abstract available, therefore our analysis is based on 128 papers. We executed the query "Word frequency" in NVivo 12 Plus version to get the top 50 most frequently occurring words, with a minimum length of 3 letters. As advised by prior research (e.g., Arts et al., 2018), our analysis used stemming (i.e., a process that converts words to their roots, so that words such as entrepreneur, entrepreneurs, entrepreneur's, entrepreneurs' are understood as "entrepreneur" by the software) and stop words removal (i.e., the elimination of words that are unrelated to research, such as "and," "the," and "toward").

Results

Our results show that CBG has had broad influence within the academic community. Specifically, 229 scholars representing 157 universities across 31 countries cited CBG in their research. We find that CBG has been especially influential to scholars in the U.S. ($N = 48$), England ($N = 13$), Sweden ($N = 8$), Italy ($N = 7$), and Denmark, China, Finland, and India with six publications each. Additionally, work citing CBG seems to be published broadly across 58 academic journals. We find that many of the publications citing CBG are placed within the field's top journals, namely: *Journal of Business Venturing* ($N = 7$), *Organization Studies* ($N = 7$), *Entrepreneurship Theory & Practice* ($N = 6$), *Strategic Entrepreneurship Journal* ($N = 4$), *Journal of Small Business Management* ($N = 4$), *Journal of Management* ($N = 3$), *Academy of Management Review* ($N = 3$), *Entrepreneurship and Regional Development* ($N = 3$), and the *Academy of Management Journal* ($N = 2$). Figure 3.1 shows the trend in total publications across time.

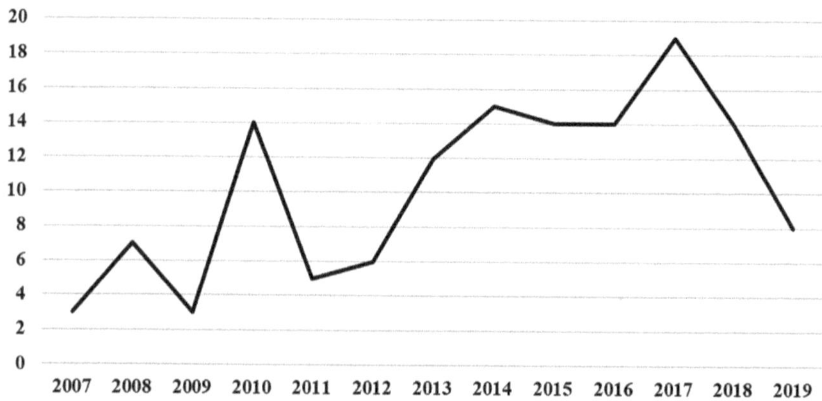

Fig. 3.1 Publications citing CBG

Results of Bibliographic Coupling

The combined bibliography of all articles in our sample includes reference to 7361 works. When we examined the degree of overlap between sampled works' bibliographies, we identified four clusters of research activity. Depicted in Fig. 3.2, these four clusters reveal the primary conversations that are motivated by the work of CBG. We will discuss each briefly in turn.

The first cluster speaks to resource constraints, institutional factors, and contextual or demographic elements of the firm that may coalesce to shape venture growth. Scholars seem to explore CBG's emphasis on creativity and recombination of resources to understand competition within emerging or resource-constrained environments (An et al., 2018). Included are studies of institutional constraints (Adomako et al., 2015) that influence the occurrence of entrepreneurship within developing

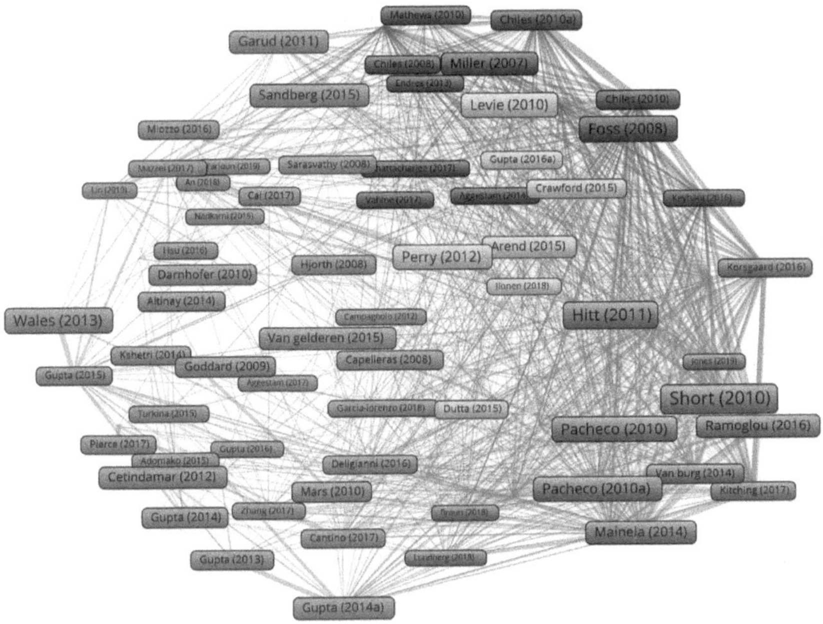

Fig. 3.2 Bibliographic network map (*Note* Only first authors are depicted to improve readability)

economies (e.g., Gupta et al., 2014). In general, scholars within this cluster seem to be interested in studies of firm growth and performance. A notable undercurrent within Cluster 1 is a focus on Entrepreneurial Orientation (Gupta & Gupta, 2015) and its interaction with executive decision-making to influence firm outcomes (Cantino et al., 2017). In summary, Cluster 1 speaks theoretically to the determinants of growth and its implications, and how individuals' creativity enable resource recombination within constrained or developing environments (Capelleras & Greene, 2008; Mazzei et al., 2017).

The second cluster "highlights the source of entrepreneurship in individuals rather than in abstract markets" (Packard, 2017, p. 536). Within this cluster, individuals' imaginativeness is central to the discussion. Specifically, scholars leveraged the insights of CBG to consider ideation and opportunity recognition within the new venture (Kier & McMullen, 2018), international (Mainela et al., 2014), and transnational contexts (Lundberg & Rehnfors, 2018). Relatedly, we find strong evidence within this cluster that CBG shaped scholars' conceptual understanding of entrepreneurial opportunities in general (Kitching & Rouse, 2017; Short et al., 2010).

The third cluster we find is more tailored to the study of radical subjectivism and Lachmannian economics. Here we find work extending that of CBG, including Chiles et al. (2010a, 2010b) who continued to refine the radical Austrian approach to entrepreneurship. Additionally, scholars seem disposed to leveraging CBG in discussing entrepreneurial firms' approach to aggregating heterogenous forms of capital (Foss et al., 2007). Within this stream, researchers have studied subjectivism in concert with resource-based theories to better understand how entrepreneurs acquire and deploy capital (Dolmans et al., 2014; Foss et al., 2008). A final theme within this cluster is the focused study of disequilibrium (Keyhani & Levesque, 2016) and its implications for strategic entrepreneurship (Mathews, 2010).

Finally, the fourth cluster that we identified is focused primarily on the study of entrepreneurial effectuation and causation. Researchers have been inspired by CBG to study the dynamic stages of entrepreneurial growth and development (Levie & Lichtenstein, 2010). Moreover, scholars have cited CBG in their attempts to both differentiate entrepreneurs' decision-making processes (Dutta et al., 2015) and use these insights to further develop the research and practice of entrepreneurship (Gupta et al., 2016; Ilonen et al., 2018). Therefore, our cumulative findings suggest CBG has been broadly influential in conversations of entrepreneurial logic and strategic decision-making.

Results of Word Cloud Analysis

The word frequency query in NVivo software resulted in a summary table, partly shown in Tables 3.1 and 3.2. Table 3.1 lists the top 30 words appearing in the titles of the citing works while Table 3.2 lists the top 30 words appearing in the abstracts. The tables also show the total count of appearances of respective words, their weighted percentage, and words that are counted together after the stemming activity. The complete list of the top 50 words appearing in the title can be seen in Fig. 3.3, while Fig. 3.4 contains the top 50 words in the abstracts of citing works, both illustrated as word clouds. While, as noted earlier, the size of the words in the word cloud depicts the count of appearances of the words, the alignment, vertical or horizontal, has no significance and merely serves an aesthetic purpose.

The word cloud analysis' results of the titles of the citing works, depicted in Table 3.1 and Fig. 3.3, show the importance of conversations around "opportunity," which appears around 26 times in the titles of work citing CBG. This is coherent with the second cluster of bibliometric analysis (Fig. 3.2), in which several papers discuss the relation between opportunity and the idea of entrepreneurship (Kitching & Rouse, 2017; Short et al., 2010). Also, the word "effectuation" appears 11 times, showing that several articles utilized CBG to further the conversation around effectuation (e.g., Arend et al., 2015; Cai et al., 2017), which is further corroborated by results from the fourth cluster of bibliometric analysis. Cumulatively, "creation," "creative," and "innovativeness" find their place in the titles 16 times to indicate the use of CBG in accentuating the role of resource creation and refinement (e.g., Chiles et al., 2010a). Other prominent themes of discussion seem to be centered around development (11 counts) and capital (11 counts). Slightly less occurring, but still dominant, research topics are dynamic capabilities, new ventures, technologies, strategy, and entrepreneurial orientation, which are in line with the clusters depicted in Fig. 3.2.

The analysis of abstracts of citing works, demonstrated in Table 3.2 and Fig. 3.4, also reflects that the focus of a significant number of conversations (e.g., Davidsson, 2015; Pacheco et al., 2010; Ramoglou & Tsang, 2016) is on "opportunity," appearing 119 times. Also, both the titles

Table 3.1 Top 30 high-frequency words appearing in the titles of publications citing CBG

Index	*Word*	*Count*	*Weighted percentage (%)*	*Words considered similar*
1.	Entrepreneurship	54	5.20	Entrepreneurship
2.	Entrepreneurial	39	3.75	Entrepreneurial
3.	Opportunity	26	2.50	Opportunities, opportunity
4.	New	13	1.25	New
5.	Theory	11	1.06	Theories, theory
6.	Effectuation	11	1.06	Effectual, effectuation
7.	Development	11	1.06	Developing, development
8.	Capital	11	1.06	Capital, capitalism
9.	Entrepreneur	10	0.96	Entrepreneur, entrepreneuring, entrepreneurs
10.	Institutional	9	0.87	Institutional, institutions
11.	Business	9	0.87	Business, businesses
12.	Role	8	0.77	Role, roles
13.	Perspective	7	0.67	Perspective
14.	Orientation	7	0.67	Orientation, oriented
15.	Evidence	7	0.67	Evidence, evidences
16.	Creation	7	0.67	Creation
17.	Context	7	0.67	Context, contexts
18.	Venture	6	0.58	Venture, ventures
19.	Technology	6	0.58	Technologies, technology
20.	Strategic	6	0.58	Strategic
21.	Organizations	6	0.58	Organic, organization, organizations, Organizing
22.	International	6	0.58	International
23.	India	6	0.58	India
24.	Future	6	0.58	Future
25.	Firm	6	0.58	Firm, firms
26.	Emerging	6	0.58	Emergence, emergent, emerging
27.	Dynamic	6	0.58	Dynamic, dynamics, dynamism
28.	Capability	6	0.58	Capabilities, capability
29.	Women	5	0.48	Women
30.	Uncertainty	5	0.48	Uncertainties, uncertainty

Table 3.2 Top 30 high-frequency words appearing in the abstracts of publications citing CBG

Index	*Word*	*Count*	*Weighted percentage (%)*	*Words considered similar*
1.	Entrepreneurship	226	1.76	Entrepreneurship, entrepreneurship'
2.	Entrepreneurial	191	1.49	Entrepreneurial, entrepreneurially
3.	Entrepreneur	133	1.04	Entrepreneur, entrepreneuring, entrepreneuring', entrepreneurs, entrepreneurs', entrepreneurs'
4.	Opportunity	119	0.93	Opportunities, opportunity
5.	Develops	102	0.80	Develop, developed, developing, development, developments, develops
6.	Process	97	0.76	Process, processes
7.	New	91	0.71	New
8.	Theory	84	0.66	Theories, theory
9.	Institutions	82	0.64	Institute, institution, institutional, institutions, institutions'
10.	Approach	76	0.59	Approach, approaches
11.	Model	76	0.59	Model, model', modeling, modelled, modelling, models
12.	Findings	72	0.56	Find, findings, finds
13.	Firms	69	0.54	Firm, firms, firms', firms'

(continued)

Table 3.2 (continued)

Index	*Word*	*Count*	*Weighted percentage (%)*	*Words considered similar*
14.	Business	64	0.50	Business, businesses
15.	Capitals	64	0.50	Capital, capitalism, capitals
16.	Implications	61	0.48	Implicated, implication, implications
17.	Manager	61	0.48	Managed, management, manager, managers, managers', managers', managing
18.	Resource	60	0.47	Resource, resources
19.	Examining	59	0.46	Examination, examinations, examine, examined, examines, examining
20.	Limited	53	0.41	Limitation, limitations, limited, limits
21.	Growth	50	0.39	Growth
22.	Industry	50	0.39	Industrial, industrialized, industries, industry
23.	Economic	49	0.38	Economic, economics
24.	Important	48	0.37	Import, importance, important
25.	Venture	47	0.37	Venture, ventures
26.	Knowledge	45	0.35	Knowledge

(continued)

Table 3.2 (continued)

Index	*Word*	*Count*	*Weighted percentage (%)*	*Words considered similar*
27.	Action	44	0.34	Action, actions
28.	Factors	44	0.34	Factor, factors
29.	Results	44	0.34	Result, resulted, resulting, results
30.	Suggest	44	0.34	Suggest, suggested, suggestions, suggests

Fig. 3.3 Word cloud of top 50 high-frequency words appearing in the titles of publications citing CBG

Fig. 3.4 Word cloud of top 50 high-frequency words appearing in the abstracts of publications citing CBG

and abstracts emphasize the contribution of CBG to further discussion on the "theory" of entrepreneurship (e.g., Bylund & McCaffrey, 2017; Packard, 2017), "institutional" constraints (e.g., Gupta et al., 2014), "resource"-based view (e.g., Foss et al., 2008), role of "capital" and "economics" in entrepreneurship (e.g., Klein, 2008; Lewin & Baetjer, 2011), and "growth" and "development" (e.g., Keyhani, 2019; Miozzo & DiVito, 2016). Subsequently, other less prominently visible themes are also identified like "knowledge," "individualism," "women," "emerging" technologies, "markets" and "environment" (e.g., Dutta et al., 2015; Erikson & Korsgaard, 2016; Gupta et al., 2013). Consequently, our findings indicate that CBG has influenced entrepreneurship scholars working in substantially varying fields, while contributing to the literature by bringing new points of discussion and raising important questions worth answering.

Discussion and Conclusion

Our research reveals that CBG provides a unique framework for entrepreneurship research, serving as a rich theoretical contribution from which researchers around the world have examined a number of topic areas. Bibliographic analysis revealed that creative imagination, capital heterogeneity, and resource recombination have all received some attention in the literature building on CBG. Word cloud analysis also showed considerable attention to CBG's idea of creation as central to the entrepreneurial process. At the same time, we did not identify any published attempts to develop measures to capture individual-level creative imagination in the way that researchers have tried to measure alertness as a key entrepreneurial characteristic (Busenitz, 1996; Tang et al., 2012). We see this as an important gap for future research to address and call for efforts to develop survey and archival measures to capture creative imagination at the individual and team level. While creation and discovery are now well-established as two opposing views of entrepreneurial action (Foss & Klein, 2017; Zahra, 2008), much less empirical research has focused on creation relative to discovery. In effect, empirical research on creation lags far behind conceptual development in this area, a notable omission that should be addressed in future research.

We were surprised that CBG's call for historical study of entrepreneurial phenomena has not yet received much attention in the literature. Some researchers have expressed interest in historical approaches to studying entrepreneurship in recent years (Wadhwani et al., 2020). Steven Klepper, who received the 2011 Global Award for Entrepreneurship Research (sometimes described as the Nobel for entrepreneurship researchers), also embraced historical analyses. Yet, the truth is that there is little traction for historically oriented inquiry in entrepreneurship (Jones & Wadhwani, 2006), and few papers that provide historical analyses are published in leading general management or field journals in entrepreneurship. We believe, as CBG noted, the use of methods and techniques from the academic discipline of history can be useful to study entrepreneurial phenomena, and we encourage more research in this area.

A key insight from CBG that we did not see discussed much in the research literature is the notion of expectations. There is considerable academic consensus around the idea of prior knowledge as influencing one's entrepreneurial activity (e.g., Shane, 2000), but CBG called for the application of human subjectivity to expectations about the future. Phelan (2005) called for entrepreneurship to be understood as a process of expectation management, as for example, between buyers and sellers regarding the future value of resources. Our bibliometric analysis and word cloud analysis revealed little enthusiasm for expectations in the extant literature. In other words, the idea of subjective expectations as influencing entrepreneurial activity has failed to gain much traction in the extant literature. We believe it is only by examining expectations that scholars can move beyond the path dependence view that dominates organizational research and instead embrace the possibility of path creation that characterizes entrepreneurial activity (Garud et al., 2010).

We see two other issues worth discussing here. First, Hjorth (2008) observed that the kind of process-oriented, context-rich qualitative research that CBG advocated was well-aligned with the Nordic tradition of entrepreneurship inquiry. Nordic research generally—and admirably—emphasizes "complexity, context, and deep understanding of the data at hand" and encourages researchers to invest in extensive data collection "rather than cranking out papers based on data that are easy to come by" (Davidsson, 2013, p. 106). A systematic exploration of the view of entrepreneurship research put forth by CBG and Nordic entrepreneurship research is outside the scope of the present inquiry, but should be a worthy endeavor for future research. Second, our research revealed CBG ideas influence effectuation research. The extent to which effectuation research can be constructively developed with CBG's disequilibrating paradigm has long attracted attention in the literature (Chiles et al., 2008; Sarasvathy & Dew, 2008). Given recent concerns about the weak epistemological and ontological foundations of effectuation research (Arend et al., 2015; Bylund & Gupta, 2017), CBG may provide the theoretical and methodological tools for clarification and validation of effectual logic in a way that has not been possible so far (Gupta et al., 2016).

In closing, CBG offer a provocative new agenda for entrepreneurship research that has resonated with scholars worldwide (as we found in our review of the extant literature); yet, several aspects of the research agenda that CBG proposed have not adequately informed ongoing inquiry in a meaningful way as we may expect. We hope our research will draw renewed attention toward the kind of passionately curious scholarship advocated by CBG, one that opens novel and exciting avenues for future inquiry about entrepreneurial phenomena.

References

Adomako, S., Danso, A., & Ampadu, E. (2015). Institutional outlook of the entrepreneurial climate in Ghana. *International Journal of Social Economics, 42*(6), 566–582.

Aguinis, H., Cummings, C., Ramani, R. S., & Cummings, T. G. (2020). "An A is an A": The new bottom line for valuing academic research. *Academy of Management Perspectives, 34*(1), 135–154.

Alvarez, S. A., & Barney, J. (2019). Has the concept of opportunities been fruitful in the field of entrepreneurship? *Academy of Management Perspectives*. https://doi.org/10.5465/amp.2018.0014.

An, W., Xu, Y., & Zhang, J. (2018). Resource constraints, innovation capability and corporate financial fraud in entrepreneurial firms. *Chinese Management Studies, 12*(1), 2–18.

Arend, R. J., Sarooghi, H., & Burkemper, A. (2015). Effectuation as ineffectual? Applying the 3E theory-assessment framework to a proposed new theory of entrepreneurship. *Academy of Management Review, 40*(4), 630–651.

Arts, S., Cassiman, B., & Gomez, J. C. (2018). Text matching to measure patent similarity. *Strategic Management Journal, 39*(1), 62–84.

Bello, D. C., & Kostova, T. (2012). From the editors: Conducting high impact international business research: The role of theory. *Journal of International Business Studies, 43*(6), 537–543.

Bergh, D. D., Perry, J., & Hanke, R. (2006). Some predictors of SMJ article impact. *Strategic Management Journal, 27*(1), 81–100.

Boyack, K. W., & Klavans, R. (2010). Co-citation analysis, bibliographic coupling, and direct citation: Which citation approach represents the research front most accurately? *Journal of the Association for Information Science and Technology, 61*(12), 2389–2404.

Busenitz, L. W. (1996). Research on entrepreneurial alertness. *Journal of Small Business Management, 34*(4), 35.

Bylund, P. L., & Gupta, V. K. (2017). Effectuation and the logic of action: A praxeological assessment of effectuation theory. *Frontiers of Entrepreneurship Research, 37*, 16.

Bylund, P. L., & McCaffrey, M. (2017). A theory of entrepreneurship and institutional uncertainty. *Journal of Business Venturing, 32*(5), 461–475.

Cai, L., Guo, R., Fei, Y., & Liu, Z. (2017). Effectuation, exploratory learning and new venture performance: Evidence from China. *Journal of Small Business Management, 55*(3), 388–403.

Cantino, V., Devalle, A., Cortese, D., Ricciardi, F., & Longo, M. (2017). Place-based network organizations and embedded entrepreneurial learning. *International Journal of Entrepreneurial Behavior & Research, 23*(3), 504–523.

Capelleras, J. L., & Greene, F. J. (2008). The determinants and growth implications of venture creation speed. *Entrepreneurship and Regional Development, 20*(4), 317–343.

Chiles, T. H., Bluedorn, A. C., & Gupta, V. K. (2007). Beyond creative destruction and entrepreneurial discovery: A radical Austrian approach to entrepreneurship. *Organization Studies, 28*(4), 467–493.

Chiles, T. H., Elias, S. R., Zarankin, T. G., & Vultee, D. M. (2013). The kaleidic world of entrepreneurs: Developing and grounding a metaphor for creative imagination. *Qualitative Research in Organizations and Management, 8*(3), 276–307.

Chiles, T. H., Gupta, V. K., & Bluedorn, A. C. (2008). On Lachmannian and effectual entrepreneurship: A rejoinder to Sarasvathy and Dew (2008). *Organization Studies, 29*(2), 247–253.

Chiles, T. H., Tuggle, C. S., McMullen, J. S., Bierman, L., & Greening, D. W. (2010a). Dynamic creation: Extending the radical Austrian approach to entrepreneurship. *Organization Studies, 31*(1), 7–46.

Chiles, T. H., Vultee, D. M., Gupta, V. K., Greening, D. W., & Tuggle, C. S. (2010b). The philosophical foundations of a radical Austrian approach to entrepreneurship. *Journal of Management Inquiry, 19*(2), 138–164.

Clark, T. A. R., & Wright, M. (2007). Reviewing journal rankings and revisiting peer reviews: Editorial perspectives. *Journal of Management Studies, 44*(4), 612.

Colquitt, J. (2013). From the editors the last three years at AMJ: Celebrating the big purple tent. *Academy of Management Journal, 56*(6), 1511–1515.

Conlon, D. E., Morgeson, F. P., McNamara, G., Wiseman, R. M., & Skilton, P. F. (2006). From the editors: Examining the impact and role of special issue and regular journal articles in the field of management. *Academy of Management Journal, 49*(5), 857–872.

David, R. J., & Han, S. K. (2004). A systematic assessment of the empirical support for transaction cost economics. *Strategic Management Journal, 25*(1), 39–58.

Davidsson, P. (2013). Some reflection on research 'schools' and geographies. *Entrepreneurship & Regional Development, 25*(1–2), 100–110.

Davidsson, P. (2015). Entrepreneurial opportunities and the entrepreneurship nexus: A re-conceptualization. *Journal of Business Venturing, 30*(5), 674–695.

Davis, M. S. (1971). That's interesting! Towards a phenomenology of sociology and a sociology of phenomenology. *Philosophy of the Social Sciences, 1*(2), 309–344.

Dietz, S. S. (2016). Using Wordle in qualitative research: A supplemental tool for case studies. *International Journal of Instructional Technology and Distance Learning., 13*(8), 23–35.

Dolmans, S. A., van Burg, E., Reymen, I. M., & Romme, A. G. L. (2014). Dynamics of resource slack and constraints: Resource positions in action. *Organization Studies, 35*(4), 511–549.

Dutta, D. K., Gwebu, K. L., & Wang, J. (2015). Personal innovativeness in technology, related knowledge and experience, and entrepreneurial intentions in emerging technology industries: A process of causation or effectuation? *International Entrepreneurship and Management Journal, 11*(3), 529–555.

Earl, P., & Littleboy, B. (2014). *G. L. S. Shackle*. Palgrave Macmillan.

Eckhardt, J. T. (2019). The distinctive domain as a durable way forward. Seminal ideas for the next twenty-five years of advances. In J. A. Katz & A. C. Corbet (Eds.), *Advances in entrepreneurship, firm emergence and growth* (Vol. 21, pp. 21–33). Emerald.

Eckhardt, J. T., & Shane, S. A. (2003). Opportunities and entrepreneurship. *Journal of Management, 29*(3), 333–349.

Elias, S. R., Chiles, T. H., Duncan, C. M., & Vultee, D. M. (2018). The aesthetics of entrepreneurship: How arts entrepreneurs and their customers co-create aesthetic value. *Organization Studies, 39*(2–3), 345–372.

Erikson, T., & Korsgaard, S. (2016). Knowledge as the source of opportunity. *Journal of Business Venturing Insights, 6*, 47–50.

Ertug, G., Gruber, M., Nyberg, A., & Steensma, H. K. (2018). From the editors: A brief primer on data visualization opportunities in management research. *Academy of Management Journal, 61*(5), 1613–1625.

Evanschitzky, H., & Goergen, M. (2018). Looking forward, looking back: British Journal of management 2000–2015. *British Journal of Management, 29*(1), 3–9.

Ferreira, J. J., Fernandes, C. I., & Kraus, S. (2019). Entrepreneurship research: Mapping intellectual structures and research trends. *Review of Managerial Science, 13*(1), 181–205.

Ferreira, M. P. (2011). A bibliometric study on Ghoshal's managing across borders. *Multinational Business Review, 19*, 357–375.

Foss, K., Foss, N. J., Klein, P. G., & Klein, S. K. (2007). The entrepreneurial organization of heterogeneous capital. *Journal of Management Studies, 44*(7), 1165–1186.

Foss, N. J., & Klein, P. G. (2017). Entrepreneurial discovery or creation? In search of the middle ground. *Academy of Management Review, 42*(4), 733–736.

Foss, N. J., Klein, P. G., Kor, Y. Y., & Mahoney, J. T. (2008). Entrepreneurship, subjectivism, and the resource-based view: Toward a new synthesis. *Strategic Entrepreneurship Journal, 2*(1), 73–94.

Garud, R., Kumaraswamy, A., & Karnøe, P. (2010). Path dependence or path creation? *Journal of Management Studies, 47*(4), 760–774.

Gloria-Palermo, S. (1999). *The evolution of the Austrian tradition: From Menger to Lachmann*. Routledge.

Gupta, A., Streb, C. K., Gupta, V. K., & Markin, E. (2015). Entrepreneurial behavior during industry emergence: An unconventional study of discovery and creation in the early PC industry. *New England Journal of Entrepreneurship, 18*(2), 61–79.

Gupta, V. K., Chiles, T. H., & McMullen, J. S. (2016). A process perspective on evaluating and conducting effectual entrepreneurship research. *Academy of Management Review, 41*(3), 540–544.

Gupta, V. K., & Dutta, D. K. . (2018). The rich legacy of Covin and Slevin (1989) and Lumpkin and Dess (1996): A constructive critical analysis of their deep impact on entrepreneurial orientation research. In G. Javadian, V. K. Gupta, D. K. Dutta, C. G. Guo, A. E. Osorio, & B. Ozkazanc-Pan (Eds.), *Foundational research in entrepreneurship studies: Insightful contributions and future pathways* (pp. 155–178). Palgrave Macmillan.

Gupta, V. K., Guo, C., Canever, M., Yim, H. R., Sraw, G. K., & Liu, M. (2014). Institutional environment for entrepreneurship in rapidly emerging major economies: The case of Brazil, China, India, and Korea. *International Entrepreneurship and Management Journal, 10*(2), 367–384.

Gupta, V. K., Guo, C. G., & Ozkazanc-Pan, B. (2018). Introduction. In G. Javadian, V. K. Gupta, D. K. Dutta, C. G. Guo, A. E. Osorio, & B. Ozkazanc-Pan (Eds.), *Foundational research in entrepreneurship studies: Insightful contributions and future pathways* (pp. 1–12). Palgrave Macmillan.

Gupta, V. K., & Gupta, A. (2015). The concept of entrepreneurial orientation. *Foundations and Trends in Entrepreneurship, 11*(2), 55–137.

Gupta, V. K., Turban, D. B., & Pareek, A. (2013). Differences between men and women in opportunity evaluation as a function of gender stereotypes and stereotype activation. *Entrepreneurship Theory and Practice, 37*(4), 771–788.

Hjorth, D. (2008). Nordic entrepreneurship research. *Entrepreneurship Theory and Practice, 32*(2), 313–338.

Ilonen, S., Heinonen, J., & Stenholm, P. (2018). Identifying and understanding entrepreneurial decision-making logics in entrepreneurship education. *International Journal of Entrepreneurial Behavior & Research, 24*(1), 59–80.

Javadian, G., Ellis, C., Gupta, A., Gupta, V. K., & Martin, J. (2020). Qualitative research in entrepreneurship studies: A state-of-science. *Journal of Entrepreneurship, 29*(2), 223–258.

Jennings, J. E., & Brush, C. G. (2013). Research on women entrepreneurs: Challenges to (and from) the broader entrepreneurship literature? *Academy of Management Annals, 7*(1), 663–715.

Jones, G., & Wadhwani, R. D. (2006). *Entrepreneurship and business history: Renewing the research agenda* (HBS Working Paper, No. 07–007).

Kessler, M. M. (1963). Bibliographic coupling extended in time: Ten case histories. *Information Storage and Retrieval, 1*(4), 169–187.

Keyhani, M. (2019). Computational modeling of entrepreneurship grounded in Austrian economics: Insights for strategic entrepreneurship and the opportunity debate. *Strategic Entrepreneurship Journal, 13*(2), 221–240.

Keyhani, M., & Levesque, M. (2016). The equilibrating and disequilibrating effects of entrepreneurship: Revisiting the central premises. *Strategic Entrepreneurship Journal, 10*(1), 65–88.

Kier, A. S., & McMullen, J. S. (2018). Entrepreneurial imaginativeness in new venture ideation. *Academy of Management Journal, 61*(6), 2265–2295.

Kitching, J., & Rouse, J. (2017). Opportunity or dead end? Rethinking the study of entrepreneurial action without a concept of opportunity. *International Small Business Journal, 35*(5), 558–577.

Klein, P. G. (2008). The mundane economics of the Austrian school. *Quarterly Journal of Austrian Economics, 11*(3–4), 165–187.

Leung, K. (2007). The glory and tyranny of citation impact: An East Asian perspective. *Academy of Management Journal, 50*(3), 510–513.

Levie, J., & Lichtenstein, B. B. (2010). A terminal assessment of stages theory: Introducing a dynamic states approach to entrepreneurship. *Entrepreneurship Theory and Practice, 34*(2), 317–350.

Lewin, P. (1997). Capital in disequilibrium: A reexamination of the capital theory of Ludwig M. Lachmann. *History of Political Economy, 29*(3), 523–548.

Lewin, P. (2019). Ludwig Lachmann and the Austrians. *Studies in Logic, Grammar and Rhetoric, 57*(1), 75–89.

Lewin, P., & Baetjer, H. (2011). The capital-based view of the firm. *Review of Austrian Economics, 24*(4), 335–354.

Low, M. B., & MacMillan, I. C. (1988). Entrepreneurship: Past research and future challenges. *Journal of Management, 14*(2), 139–161.

Lundberg, H., & Rehnfors, A. (2018). Transnational entrepreneurship: Opportunity identification and venture creation. *Journal of International Entrepreneurship, 16*(2), 150–175.

Mainela, T., Puhakka, V., & Servais, P. (2014). The concept of international opportunity in international entrepreneurship: A review and a research agenda. *International Journal of Management Reviews, 16*(1), 105–129.

Mariano, S., & Awazu, Y. (2016). Artifacts in knowledge management research: A systematic literature review and future research directions. *Journal of Knowledge Management, 20*(6), 1333–1352.

Mathews, J. A. (2010). Lachmannian insights into strategic entrepreneurship: Resources, activities and routines in a disequilibrium world. *Organization Studies, 31*(2), 219–244.

Mazzei, M. J., Ketchen, D. J., & Shook, C. L. (2017). Understanding strategic entrepreneurship: A "theoretical toolbox" approach. *International Entrepreneurship and Management Journal, 13*(2), 631–663.
McNaught, C., & Lam, P. (2010). Using Wordle as a supplementary research tool. *Qualitative Report, 15*(3), 630–643.
Merigó, J. M., & Yang, J. B. (2017). A bibliometric analysis of operations research and management science. *Omega, 73*, 37–48.
Meyer, M., Grant, K., Morlacchi, P., & Weckowska, D. (2014). Triple Helix indicators as an emergent area of enquiry: A bibliometric perspective. *Scientometrics, 99*(1), 151–174.
Mingers, J., & Lipitakis, E. (2010). Counting the citations: A comparison of Web of Science and Google Scholar in the field of business and management. *Scientometrics, 85*(2), 613–625.
Miozzo, M., & DiVito, L. (2016). Growing fast or slow?: Understanding the variety of paths and the speed of early growth of entrepreneurial science-based firms. *Research Policy, 45*(5), 964–986.
Nightingale, P., & Coad, A. (2014). Muppets and gazelles: Political and methodological biases in entrepreneurship research. *Industrial and Corporate Change, 23*(1), 113–143.
Pacheco, D. F., Dean, T. J., & Payne, D. S. (2010). Escaping the green prison: Entrepreneurship and the creation of opportunities for sustainable development. *Journal of Business Venturing, 25*(5), 464–480.
Packard, M. D. (2017). Where did interpretivism go in the theory of entrepreneurship? *Journal of Business Venturing, 32*(5), 536–549.
Phelan, S. E. (2005). Entrepreneurship as expectations management. *New England Journal of Entrepreneurship, 8*(1), 7.
Phelan, S. E. (2016). Austrian theories of entrepreneurship: Insights from complexity theory. *The Review of Austrian Economics, 29*(3), 277–297.
Podsakoff, P. M., MacKenzie, S. B., Podsakoff, N. P., & Bachrach, D. G. (2008). Scholarly influence in the field of management: A bibliometric analysis of the determinants of university and author impact in the management literature in the past quarter century. *Journal of Management, 34*(4), 641–720.
Ramoglou, S., & Tsang, E. W. (2016). A realist perspective of entrepreneurship: Opportunities as propensities. *Academy of Management Review, 41*(3), 410–434.
Sarasvathy, S. D., & Dew, N. (2008). Is effectuation Lachmannian? A response to Chiles, Bluedorn, and Gupta (2007). *Organization Studies, 29*(2), 239–245.
Schilling, M. A., & Green, E. (2011). Recombinant search and breakthrough idea generation: An analysis of high impact papers in the social sciences. *Research Policy, 40*(10), 1321–1331.
Shackle, L. S. (1972). *Epistemics and economics: A critique of economic doctrines*. Cambridge University Press.

Shane, S. (2000). Prior knowledge and the discovery of entrepreneurial opportunities. *Organization Science, 11*(4), 448–469.

Shane, S. (2012). Reflections on the 2010 AMR decade award: Delivering on the promise of entrepreneurship as a field of research. *Academy of Management Review, 37*(1), 10–20.

Shepherd, D. A. (2015). Party On! A call for entrepreneurship research that is more interactive, activity based, cognitively hot, compassionate, and prosocial. *Journal of Business Venturing, 30*(4), 489–507.

Shepherd, D. A. (2016). *Decision making in entrepreneurship: Selected joint papers of Dean A. Shepherd*. Edward Elgar.

Short, J. (2009). The art of writing a review article. *Journal of Management, 35*(6), 1312–1317.

Short, J. C., Ketchen, D. J., Jr., Shook, C. L., & Ireland, R. D. (2010). The concept of "opportunity" in entrepreneurship research: Past accomplishments and future challenges. *Journal of Management, 36*(1), 40–65.

Storr, V. H. (2019). Ludwig Lachmann's peculiar status within Austrian economics. *The Review of Austrian Economics, 32*(1), 63–75.

Streb, C., & Gupta, V. K. (2011). Methodology of entrepreneurship research in a radical subjectivist paradigm. In *Entrepreneurship, growth and economic development: Frontiers in European entrepreneurship research* (pp. 262–288). Edward Elgar.

Tang, J., Kacmar, K. M. M., & Busenitz, L. (2012). Entrepreneurial alertness in the pursuit of new opportunities. *Journal of Business Venturing, 27*(1), 77–94.

Tihanyi, L. (2020). Academy of Management Journal in 2020 and beyond. *Academy of Management Journal, 63*(1), 1–6.

Vaughn, K. I. (1998). *Austrian economics in America: The migration of a tradition*. Cambridge University Press.

Venkataraman, S. (1997). The distinctive domain of entrepreneurship research: An editor's perspective. In J. A. Katz (Ed.), *Advances in entrepreneurship, firm emergence and growth* (Vol. 3, pp. 119–138). Emerald.

Vogel, R., & Güttel, W. H. (2013). The dynamic capability view in strategic management: A bibliometric review. *International Journal of Management Reviews, 15*(4), 423–446.

Wadhwani, R. D., Kirsch, D., Welter, F., Gartner, W. B., & Jones, G. G. (2020). Context, time, and change: Historical approaches to entrepreneurship research. *Strategic Entrepreneurship Journal, 14*(1), 3–19.

Waltman, L., van Eck, N. J., & Noyons, E. C. (2010). A unified approach to mapping and clustering of bibliometric networks. *Journal of Informetrics, 4*(4), 629–635.

Wiklund, J., Davidsson, P., Audretsch, D. B., & Karlsson, C. (2011). The future of entrepreneurship research. *Entrepreneurship Theory and Practice, 35*(1), 1–9.

Wiklund, J., Wright, M., & Zahra, S. A. (2019). Conquering relevance: Entrepreneurship research's grand challenge. *Entrepreneurship Theory and Practice, 43*(3), 419–436.

Zahra, S. A. (2008). The virtuous cycle of discovery and creation of entrepreneurial opportunities. *Strategic Entrepreneurship Journal, 2*(3), 243–257.

Zhou, Z., & Mi, C. (2017). Social responsibility research within the context of megaproject management: Trends, gaps and opportunities. *International Journal of Project Management, 35*(7), 1378–1390.

CHAPTER 4

A Reflection on "Emerging Issues in Corporate Entrepreneurship" by Dess, Ireland, Zahra, Floyd, Janney, and Lane (2003, JOM)

Qin Yang and Grace Chun Guo

Introduction

Dess et al. (2003) anchor their work on the early definition of CE as presented by Sharma and Chrisman (1999). Accordingly, CE is understood as "[...] the process whereby an individual or a group of individuals, in association with an existing organization, create a new organization or instigate renewal or innovation within that organization" (p. 18). The connection with the work of Sharma and Chrisman (1999) allows

Q. Yang (✉)
Robert Morris University, Moon Township, PA, USA
e-mail: yang@rmu.edu

G. C. Guo
Sacred Heart University, Fairfield, CT, USA
e-mail: chun-guog@sacredheart.edu

A. E. Osorio et al. (eds.), *Modern Classics in Entrepreneurship Studies*,
https://doi.org/10.1007/978-3-030-61029-6_4

Dess et al. (2003) to build their research on the basis of organizational learning theory. This framework is core to the CE argument; when firms initiate CE activities, they are exposed to "new and diverse stimuli" which "induces experimentation" and "foster learning by doing" in the whole process (p. 352). In other words, effective CE is "a knowledge enabler" (p. 353) that allows firms to develop new knowledge and innovations to outperform their competitors. Through these ideas, Dess et al. (2003) identify the relationship between CE and new knowledge creation and the mediating role of organizational learning, highlighting the importance of entrepreneurial leadership and its role in fostering social exchanges across multiple levels of management to further stimulate (or impede) organizational learning in firms' domestic and international operations. Further, Dess et al. (2003) point out that special attention should be directed to how social, human, and intellectual capital could compel these outcomes. The impact of Dess et al.'s (2003) article is evident in recent empirical studies on the content and structure of CE, the leadership role in promoting CE, as well as in CE and internationalization, and CE engaged by emerging market firms. Below we provide a specific discussion on Dess et al.'s (2003) article in each of these four research streams and its impact on later CE research.

Stream 1: The Mediating Role of Organizational Learning & CE

Based on the knowledge-based view, Dess et al. (2003) propose that organizational learning (i.e., acquisitive learning and experimental learning) mediates the relationship between different forms of CE and the development of new knowledge components (i.e., technical, integrative, and exploitative knowledge). Hence, the firms' CE efforts vary with the four types of CE forms: (1) sustained regeneration, (2) organizational rejuvenation, (3) strategic renewal, and (4) domain redefinition. Matching the four types of CE forms, the firms' four categories of efforts include product innovation, process and administrative innovation, exploitation of existing opportunities to reposition, and exploration of new areas.

Taking a closer look at the relationships between CE forms and efforts, Dess et al. propose that the different types of CE efforts impact organizational learning differently. For instance, sustained regeneration has a stronger effect on acquisitive learning rather than on experimental learning. Moreover, to maximize the benefit of the new knowledge components, different implementation focuses (i.e., leveraging knowledge, recombining and extending knowledge, and importing new knowledge to value-creating activities) are required. For instance, when firms apply new technical knowledge, the implementation focus should be on how to leverage knowledge; when firms apply new integrative knowledge, the focus should be on recombining and extending knowledge; and when firms apply exploitative knowledge, the focus should be on importing new knowledge to value-creating activities. While insightful, these propositions from Dess et al. (2003) still need to be tested empirically, thus generating avenues of research that can extend the explanatory power of CE.

Stream 2: Entrepreneurial Leadership & CE

By viewing CE as a system of managerial roles and social exchange, Dess et al. (2003) argue that entrepreneurial leadership plays an important role in resolving conflicts between firms' old and new priorities and in managing the organizational learning process. Dess et al. (2003) maintain that the pursuit of different CE types requires aligned managerial acceptance of new initiatives and change efforts at the top, middle, and operational levels of organizations. Nine strategic roles (e.g., directing, recognizing, implementing, synthesizing and facilitating, conforming, experimenting, and so on) performed by managers are categorized within three levels. These nine roles facilitate CE efforts as they involve information processing and action taking within the organization. Further, these strategic roles can promote CE by creating sub-processes, including competence deployment, modification, and definition. The combination of these sub-processes drives the four types of CE. For example, firms engaged in sustained regeneration and aimed to develop a steady source of new product introductions can be best supported by a combination of competence deployment and competence modification. Moreover, as roles and role expectations of managers determine how well the organizations engage in CE activities, it is necessary to reduce strategic role conflicts within organizations themselves. Dess et al. (2003) further suggest that three control mechanisms (i.e., bureaucratic, clan, and market controls) may help to develop dominant logic consensus and to enhance trust among managers across all organizational levels. Dess et al. (2003) further argue that only when the three control mechanisms align with the corresponding CE types, role dissensus can be addressed, and organizational trust could be reinforced to deal with the uncertainties in CE. These ideas, although intuitive, require further corroboration, thus creating the opportunity for an extended research agenda in this stream.

Stream 3: Global Markets & CE

Dess et al. (2003) maintain that "global markets require companies to be entrepreneurial in deciding when, how, and where to expand international" (p. 363). Hence CE provides an opportunity to establish new ventures in the internationalization of the established companies. Dess et al. (2003) develop a two-by-two (content vs. process and new venture vs. established companies) typology to categorize studies done on CE and internationalization. In their typology, Dess et al. (2003) maintain that while there is some research on the content of new ventures' international efforts, there is no study examining startup firms' entrepreneurial activities after they go international. As to the entrepreneurial processes of new ventures (global startups), the lack of systematic investigation on the different types of CE and their impact on the evolution, growth, and outcome of these firms presents an interesting research opportunity.

Furthermore, the evidence of the link between startups' CE activities and organizational learning is missing. Some researchers propose that CE is positively related to the successful performance of multinational corporations (MNCs). However, how firms apply CE to leverage their capabilities in internationalization to achieve superior performance remains unclear. As to the processes of CE in MNCs, Dess et al. (2003) summarize three dominant themes: managers' roles in stimulating and fostering CE; leveraging subsidiary knowledge to the overall organization; and the effect of national culture on CE. In sum, Dess et al. (2003) consider that the association between CE and internationalization is an emerging subject and provides suggestions for future research in this stream.

Stream 4: Multiple Measures of Economic Outcomes Should Be Included in the CE Research

To develop an in-depth understanding of CE, Dess et al. (2003) discuss the importance of reassessing the dependent variables in the CE literature. In concrete, Dess et al. (2003) argue that multiple measures of economic outcomes such as profitability and sales growth should be included in the

CE research. Furthermore, Dess et al. (2003) suggest that more sophisticated measures, such as economic value added (EVA) and market value added (MVA) should also be considered when measuring the financial performance of the new ventures. Researchers need to pay close attention to the lag effects to reflect the temporal nature of the outcomes of CE initiatives, such as investment in R&D and new product development.

In addition, Dess et al. (2003) propose that the stakeholder perspectives should be incorporated in the CE research and that the balanced scorecard approach could provide important implications for how to study CE activities that must satisfy criteria weighted differently by different stakeholders. This approach's problem is "ignoring the learning outcomes of the various CE types" (p. 371). Dess et al. (2003) argue that learning requires different capital, and they discuss the increasing role of different forms of capital (human, social, and intellectual) in the context of CE research and new ventures. Testing the validity of these ideas call for future research in this stream.

A Modern Jewel in Entrepreneurship: Impact and Highlights

Dess et al. (2003) research proposes important emerging issues in CE based on the organizational learning theory. This work points out gaps in the literature while providing new directions for researchers. The 981 google citations (as of August 15, 2020) show how Dess et al. (2003) have inspired many scholars to conduct studies on the related topics of CE later. The following sections introduce some valuable research development based on the emerging issues they suggest.

Theoretical and Empirical Development of CE Forms, Organizational Learning, Knowledge, and Implementation

As organizations are considered as a collective entity of learning, it is recognized that organizational capabilities of knowledge management determine how successful their entrepreneurial activities are. More research has been done on studying the relationships among CE forms, organizational learning, knowledge, and implementation in recent years. For example, in 2009, the *Journal of Business Venturing* (JBV) published a special issue on CE to enrich our understanding of CE with the advanced theoretical background and empirical findings. This special issue was largely built on Dess et al.'s (2003) work. The co-editors Phan et al. (2009) called for more research on the processes and knowledge-based resources and capabilities involved in CE. Studies included in this special issue examined issues such as types of organizational learning (Burgers et al., 2009), capability development (Yang et al., 2009), managerial roles (Hornsby et al., 2009), and the relationship between the board of directors and absorptive capability in threshold firms (Zahra et al., 2009). In addition, other scholars (e.g., Guo et al., 2014; Yiu et al., 2007) empirically test how CE provides firms in emerging markets a viable means to transit into market-oriented ones and catch up with their global competitors. Some empirical studies have examined CE as resource capital configuration (e.g., Yiu & Lau, 2008) while also providing evidence of the impact of transformational leaders on promoting CE (e.g., Ling et al., 2008).

More recently, Nielsen (2015) uses the framework of Dess et al. (2003) to perform a comprehensive analysis of the interdependent relationship among CE, organizational learning, knowledge, and implementation. She suggests that "knowledge is not only a result of organizational learning and CE but also the trigger of future entrepreneurial activities" (p. 199). Two major forms of CE are categorized: creating new ventures and strategic entrepreneurship (Nielsen, 2015). The former form includes expansion of existing business portfolio by creating "ventures in new areas of competence, adding up new, but related business activities, as well as investing in external promising startups" (p. 202), internal corporate ventures, and external joint ventures. The latter form incorporates strategic initiatives ranging from strategic renewal to sustainable regeneration to business domain redefinition to organizational rejuvenation to business model restructuring. These wide ranges of initiatives may or may not lead to the creation of new ventures (Morris et al., 2011). Nielsen (2015) agrees that organizational learning is a key step to transform CE into knowledge and superior performance. Still, Nielsen (2015) does not elaborate on how each type of CE form may affect the learning types. Except for the acquisitive type (learning before doing) and experimental (learning by doing) type of learning, Nielsen (2015) empathizes the importance of an organization nurturing learning. In other words, organizations should establish a system to incorporate "intuition, the interpretation, integration and institutionalization of knowledge at the individual, group and organization levels" (p. 204). Nielsen (2015) points out that a learning organization has shared leadership, a culture of innovation, a strategic focus on customers, organic organizational design, and intensive use of information. Further, she suggests that organizational learning creates knowledge through the interaction of employees' cognitive structure and the learning contexts. This "experimental learning is believed to have a superior positive effect since it is built upon organizational experience. Experimental learning contributes to the development of the knowledge base and human resources, it is unique and complicated to replicate" (Nielsen, 2015, p. 207). She argues that technical knowledge mainly results from acquisitive learning, integrative knowledge from the joint effect of acquisitive and experimental learning, and exploitative knowledge from the effective implementation of technical and integrative knowledge, which is slightly different from the propositions of Dess et al. (2003). The implementation of technical knowledge corresponds to product line extension, integrative knowledge to new platform development, and exploitative knowledge to new business creation. In sum, Nielsen's (2015) study provides an in-depth elaboration of Dess et al.'s framework.

Turner and Pennington (2015) empirically examined how CE enables innovation to emerge through organizational learning within organization networks. Turner and Pennington suggest that "CE offers a mechanism for organizations to cope with increasing complexity and high-velocity change in the external environment through continual exploration, exploitation, and internal adaption where innovation, or the development of knowledge that can be translated into new products, services, processes, administrative systems, or programs pertaining to an organization, its affiliates, and customers, lies at the heart of its practice" (p. 448). Thus, they examine the whole mechanism from CE antecedents, information processing, knowledge sharing, and organizational learning to innovation. By adopting a MOA (Motivation, Opportunity, and Ability) framework, Turner and Pennington (2015) effectively explain how long-term initiatives could drive organizational learning and predict entrepreneurial implementation in the presence of knowledge. First, they indicate that CE information processing is dependent on CE antecedents (CE structural variables), which include such factors as individual or unit's performance and rewards, competitive intensity, entrepreneurial beliefs, values, and attitudes; management support, organizational structure, worker autonomy, organizational culture; work discretion, know-how/capability, resources, time availability, and relationship. Then, the MOA framework (CE functional variables) is applied to explain the information processing and to integrate the multi-level factors like the environmental stimulus, internal coordination, and organizational desire to capture the essence of CE behavior. Next, they develop hypotheses about the long-term orientation of CE, MOA, knowledge sharing, and organizational learning. Using survey data collected from 200 franchise operators of a single large hybrid organization, Turner and Pennington (2015) find that the long-term orientation is positively associated with MOA; motivation and opportunity enhance knowledge sharing; and knowledge sharing leads to organizational learning and thus the outcome. In sum, different from Dess et al. (2003), Turner and Pennington (2015) investigate CE initiatives with structural and process approaches, which complement the tools of traditional measures of CE. Besides, they prove the roles of organizational learning and knowledge in the context of CE empirically, corresponding to the call of research directions of Dess et al. (2003).

Entrepreneurial Leadership: The Roles of Control, Consensus, and Trust

After Dess et al. (2003) identified entrepreneurship leadership as an emerging research trend, more research has paid attention to the CE context's strategic leaders. As Morris et al. (2011) have described, CE is "a vision-mediated process where change must be institutionalized as the organization's goal" (p. 454). Organizations should take a long-term orientation fueling by persistent transformation (Turner & Pennington, 2015). Corporate transformation requires an integrative leadership support and employees' engagement (Kuratko & Hoskinson, 2019) because "Corporate entrepreneurial activity involves the firm and its managers' use of new resources, interactions with new customers, involvements with new markets and/or with new combinations of its existing resource portfolio, customer base, and served markets" (Kuratko & Neubert, 2019, p. 90).

Since lack of managerial coordination at all levels within the organization is an important barrier for CE, Hornsby et al. (2009) suggest that alignments should be created in evaluation and reward systems to achieve consensus in the CE initiatives and behavior across organizational levels. Hornsby et al. (2009) examine the relationship of perceived CE antecedents (management support, work discretion, rewards and reinforcement, time availability, flexible organizational boundaries) and CE implementation at different management levels (senior, middle, and first levels). After analyzing a sample of 458 managers, Hornsby et al. (2009) find that managers at different levels play different roles by providing more or less structural ability to implement CE initiatives. Their results also find that senior and middle-level managers have greater structural ability to provide entrepreneurial conditions and implement CE ideas than first-level managers, which "offer a counter-weight to this "bottom–up" process" (p. 238). The bottom-up process explains that innovations usually initiate from a lower level to a higher level. This study proves that, in general, CE can be applied to all level managers. It confirms the importance of managerial roles in the CE context, especially "managers at higher levels were better able to make the most of top management support and of work discretion." (Hornsby et al., 2009, p. 244). It advances our understanding of entrepreneurship leadership and the CE process with some empirical evidence.

Responding to calls for "more research into the role of personal and organizational networks in CE" (Dess et al., p. 307), Glaser et al. (2015) study why and how the hierarchical differences influenced managers' capability to foster strategic renewal in their business units. Managers play different roles in CE activities based on their positions within the organizational hierarchy (e.g., Hornsby et al., 2009; Ireland et al., 2009). Managers' accessible authority and resources in the CE contexts may vary, and their effect on CE implementation is different. Glaser et al. (2015) investigate the impact of boundary-spanning at top and middle-level managers on CE's strategic renewal form. Exploratory innovation of business units, which refers to experimenting with new product-market combinations and building new skills and capabilities, is the key underlying activity of strategic renewal. Taking a configurational perspective of social exchanges at multiple levels, Glaser et al. (2015) analyze data collected from 72 top managers (TMs) and 397 middle managers (MMs) operating in 34 units of a multinational organization. Results show that TMs have a greater structural ability to leverage boundary-spanning activities and implement CE ideas than MMs. Glaser et al. (2015) find that TMT's boundary-spanning activities spur MMs' role conflict due to information asymmetry, signal confusion, and inconsistent expectations. MMs' role conflict is negatively related to exploratory innovation. Last, fit in terms of overlapping boundary-spanning ties between TMs and MMs reduces the conflict and helps to coordinate the joint efforts to initiate and implement exploratory innovation. Glaser et al.'s study not only furthers the empirical testing of managers' roles and CE form but also examines the interaction of managers across different levels. It proves the top-down perspective on CE suggested by Hornsby et al. (2009) and assesses the cascading effect of roles and activities at one hierarchical level on roles and activities at other levels. In sum, this research provides empirical evidence of the relationship between managers' roles and CE forms. It proves that dominant consensus and alignment across different levels of managers contribute to CE implementation.

Yuan et al. (2017) examine how CEOs' perceptions towards ambivalent environmental changes affect CE activities. Based on the heuristic-systematic model and an information processing perspective, they analyze data from 170 firms in China during the global economic crisis since 2008 and find that firms' market capabilities moderate the relationship between ambivalence and CE. That is, organizations with strong market capabilities are more likely to adopt CE when their CEOs perceive environmental change ambivalent. Just as Dess et al. (2003) suggest, the strong market capabilities may help managers evaluate new ideas and opportunities with objective criteria and address the potential role conflict in competence definition.

Some research focuses on the control mechanisms, and their roles in CE as control systems not only provide strategic directions to CE efforts but also exert influence on strategic implementation through resource utilization and behavior monitoring. Morris et al. (2006) empirically test the relationship between the control system and CE. They identify three control dimensions (administrative formality/informality, managerial flexibility/inflexibility, budgetary tightness/looseness) and link them with firms' level of entrepreneurial orientation, which is measured with innovativeness, risk-taking, and proactiveness. Their findings empirically support the effect of control systems on CE. Moreover, the relationships are complex, and intermediate or balanced control systems (intermediate informality, high discretion, and intermediate budgetary) are more conducive to CE.

CE in International Firms

Dess et al. (2003) note that many studies emphasize the internationalization process rather than entrepreneurial issues in the literature of CE in large MNEs. In recent years, this condition has been much improved. For instance, Luo et al. (2005) investigate the innovation, venturing, and proactiveness of some Chinese firms, and their results show that joint venture firms engage in more CE activities than traditional state-owned firms. In other words, international presence makes firms more active in taking entrepreneurial activities. Some recognize that continued internationalization requires a high-level resource commitment and a proactive attitude towards opportunities, leading to risk-taking behavior (e.g., Barringer et al., 2005; De Clercq et al., 2005; Johanson & Vahlne, 2006). As CE acts as a configurational mechanism to mediate the relationship of external resources and firm performance (Yiu & Lau, 2008), emerging market firms use international growth to leverage, link and learn to overcome resource advantages, and develop new products (Jiang et al., 2016).

Except for a few studies, not much progress has been made to unfold the content and CE process in new ventures (international startups or small firms). Naldi et al. (2015) conduct a study on how established small and medium-sized enterprises (SMEs) carry out CE in international markets based on Stevenson's opportunity-based conceptualization of entrepreneurial management (Stevenson, 1984; Stevenson & Gumpert, 1985; Stevenson & Jarillo, 1990). Stevenson's framework depicts six key dimensions of entrepreneurial management: management structure, reward philosophy, strategic orientation, growth orientation, resource orientation, and entrepreneurial culture. Naldi et al. (2015) hypothesize that these dimensions of entrepreneurial management enhance SMEs' CE in foreign markets. The international CE activities are measured by new international market development and new product development in international markets. Collecting data from 111 Swedish SMEs with international operations across three years, they find that entrepreneurial management structure, strategic orientation, and culture affect international CE positively, while resource orientation and reward system impact international CE negatively. These results highlight how important it is for SMEs to engage in CE activities to pursue opportunities overseas. In addition, international CE requires a higher level of resource commitment than international entrepreneurship (initial international activities).

In sum, this study tests how SMEs foster CE activities in the international markets, extending our understanding of the international CE content of startup or small firms.

Lee and Williams (2007) develop a new theoretical perspective on dispersed entrepreneurship in established large MNCs. Considering MNCs as entrepreneurial communities, this research not only investigates how knowledge in entrepreneurial initiatives is created, shared, and utilized but also the antecedents and consequences of these communities in MNCs. Through these communities, knowledge and ideas are created and shared in the intra- and inter-MNC networks, which promote the entrepreneurial spirit and organizational capabilities. Lee and Williams (2007) propose four stages of the entrepreneurial community evolvement. First, the antecedents of the community formation: the existence of dispersed individuals who are willing to participate in idea generation and knowledge sharing in various geographical locations; second, high-boundary porosity (the ease that dispersed actors come together), which allows dispersed actors to form a group with a focal idea or opportunity; third, community development, which includes changing members (joining, leaving, and changing of participation intensity) and constant refining of focal idea and boundary porosity; and four, legacy stage, which means as an entrepreneurial community dissolves, residues are deployed for new community practice. The first two stages explain the pre-conditions of the entrepreneurial community. If the perceived opportunities by the dispersed actors cannot achieve a critical mass, the community dissolves quickly. During the third stage, when critical community mass in terms of alignment between the focal point and members is achieved, the approval and investment proceed, and learning becomes tangible and embedded. If the alignment cannot be achieved, the investment is not gained even though knowledge flows still occur across borders. At stage four, the consequence is the establishment of the MNC-external environment interface. This "conceptualization of the entrepreneurial community is consistent with the heterarchical view of the MNC" (Lee & Williams, 2007, p. 514), that is, knowledge may be generated from any MNC domains like "local-internal, global/regional-internal, local-external, and global/regional-external" (Lee & Williams, 2007, p. 515). It also indicates that organizational learning is a key outcome of CE in MNCs. And managers in MNCs can promote CE "(1) by allowing high-boundary porosity situations, (2) by supporting associate membership, and (3) by identifying and nurturing community leaders" (Lee & Williams, 2007, p. 516). This study extends the research on the CE process in established MNCs by exploring the evolvement path of the entrepreneurial community.

Later Williams and Lee (2011) develop another work on entrepreneurship within MNCs based on knowledge coordination. They comprise two dimensions of entrepreneurship (headquarter driven/dispersed unit driven; internal resources/external resources used in the entrepreneurial endeavor) and develop a framework of four entrepreneurship activity contexts; then the difference of knowledge (knowledge of opportunities, knowledge of the solution, learning from outcomes of initiatives) is identified for each different context. Finally, they propose the following elements that make inter-contextual knowledge coordination occur: "interdependence with strategic partners, embeddedness in local host country networks, internal empowerment of subsidiaries, and brokering of knowledge arising in external contexts" (Williams & Lee, 2011, p. 261). This article focuses on the interaction of headquarters and subsidiaries in multiple entrepreneurship contexts and how entrepreneurial knowledge coordination takes place in MNCs.

Webb et al. (2010) examine the entrepreneurship process in the base of the pyramid (BOP) markets, which are usually located in the least developed countries or rural regions of developing countries and characterized with high inter-and intra-institutional distance, formal institutional voids, and high knowledge gaps. They suggest that entrepreneurial activities through which MNCs move from one CE stage to another stage are quite different when they operate in the BOP markets. These MNCs "do not discover opportunities but rather create them (Alvarez & Barney, 2007) as they exploit ideas, incorporate feedback, learn, and transform ideas into opportunities" (Webb et al., 2010, p. 574). This opportunity creation process usually involves local individuals and entities, and Webb et al. (2010) suggest that non-government organizations (NGO) serve a vital role in helping MNCs' opportunity recognition and exploitation through NGOs' knowledge of the local environment and their local networks. This article enriches our understanding of MNCs' CE process in different host country contexts, which is not quite focused on by many researchers.

Multiple Measurements of CE Outcome and the Roles of Capital

Entrepreneurship benefits firms to not only achieve innovations and financial success but also create values for consumers and wealth for stakeholders. At the social level, it could improve local economic growth and employment and help technology advancement (Ireland & Webb, 2007). As a result, organizational performance metrics measuring stakeholder value attract the attention of entrepreneurship scholars (e.g., Heath & Palenchar, 2009). Stakeholder value usually measures "the degree to which corporate activities generate value for key stakeholders such as customers, buyers, suppliers, local government, community residents, and the natural environment" (Shahzad et al., 2016, p. 273).

Responding to Dess et al.'s (2003) call for exploring CE outcomes with a balanced scorecard approach, Shahzad et al. (2016) study the effect of firm entrepreneurial orientation on stakeholder value. Entrepreneurial orientation captures a firm's entrepreneurial posture, management philosophy, and behavioral or practice directions. In their work, Shahzad et al. (2016) consider stakeholder values as "corporate activities directed towards managing relations with stakeholders" (p. 278). Five primary stakeholders groups are identified, including: "community relations (e.g., charitable giving, support for education and housing, compliance with federal, state, or local government), employee relations (e.g., worker health and safety plus union issues), product quality (a proxy for customer relations), workforce diversity (e.g., record on minority discrimination, treatment of the differently abled), and environmental performance" (Shahzad et al., 2016, p. 278). Following previous empirical research, a composite measure of stakeholder value is adopted. After analyzing 1015 public US firms, they conclude that higher innovativeness, risk-taking and proactiveness are positively associated with stakeholder value. This research advances the literature on non-financial outcomes of entrepreneurship and provides empirical support of CE's benefits to stakeholders.

The role of multiple forms of capital in CE has also attracted increasing attention. For instance, De Clercq et al. (2013) analyze data from the managers of 232 firms and find that the two aspects of social capital (goal congruence and trust) enhanced internal knowledge sharing, which result in high levels of entrepreneurial orientation measured by innovation, proactiveness, and risk-taking. Empirical support shows that consensus and trust among managers improve knowledge sharing due to the uncertainty decrease of managerial interactions.

Alpkan et al. (2010) explore how human capital plays a moderating role in the relationship between the internal supportive environment and CE activities. Human capital is a key indicator of organizational learning since it indicates the knowledge, skills, and abilities embedded in individuals and contributes to firms' competence of entrepreneurship. Using data from 184 manufacturing firms in Turkey, Alpkan et al. (2010) test the moderating effect of human capital on the relationship between supportive organizational environment (i.e., management support, time availability, work discretion/organizational structures, incentives and rewards, and tolerance for risk-taking) and firm innovative performance, which is measured with items on product and process innovations. Results show that an organizational supportive environment has a strong effect on innovative performance when the human capital is low, but when both human capital and supportive environment are high, the increase of innovativeness is not significant. They draw an implication that human capital may be complementary to a supportive environment when managers have limited time and resources to improve CE outcomes.

Mehdivand et al. (2012) investigate the relationship of intellectual capital, entrepreneurial orientation, and firm performance by analyzing 91 Iranian nano-businesses. They adopt the definition of intellectual capital as "the total stocks of all intangible assets and capabilities in a company" (Mehdivand et al., 2012, p. 148). Three basic dimensions of intellectual capital are examined: human capital, which refers to employees' knowledge, skills, experiences, capabilities, and so on; structural capital, which is "the sum of all non-human storehouses of knowledge" (Mehdivand et al., 2012, p. 148); and relational capital, which represents intangible assets embedded in external associations such as customers, suppliers, and so on. Mehdivand et al. (2012) argue that intellectual capital affects entrepreneurial orientation and performance directly because it can increase firms' knowledge-based resources and organizational readiness for entrepreneurial activities, thus improving CE. In addition, as a most important intangible asset, intellectual capital impacts how resources are managed and developed as well as how the stakeholders' interests are leveraged, both of which determine business performance. They measure customer performance (customer acquisition and retention) and product performance (sales and market share of products). Results show that entrepreneurial orientation mediates the relationship between intellectual capital and firm performance. Human capital and relational capital affect firm performance both directly and indirectly, while structural capital only affects firm performance through entrepreneurial orientation. This article not only measures the firms' entrepreneurial performance from a stakeholder perspective but also explains how intellectual capital affected entrepreneurship in established firms.

Final Thoughts

Taken together, Dess et al. (2003) provide promising directions for research in CE. As we discussed above, researchers have been working towards these directions. We observe some further development of CE research related to the four streams. However, much is concentrated on organizational learning and entrepreneurial leadership. The research on internationalization is much less, in which CE in MNCs get more focus than CE in global startups. The process study of CE and internationalization is also in short. As to the CE outcome from a stakeholder perspective, we see little work except for the ones we mentioned above (Heath & Palenchar, 2009; Shahzad et al., 2016). In the following section, we summarize more research development in the four streams and then develop some potential research directions for the future.

Some Further Research Development in the Four Streams

Some researchers incorporate environmental factors in the relationship of CE and organizational learning. Sambrook and Roberts (2005) highlight the dynamic interrelated relationship of four key elements: CE, organizational learning, change of external environment (e.g., economic, social-cultural, technological environment, etc.), and change of internal environment (e.g., strategy, structure, organizational culture, etc.). They suggest examining CE and organizational learning from broad, multilevel, and dynamic perspectives. Some further investigate a reciprocal relationship between CE and inter-organizational learning. For instance, Thorgren et al. (2009) obtain empirical support that firms with a high level of CE stimulate high knowledge transfer among inter-firm networks, and extensive knowledge transfer provides more opportunities and resources for individual firms to take entrepreneurial activities. Evidently these researchers attempt to incorporate more factors in studying CE, organizational learning, and knowledge in the CE process.

Some research on entrepreneurial leadership shift focus to the underlying mechanisms of how leadership impacts CE. Chen and Nadkarni (2017) provide empirical support that CEO's temporal dispositions (time urgency and pacing style) directly influence temporal leadership (how top managers manage temporal aspects of their activities), and thus firm CE activities. Ling et al. (2008) empirically test that transformational CEOs impact TMTs' behavioral integration, risk propensity, decentralization of responsibilities, and long-term compensation affect firm CE consequently. Shafique and Kalyar (2018) find transformational leadership affects CE positively both directly and through absorptive capacity. Chen et al. (2014) prove that CE mediates the relationship between CEOs' transformational leadership and firm innovation performance. In addition, technology orientation moderates the CEOs' transformational leadership-CE linkage significantly. Heavy and Simsek (2013) examine TMT composition's impact in terms of human capital and social capital on CE. More, Heavy and Simsek (2013) test whether a team's level of perceived technological uncertainty moderates the TMT effect on CE. They find that smaller size TMT are more likely to engage in CE, which could be explained by easy-to-make consensus, more agile and focused, and thus more efficient.

Only a few researchers further explore CE in established MNCs. Boone et al. (2019) connect strategic leadership and CE in MNCs and underscore the importance of corporate headquarters and TMTs. After analyzing MNCs from 20 countries across ten years, Boone et al. (2019) figure out that TMTs with diverse nationalities engage more in CE and lead to better innovation performance only in such circumstances as equal distribution of power and low hierarchy. Some focus on the contribution of subsidiaries' entrepreneurship (e.g., Scott et al., 2010). O'Brien et al. (2019) argue that subsidiary managers are the key actors to translate the benefits of subsidiary entrepreneurship for CE outcomes. Specifically, O'Brien et al. (2019) prove that subsidiary managers' micro-level activities help realize the benefits of subsidiary entrepreneurship by facilitating subsidiary adaptability and enabling embeddedness in the local environment.

There is still a lack of research on CE performance with measurements of stakeholders. Zellweger and Nason (2008) suggest that different performance outcomes are interrelated. Zellweger and Nason (2008) extract four stakeholder levels of analysis (individual, family, organization, and society) and categorize four types of performance relationships (overlapping, causal, synergistic, and substitutional). They conclude that understanding the performance relationships can help to increase organizational effectiveness in satisfying multiple stakeholders. As to the effect of multiple forms of capital on CE, we see more empirical studies in recent years (e.g., Hayton, 2005a, 2005b). Simsek and Heavy (2011) find that knowledge-based capital (human capital, relational capital, and organizational capital) mediate the relationship between CE and performance.

Future Research Expectations

Despite the achievement researchers have made in these years, the current research on CE in the four streams is still fragmented and limited. More theoretical and empirical research is needed to unravel the loop of CE, organizational learning, and knowledge outcome. For example, how the inter-firm and intra-firm networks play roles in the CE-learning-knowledge loop is an interesting topic. How CE affects firms' external network and internal network and their knowledge strategies? What CE forms affect the inter-firm and intra-firm knowledge transfer and thus knowledge outcome? How CE drives multi-level (individual, group, and firm), organizational members to engage in learning and create/exploit knowledge?

We expect more research on entrepreneurial leadership, such as the effect of different leadership styles on CE; the compositional characteristics of TMT; the interaction of CEOs and TMTs; the influence of environmental factors on managerial roles in CE at different levels; the combined effect of TMT and control mechanisms on CE; organizational changes in leadership, strategies, structure, and resources and the effect on CE. We suggest that a knowledge-based view could be considered in entrepreneurial leadership. For instance, how firm leaders facilitate CE through successful knowledge management? What are the roles that multiple-level managers play in promoting knowledge transfer in the CE process? In addition, with the emergence of research on collective CE (e.g., Doh et al., 2019; Santos & Spann, 2011), which refers to the utilization of employees and outside partners to source and commercialize ideas in a corporate setting. Thus, the roles managers play to achieve collective CE is another interesting topic to study.

The field of CE and internationalization is still quite underexplored, especially CE in international new ventures and small firms. How knowledge flows in established MNCs/global startups interact with CE and affect innovation? Whether the CE content and process are different between established firms and small new firms in the international contexts? How CE varies at different stages of the internationalization process? In addition, examining how host country contexts affect CE is also important. Finally, the measurements of CE performance from a stakeholder perspective is still to be developed. Besides, the relationships of performance outcomes affect on stakeholder satisfaction could be studied. In summary, there is still a long way to go on this path. We look forward to seeing more research on explaining and elaborating the unclear or unexplored fields in CE in the future.

References

Alpkan, L., Bulut, C., Gunday, G., Ulusoy, G., & Kilic, K. (2010). Organizational support for intrapreneurship and its interaction with human capital to enhance innovative performance. *Management Decision, 48*(5), 732–755.

Alvarez, S. A. & Barney, J. B. (2007). Discovery and creation: Alternative theories of entrepreneurial action. *Strategic Entrepreneurship Journal, 1*(1/2), 11–26.

Barringer, B. R., Jones, F. F., & Neubaum, D. O. (2005). A quantitative content analysis of the characteristics of rapid-growth firms and their founders. *Journal of Business Venturing, 20*(5), 663–687.

Boone, C., Lokshin, B., Guenter, H., & Belderbos, R. (2019). Top management team nationality diversity, corporate entrepreneurship, and innovation in multinational firms. *Strategic Management Journal, 40*(2), 277–302.

Burgelman, R. A. (1983). A process model of internal corporate venturing in the diversified major firm. *Administrative Science Quarterly, 28*(2), 223–244.

Burgers, J. H., Jansen, J. J. P., Van den Bosch, F. A. J., & Volberda, H. W. (2009). Structural differentiation and corporate venturing: The moderating role of formal and informal integration mechanisms. *Journal of Business Venturing, 24*(3), 206–220.

Chen, J., & Nadkarni, S. (2017). It's about time! CEOs' temporal dispositions, temporal leadership, and corporate entrepreneurship. *Administrative Science Quarterly, 62*(1), 31–66.

Chen, Y., Tang, G., Jin, J., Xie, Q., & Li, J. (2014). CEOs' transformational leadership and product innovation performance: The roles of corporate entrepreneurship and technology orientation. *Journal of Product Innovation Management, 31*(1), 2–17.

Covin, J. G., & Miles, M. P. (1999). Corporate entrepreneurship and the pursuit of competitive advantage. *Entrepreneurship Theory and Practice, 23*(3), 47–63.

De Clercq, D., Dimov, D., & Thongpapanl, N. (2013). Organizational social capital, formalization, and internal knowledge sharing in entrepreneurial orientation formation. *Entrepreneurship Theory and Practice, 37*(3), 505–537.
De Clercq, D., Sapienza, H. J., & Crijns, H. (2005). The internationalization of small and medium-sized firms. *Small Business Economics, 24*(4), 409–419.
Dess, G. G., Ireland, R. D., Zahra, S. A., Floyd, S. W., Janney, J. J., & Lane, P. J. (2003). Emerging issues in corporate entrepreneurship. *Journal of Management, 29*(3), 351–378.
Doh, J., Tashman, P., & Benischke, M. (2019). Adapting to grand environmental challenges through collective entrepreneurship. *Academy of Management Perspectives, 33*(4), 450–468.
Glaser, L., Fourné, S. P. L., & Elfring, T. (2015). Achieving strategic renewal: The multi-level influences of top and middle managers' boundary-spanning. *Small Business Economics, 45*, 305–327.
Guo, C., Jiang, C., & Yang, Q. (2014). The development of organizational capabilities and corporate entrepreneurial processes: The case of Chinese automobile firms. *Thunderbird International Business Review, 56*(6), 483–500.
Guth, W., & Ginsberg, A. (1990). Guest editor's introduction: Corporate entrepreneurship. *Strategic Management Journal, 11*(Summer Special Issue), 5–15.
Hayton, J. C. (2005a). Promoting corporate entrepreneurship through human resource management practices: A review of empirical research. *Human Resource Management Review, 15*(1), 21–41.
Hayton, J. C. (2005b). Competing in the new economy: The effect of intellectual capital on corporate entrepreneurship in high-technology new ventures. *R&D Management, 35*(2), 137–155.
Heath, R. L., & Palenchar, M. J. (2009). *Strategic issues management: Organizations and public policy challenges*. Sage.
Heavy, C., & Simsek, Z. (2013). Top management compositional effects on corporate entrepreneurship: The moderating role of perceived technological uncertainty. *Journal of Product Innovation Management, 30*(5), 837–855.
Hornsby, J. S., Kuratko, D. F., Shepherd, D. A., & Bott, J. P. (2009). Managers' corporate entrepreneurial actions: Examining perception and position. *Journal of Business Venturing, 24*(3), 236–247.
Ireland, R. D., & Webb, J. W. (2007). A cross-disciplinary exploration of entrepreneurship research. *Journal of Management, 33*(6), 891–927.
Ireland, R. D., Covin, J. G., Donald, F., & Kuratko, D. F. (2009). Conceptualizing corporate entrepreneurship strategy. *Entrepreneurship Theory and Practice, 33*(1), 19–46.
Jiang, C. X., Yang, Q., Song, S., & Annavarjula, M. (2016). Emerging markets firms' catch-up strategy in new product development: Cases of Chinese companies. *International Journal of Business and Emerging Markets, 8*(3), 324–339.

Johanson, J., & Vahlne, J. E. (2006). Commitment and opportunity development in the internationalization process: A note on the Uppsala internationalization process model. *Management International Review, 46*(2), 1–14.

Kuratko, D. F., & Hoskinson, S. (2019). *The challenges of corporate entrepreneurship in the disruptive age* (First ed.). Emerald Publishing Limited.

Kuratko, D. F., & Neubert, E. (2019). Corporate entrepreneurial leadership: Addressing critical challenges in a disruptive age. In D. F. Kuratko & S. Hoskinson (Eds.), *The challenges of corporate entrepreneurship in the disruptive age* (Vol. 28, pp. 89–109). Emerald Publishing Limited.

Lee, S. H., & Williams, C. (2007). Dispersed entrepreneurship within multinational corporations: A community perspective. *Journal of World Business, 42*(4), 505–519.

Ling, Y., Simesek, Z., M., Lubatkin, M. H., & Veiga, J. F. (2008). Transformational leadership's role in promoting corporate entrepreneurship: Examining the CEO-TMT interface. *Academy of Management Journal, 51*(3), 557–576.

Luo, X., Zhou, L., & Liu, S. S. (2005). Entrepreneurial firms in the context of China's transition economy: An integrative framework and empirical examination. *Journal of Business Research, 58*(3), 277–284.

Mehdivand, M., Reza Zali, M., Madhoshi, M., & Kordnaeij, A. (2012). Intellectual capital and nano-business performance: The moderating role of entrepreneurial orientation. *European Journal of Economics, Finance and Administrative Science, 52*, 147–162.

Morris, M. H., Allen, J., Schindehutte, M., & Avila, R. (2006). Balanced management control systems as a mechanism for achieving corporate entrepreneurship. *Journal of Managerial Issues, 18*(4), 468–493.

Morris, M. H., Kuratko, D. F., & Covin, J. G. (2011). *Corporate entrepreneurship and innovation* (3rd ed.). South-Western, Cengage Learning.

Naldi, L., Achtenhagen, L., & Davidsson, P. (2015). International corporate entrepreneurship among SMEs: A test of Stevenson's notion of entrepreneurial management. *Journal of Small Business Management, 53*(3), 780–800.

Nielsen, J. E. (2015). Corporate entrepreneurship, organizational learning and knowledge implementation. *Ekonomski Horizonti, 17*(3), 203–217.

O'Brien, D., Sharkey Scott, P., Andersson, U., Ambos, T., & Fu, N. (2019). The microfoundations of subsidiary initiatives: How subsidiary manager activities unlock entrepreneurship. *Global Strategy Journal, 9*(1), 66–91.

Phan, P. H., Wright, M., Ucbasaran, D., & Tan, W. (2009). Corporate entrepreneurship: Current research and future directions. *Journal of Business Venturing, 24*, 197–205.

Sambrook, S., & Roberts, C. (2005). Corporate entrepreneurship and organizational learning: A review of the literature and the development of a conceptual framework. *Strategic Change, 14*(3), 141–155.

Santos, R., & Spann, M. (2011). Collective entrepreneurship at Qualcomm: Combining collective and entrepreneurial practices to turn employee ideas into action. *R&D Management, 41*(5), 443–456.

Scott, P., Gibbons, P., & Coughlan, J. (2010). Developing subsidiary contribution to the MNC—subsidiary entrepreneurship and strategy creativity. *Journal of International Management, 16*(4), 328–339.

Shafique, I., & Kalyar, M. (2018). Linking transformational leadership, absorptive capacity, and corporate entrepreneurship. *Administrative Science, 8*(2), 1–17.

Shahzad, A. M., Wales, W. J., Sharfman, M. P., & Stein, C. M. (2016). Casting a wider performance net: The role of entrepreneurial orientation in boosting overall firm stakeholder value. *Journal of Management and Organization, 22*(2), 272–290.

Sharma, P., & Chrisman, J. J. (1999). Toward a reconciliation of the definitional issues in the field of corporate entrepreneurship. *Entrepreneurship Theory and Practice, 23*(3), 11–27.

Simsek, Z., & Heavy, C. (2011). The mediating role of knowledge-based capital for corporate entrepreneurship effects on performance: A study of small- to medium-sized firms. *Strategic Entrepreneurship Journal, 5*(1), 81–100.

Stevenson, H. H. (1984). A perspective of entrepreneurship. In H. H. Stevenson, M. J. Roverts, & H. Grousbeck (Eds), *New business venture and the entrepreneur*. Harvard Business School.

Stevenson, H. H., & Gumpert, D. (1985). The heart of entrepreneurship. *Harvard Business Review, 63*(2), 85–94.

Stevenson, H. H., & Jarillo, J. C. (1990). A paradigm of entrepreneurship: Entrepreneurial management. *Strategic Management Journal, 11*(4), 17–27.

Thorgren, S., Örtqvist, D., & Wincent, J. (2009). A cause-effect study of inter-firm networking and corporate entrepreneurship: Initial evidence of self-enforcing spirals. *Journal of Developmental Entrepreneurship, 14*(4), 355–373.

Turner, T., & Pennington, W. W. (2015). Organizational networks and the process of corporate entrepreneurship: How the motivation, opportunity, and ability to act affect firm knowledge, learning, and innovation. *Small Business Economics, 45*, 447–463.

Webb, J. W., Kistruck, G. M., Ireland, R. D., & Ketchen, D. J. (2010). The entrepreneurship process in base of the pyramid markets: The case of multinational enterprise/non-government organization alliances. *Entrepreneurship: Theory & Practice, 34*(3), 555–581.

Willimas, C., & Lee, S. H. (2011). Entrepreneurial context and knowledge coordination within the multinational corporation. *Journal of World Business, 46*(2), 253–264.

Yang, Y., Narayanan, V. K., & Zahra, S. (2009). Developing the selection and valuation capabilities through learning: The case of corporate venture capital. *Journal of Business Venturing, 24*(3), 261–273.

Yiu, D., & Lau, C. M. (2008). Corporate entrepreneurship as resource capital configuration in emerging market firms. *Entrepreneurship Theory and Practice, 32*(1), 37–58.

Yiu, D. W., Lau, C. M., & Bruton, G. D. (2007). International venturing by emerging economy firms: The effects of firm capabilities, home country networks, and corporate entrepreneurship. *Journal of International Business Studies, 38*(4), 519–540.

Yuan, W., Bao, Y., & Olson, B. J. (2017). CEOs' ambivalent interpretations, organizational market capabilities, and corporate entrepreneurship as responses to strategic issues. *Journal of World Business, 52*(2), 312–326.

Zahra, S. A. (1995). Corporate entrepreneurship and financial performance: The case of management leveraged buyouts. *Journal of Business Venturing, 10*(3), 225–247.

Zahra, S. A. (1996). Governance, ownership, and corporate entrepreneurship: The moderating impact of industry technological opportunities. *Academy of Management Journal, 39*(6), 1713–1735.

Zahra, S. A., Filatotchev, I., & Wright, M. (2009). How do threshold firms sustain corporate entrepreneurship? The role of boards and absorptive capacity. *Journal of Business Venturing, 24*(3), 248–260.

Zellweger, T. M. & Nason, R. S. (2008). A stakeholder perspective on family firm performance. *Family Business Review, 21*(3), 203–216.

CHAPTER 5

Entrepreneurial Alertness and Opportunity Identification: Suggestions for the Next Generation

Connie Marie Gaglio, Susan J. Winter, and Jerome A. Katz

Introduction

Mark Twain once said that he never saw an opportunity until it ceased to be one. Some people are surprised by a new product or service because they themselves had thought of it but dismissed the idea out of hand. The question of why some people see and act on opportunities (i.e., entrepreneurs) while others do not remains as vital a question today as it

C. M. Gaglio (✉)
San Francisco State University, San Francisco, CA, USA
e-mail: cgaglio@sfsu.edu

S. J. Winter
University of Maryland, College Park, MD, USA

J. A. Katz
Saint Louis University, St. Louis, MO, USA

A. E. Osorio et al. (eds.), *Modern Classics in Entrepreneurship Studies*,
https://doi.org/10.1007/978-3-030-61029-6_5

was in the 1980s, when entrepreneurship was reborn as an academic discipline, and is especially important since Shane and Venkataraman (2000) declared the study of opportunity as *the* question for the discipline.

Kirzner (1979) proposed "entrepreneurial alertness" as the unique point of difference. While his claim seemed intriguing, its impact was limited partly because his musings did not naturally lend themselves to empirical testing. However, Gaglio and Katz (2001) realized that the application of social cognition theory not only made the idea of entrepreneurial alertness plausible but also enabled rigorous empirical testing of his theory. They reconceptualized alertness as a distinctive way of perceiving and interpreting information. Their hope was that investigating opportunity identification through this lens would de-mystify it.

The article was influential in developing several research streams in opportunity identification and entrepreneurial cognition, resulting in over a thousand academic articles and books. The entrepreneurial opportunity identification process is now considered one of the five core constructs for the discipline (Chandra, 2018).

We were tasked with assessing the impact of our article and indeed our first draft covered all the key issues associated with such a task. We found that (1) we were rehashing ground already covered elsewhere; (2) it read like a handbook chapter; and (3) *most importantly*, it obscured the single development of utmost importance in the entrepreneurship discipline—that is, the transition from a data-poor to a data-rich environment (Borgman, 2010). How could we claim to know something about alertness if we, ourselves, were not alert to and discussed this development?

Therefore, this chapter begins with a brief review of the central thesis presented in our 2001 article, *The Psychological Basis of Opportunity Identification: Entrepreneurial Alertness* with an eye toward the limitations of the data-poor environment of the period, and then examine the theoretical and empirical contributions and problems associated with investigating alertness over the years. We then turn attention to what is possible now and in the future as the discipline exists in a more data-rich environment. We are excited by the possibilities and hope to persuade investigators, especially the next generation, to explore our suggestions.

Forging a Discipline in a Data-Poor Environment

The fundamental questions any new discipline must address include how we define the phenomenon of interest and why it requires a new discipline. If this can be achieved, the next question is how to approach understanding it.

Defining Entrepreneurial Opportunities. The phenomenon of interest is entrepreneurial opportunities: What they are? How they come into being? etc. In their justification for entrepreneurship as a unique academic discipline devoted to the study of entrepreneurial opportunities, Shane and Venkataraman (2000) define entrepreneurial opportunities as "those situations in which goods, services, raw materials, and organizing methods can be introduced and sold at greater than their cost of production" (p. 220).

While most in the field embraced their stipulation that entrepreneurial opportunities represent a core discipline concept, many did not embrace their definition of what constitutes an entrepreneurial opportunity. Aware of a potentially data-poor environment, elegantly called "idiosyncratic milieus" (MacMillan & Katz, 1992), investigators were concerned about insufficient sample sizes and the inability to produce robust research results. Gaglio (1997a) fretted that Schumpeter's or Kirzner's entrepreneurial opportunity was a randomly occurring and rare event.

Twenty plus years later, scholars continue to debate the definition of an entrepreneurial opportunity: Does it represent the opportunity for a new product or to start a new business? Does it refer to radical innovations or variations of existing offerings? Is it discovered or created? Is it objective or subjective? Dimov (2011) and Hansen et al. (2016) carefully review these issues and conclude that the concept is a multi-headed beast hindering advancement in the field. Davidsson (2015) suggests that the field abandon the concept, but his suggested remedy simply introduces a new label.

Gaglio and Winter (2017) believe that the debate will continue into the foreseeable future because it has become a political issue reflecting the various needs and interests of several communities of interest. However, they also observe that, with few exceptions, the opportunity to start a business is the default operational definition of an entrepreneurial opportunity. In the data-poor environment, this is understandable as small business owners and new venture founders were groups that were easier to identify and locate than were those more ephemeral entrepreneurial business opportunities. The exemplar of entrepreneurial opportunities at the millennium (i.e., Apple) started as a new product (i.e., the Apple II) presented to the marketplace through a new venture. Nevertheless, this default setting is disconcerting and dangerous for the discipline; Shane and Venkataraman explicitly warned that such a definition demotes entrepreneurship to an applied research setting for organizational and management theory, not something in need of its own academic discipline. Knowing that the debate will continue regardless, Gaglio and Dimov (2019) implore investigators to specify whether they are looking at product/service opportunities, venture opportunities, or the creation of an entirely new industry and to make sure respondents know which is the focus of the investigator's questions.

Approaching the Study of Entrepreneurial Opportunities. One of Gaglio and Katz's objectives was to trace the theoretical antecedents of entrepreneurial opportunities from Economics and explore these existing theories as a way of increasing the academic legitimacy of the new field of Entrepreneurship. At the time, mainstream economists considered entrepreneurial opportunities an exogenous variable of no theoretical importance. Two outliers from the Austrian School of economics, Schumpeter and Kirzner, not only considered entrepreneurial opportunities theoretically necessary but the actual catalyst for the economic market. Schumpeter (1950) favors exploring the impact of entrepreneurial opportunities (creative destruction) and attributed their origins and processes to heroic efforts by creative men. Kirzner (1979, 1985) questions how entrepreneurs discover their opportunities and hypothesized a unique ability, entrepreneurial alertness.

Kirzner defined entrepreneurial alertness as "the ability to notice without search opportunities that have hitherto been overlooked" (1979, p. 48) or as "a motivated propensity of man to formulate an image of the future" (1985, p. 56). His theory of alertness depends on a person breaking and re-creating the existing means-ends framework (i.e., the chain of events/conditions that results in the current way of doing things) for an industry, an economy, or even a society. These stipulations clearly cast alertness as a set of cognitive processes, so Gaglio and Katz's application of social cognition theory is simply an exploration of the details. Application of social cognition theory provided the fledgling discipline the potential for rigorous theoretical development and testing; to that end, Gaglio and Katz outlined a research agenda and testable propositions.

Figure 5.1 depicts Gaglio and Katz's cognitive theory of alertness which begins with a person in a situation. The situation's unexpectedness motivates or prompts the type of cognitive processing to be used.

Specifically, the person begins looking for signals or cues that market conditions in the situation have, are, or will be changing in significant ways compared to the person's previous understanding of the situation. In other words, the alert person starts to assess market conditions to determine if assumptions about how things work (the means-ends framework) are still valid. Even if one notices signals or cues of change, what really matters is what the alert person does with that perceptual knowledge. Some will start to imagine how to take advantage of the situation, which typically requires small or large changes in his/her assumptions about the way things work resulting in altering or breaking the existing means-ends framework. Further thinking about the new way things may be working leads to opportunities no one else has seen or enacted—that is, to the identification of *entrepreneurial* opportunities.

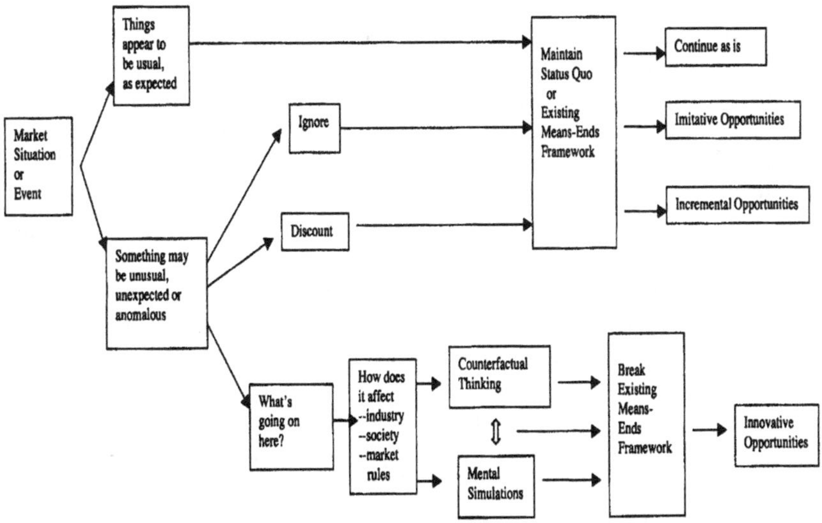

Fig. 5.1 Alertness and the opportunity identification process (Reprinted by permission from Springer Nature: Nature/Springer/Palgrave, *Journal of Small Business Economics*, The psychological basis of opportunity identification: Entrepreneurial alertness, Gaglio and Katz [2001, p. 99])

Several psychological concepts are embedded in this account:

1. Motivation—a conscious or unconscious reason/impulse to engage in additional mental effort;
2. Accurate perceptions—the cues and signals are not delusions;
3. Accurate interpretation—the cues and signals indicate a need to challenge the assumptions about the way things work;
4. Sensemaking—taking interpretations to the next step of integrating the cues and signals into a plausible alternative set of assumptions or a new means-ends framework;
5. Imagination—going even further by speculating or predicting likely outcomes and consequences if the new means-ends framework is a more accurate or useful account of the situation and market conditions.

Items 2–5 require that a person already have assumptions about the way things work; cognitive psychologists (Fiske & Taylor, 1991) refer to this set of assumptions as a *schema* or mental model which everyone develops based on experience (personal or role modeled), education, imagination, or a combination of these. Schema direct our attention and interpretation and facilitate or impede sensemaking and imagination. Gaglio (1997a) and the Gaglio and Katz article provides detailed explanations of schema formation, activation, and change. Kirzner (1979) stressed that alertness was rather effortless (notice without search) which the diagram and description above would seem to refute. In their book outlining the basic precepts and research about social cognition and schema theory, Fiske and Taylor (1991) report that cognitive psychologists have observed that some people seem to develop a habit or default setting of using one schema to guide cognitive process, which they call a *chronic schema.* According to psychologists, chronic schema may look and feel effortless but apparently have the advantage that they are not only speedy but more accurate—regardless of the amount of information to be perceived and interpreted. This led Gaglio and Katz to propose that entrepreneurial alertness was probably a chronic schema. If accurate, this would suggest that some individuals will naturally and consistently look at the world through a lens of entrepreneurial alertness.

Theoretical Explorations

Contemporary theoretical development in Economics focuses on expanding economic theory in general to accommodate the disruptive events of the Digital Revolution (Casson & Wadeson, 2007; Manne, 2014; Minniti & Lévesque, 2008). Along these lines, Schumpeter and Kirzner are being re-examined (Betta et al., 2010; Endres & Woods, 2010; Gerschlager, 2012).

Within the entrepreneurship discipline, the Gaglio and Katz paper identified the fundamental elements of a theory of entrepreneurial alertness and suggested how to operationalize those elements. Since then, activity along several theoretically driven fronts in the field grew: Dimensionality, Objectivity, Benefit, Knowledge, Mental Models, and Alternative Perspectives.

Dimensionality. Kirzner (1979, 1985) describes alertness in terms of two dimensions: (1) noticing and (2) breaking the means-end framework. Tang et al. (2012) recast alertness with three dimensions: (1) scanning and searching; (2) association and connection; and (3) evaluation and judgment. Their distinction makes logical sense because in order to get from Kirzner's noticing to breaking the means-ends framework requires that the entrepreneur engages in some form of interpretation, which Tang et al. capture in their second behavioral dimension.

Entrepreneurship scholars who define entrepreneurial opportunity as new ventures tend to focus on the evaluative dimension without providing any explanation of the origins of the idea. Summaries of the theoretical and empirical work in this vein can be found in the many reviews of opportunity identification/recognition.[1]

Scholars pursuing a theory of alertness believe that the further development required an understanding of whether it involves deliberate search or effortless discovery (Fiet, 2002; Tang & Khan, 2007). Over time, the debate about effort evolved into a debate about the ontological nature of entrepreneurial opportunities.

Objectivity. Scholars in both Economics and Entrepreneurship believed it was important to determine whether the entrepreneurial opportunities arising from alertness were objective or subjective. As a cognitive process, alertness is inherently subjective but social cognition theory holds that market conditions are socially constructed and not the

[1] See Busenitz et al. (2014), Crump et al. (2011), Welter and Alvarez (2015).

province of a single person. Sautet (2018) observes that, at least from an economist's perspective, the perception and interpretation of market conditions requires the realization that such conditions exist so treating them as "objective" is useful for theoretical exploration. Pelly (2017) details the logical flaws of a purely objective or purely subjective theory and offers a way to bridge the two.

Benefit. Kirzner (1979) argued that an essential feature of an economic situation is whether it affords the person the chance to benefit from it and retain control of that benefit.[2] Gaglio and Katz accept Kirzner's argument as a necessary condition that increases the likelihood of a person deploying his/her alertness. However, as will be discussed in the section on Empirical Explorations, preliminary evidence calls this assumption into question.

Knowledge. Several works argue that association with prior knowledge is an essential component both for understanding what the existing means-ends framework is and for creating interpretations of what is noticed (Arentz et al., 2013; Dimov, 2007; Shepherd & DeTienne, 2005). Shane (2000) suggests that, at the very least, one must have a knowledge of markets, ways to serve those markets, and possible customer needs. Other scholars suggest that knowledge of long-run trends, resource gaps, and depletion rates as well as knowledge of the characteristics of gain and how to detect it are also necessary (Archichvili et al., 2003; Berglund, 2007; Casson & Wadeson, 2007; Hsieh et al., 2007; Ko & Butler, 2007).

Mental Models. Mental simulations and counterfactual thinking have been proposed as mental processes that explain how association leads to breaking the means-ends framework (Gaglio, 2004). Pattern recognition (Barron & Ensley, 2006), structural alignment (Grégoire, Barr, & Shepherd, 2010), and problematizing (Endres & Woods, 2007) have also been proposed as underlying cognitive processes that culminate in changes to or destruction of means-ends frameworks. All are plausible and await empirical support based on the observation of real-time cognitive processing rather than respondent self-reflection. Inclusion of techniques such as cognitive mapping (Brännback & Carsrud, 2017) as part of the data analysis will greatly improve our understanding of whether and how association facilitates alertness.

[2] A benefit can be financial, psychological, social, or any combination of the these.

Alternative Theories. Alertness is not the only theory for conceptualizing how entrepreneurial opportunities come into being. Creativity (Chen et al., 2018; Hansen et al., 2011), bricolage (Baker & Nelson, 2005), effectuation (Sarasvathy, 2001), and situated attention (Valliere, 2013) have been proposed as theories describing a process by which opportunities are created rather than noticed. Creativity theory remains intuitively appealing, especially in the light of Schumpeter's characterizations of "creative destruction." However, we do not consider this approach particularly useful as it puts opportunity identification back into the black box we sought to explore.

Bricolage and effectuation provide a plausible route for the opportunity to create a business offering a product or service, which neither Schumpeter nor Kirzner seek to address but some communities of interest in entrepreneurship find essential. Gaglio and Katz proposed a social cognitive approach precisely because, ultimately, any theory of entrepreneurial opportunities must account for the thinking that precedes action, so we look forward to elaboration on the underlying cognitive processes for bricolage and effectuation.

Valliere's (2013) idea of situated attention directly challenges our model. He argues that our description of alertness as its own schema overcomplicates the process; whereas the socio-cognitive process of situated attention can also account for identification of opportunities. This idea is an attractive one and deserves further exploration as an underlying dynamic. However, we challenge the belief that this theory simplifies alertness as he posits an entrepreneurial expertise schema, an entrepreneurial practice schema, and an entrepreneurial intention schema as predecessors to situated alertness. We are also concerned that this theory may exclude people whose alertness notices an idea and who only then develop or acquire entrepreneurial schema. Nevertheless, we would like to see an empirical investigation of these competing theories.

Most importantly, the discipline must heed Valliere's (2013) admonition that a theory of entrepreneurial alertness must account for its origins, antecedents, and dynamics/mechanisms. He presents a challenge difficult to meet in a data-impoverished environment. We expect that the next generation of scholars who live and are working in a data-rich environment will rise to the challenge.

Empirical Explorations

As noted earlier, the entrepreneurship discipline started in an impoverished data environment. There were relatively few opportunities to study the phenomena of interest *in situ* because they were less common and because contemporaneous data about entrepreneurial concepts and processes was seldom captured. The most accessible data sources were self-reports of small business owners and those starting new businesses. We know a lot about how these particular groups grapple with opportunity selection and opportunity exploitation and the reader is referred to several excellent reviews and books for the empirical record.[3]

Self-Reports. The majority of entrepreneurial alertness studies rely on the self-reports of study participants who are usually small business owners or venture founders. However, some of the more interesting and exciting findings come from alternative methods such as experiments (Arentz et al., 2013), simulations (Bonney et al., 2016), and analysis of historical records like websites, media interviews, e-mails, VC pitch slides, etc. (Gartner, 2010; Ziegler et al., 1992). Self-report studies use either questionnaires or interviews. Both data collection techniques have advantages, but their ability to accurately capture the phenomena of interest is inherently severely limited due to issues with instrumentation and measurement.

Self-report questionnaires have the advantage of being efficient, affordable, and familiar. However, they do pose serious problems. Entrepreneurship alertness studies generally rely on a scale of self-perceived alertness behaviors that was developed by the investigator and used only once, which limits our ability to assess their validity or compare results across studies. Tang et al.'s scale (2012) mentioned earlier is a notable exception in that it was used several times.

Self-report also presumes that most respondents are accurately aware of their alertness activity. If we accept this questionable premise, studies indicate that:

[3] Brännback and Carsrud (2009, 2017), Busenitz et al. (2014), Crump et al. (2011), Gaglio and Dimov (2019), Gaglio and Winter (2009, 2017), Short et al. (2010), Welter and Alvarez (2015).

- individuals are more likely to engage their alertness ability if they perceive the social environment to be abundant in the necessary resources and social support (Tang, 2008);
- the amount of scanning and what is scanned is influenced by the perception of the degree of change or turbulence (Tang, 2007); more volatile environments are scanned more frequently than less volatile environments;
- respondents report that they perceive themselves as connecting the dots among diverse pieces of information (Baron, 2006)
- respondents express preferences to start businesses when they believe there is an information asymmetry in their favor (Minniti, 2004).[4]

In addition, unless ingeniously designed (e.g., Kahneman & Tversky, 1979), the investigator is not capturing the respondents' cognitive processes; he/she is capturing respondents' perceptions of probable associated behaviors and outcomes. These questionnaires also tend to conflate the product/service opportunity and the opportunity to start a business. The cognitive processes associated with each of these opportunities probably have some overlap but there is evidence suggesting they are not identical (Dimov, 2007; Haynie et al., 2009). Most problematic, however, is that the use of scales casts alertness as a static skill or trait rather than the dynamic cognitive process that Kirzner (1979, 1985) and Gaglio and Katz (2001) conceptualize.

Several investigators opted to interview groups of entrepreneurs/CEOs as well as a comparison group of corporate senior management. This method still has all of the shortcomings outlined above but has the advantage that the entrepreneur or senior executive can explain his/her perception of his/her thinking process instead of the investigator inferring that process. These explanations offer food for thought about potential cognitive processes that merit further investigation. For example, Dyer et al. (2008) found that the entrepreneurs interviewed were *deliberately* looking to disrupt the status-quo, whatever that might mean. They were also more likely to ask "what if" type questions (counterfactual reasoning) than their corporate counterparts. Maine and Dos Santos (2015) found that entrepreneurs might use different

[4] These issues have also been explored in the context of opportunity identification/recognition without references. Interested scholars can examine the summaries mentioned in Footnote 3.

paths to alertness depending on the level of situational constraints; under high constraints, their descriptions conformed to the discovery process whereas under lower constraints, the reasoning seemed more aligned with the creation process. This finding might have implications for resolving differences between alertness and effectuation/bricolage models mentioned earlier.

Gaglio and Katz argued that because socio-cognitive processes drive all perception and thinking of all people, if investigators could create the right conditions to induce and observe those processes, then the sampling frame need not be restricted to samples of small business owners, new venture founders, or entrepreneurs. Preliminary experiments and simulations could use graduate students or any group of adults. The results from these studies might rule out or rule in useful techniques and variables to be used in later studies with verifiable entrepreneurs. Several investigators have designed experiments and simulations in order to observe the use of alertness cognitive processes in real time (Dew et al., 2011; Dimov, 2007; Grégoire, Shepherd, & Lambert, 2010; Newell & Holian, 2017; Shepherd & DeTienne, 2005). These methods have also been coupled with think-aloud protocols, including some that used scenarios (Grégoire, Barr, & Shepherd, 2010). Analysis of these studies reveals evidence of alertness; doubts about whether benefit motivates alertness; and the critical importance of interpretation.

Evidence of Alertness. The Digital Revolution and its associated "winner take all" reward system provides face validity for the existence of alertness, which is a necessary but insufficient justification for the concept. Roundy et al. (2018) quasi-experiment using an episode of environmental turbulence in North Arlington, Texas, confirmed the expectation that some people demonstrated alertness while others did not. Of more importance for the theory of alertness, they concluded that alertness is a dimension separate from the traditional management opportunity/threat perceptual categories, which were also evident. The authors state that they developed a strong sense that there is something about how opportunities were spotted that contributed to reported alertness. While we are excited that they recognized the opportunity to use a real-world situation, their work, like most empirical investigations of entrepreneurial alertness, relies on self-reports which is more evidence of a claim to alertness rather than evidence of alertness itself.

Arentz et al. (2013) created an experiment to test the importance of prior knowledge but their most interesting finding was the appearance of alertness. In their experiment, half of the participants were given information priming their sensitivity to a "hidden in plain sight" arbitrage opportunity while the other half did not receive any prior information.[5] Results confirmed their expectations regarding prior knowledge: More participants in the primed condition found the arbitrage opportunity but, more importantly, more than half of the respondents in the primed condition did *not* find the arbitrage opportunity while nearly 20% in the non-primed condition did!

Additional experiments and simulations provide rigorous empirical evidence that alertness exists; that some people have it while others do not; and that it can be activated in study conditions (Bonney et al., 2016; Demmert & Klein, 2003; Kitzmann & Schiereck, 2005). However, it should be noted that these studies were designed based on an assumption that alertness is triggered by situational anomalies or gaps. This assumption is consistent with both economic and social cognition theory but theoretical rigor requires that this assumption must also be empirically challenged.

Is Benefit a Real Motivator? As noted earlier, Kirzner (1979) argues that a person will not activate alertness unless he/she believes in the possibility of some kind of personal benefit (financial or otherwise). However, Demmert and Klein's (2003) experiment found support for alertness but not for financial benefit. They question whether they adequately operationalized the concept of benefit as financial gain. Kitzmann and Schiereck (2005) conducted an altered replication of this study, changing the financial incentives but found similar results both for alertness and the role of benefit. These investigators questioned whether the actual task and instructions used in both experiments over-emphasized solving a specific problem, which Kirzner felt could be the result of alertness but not necessarily its prompt. It is also possible that benefit is not as influential as Kirzner thought. However, questioning the validity of the experimental task should not be so easily dismissed. Market simulations varying the financial incentives and exploring other kinds of benefits could better address the theoretical construct.

Interpretation of Perceptions Matters. An important component of alertness is interpreting perceptions and determining what to do. In one of the earliest experiments involving alertness, Gaglio (1997b) found that

[5] Kirzner typically referred to arbitrage when explaining alertness.

the essential difference between those who found embedded opportunities and those who did not was that finders did not categorically dismiss anomalous information whereas non-finders did. Surprisingly, those who did not find an opportunity made note of the anomalous information, but engaged in a series of rationalizations to discount or dismiss the value of that perception, which suggests that as we look at mechanisms, we should look at what does *not* happen along with what does.

Shane (2000) conducted a quasi-experiment examining the influence of prior knowledge and found that an individual's unique store of knowledge influences alertness in two ways. First, it led participants to interpret the market event in different ways which led some to identify an opportunity and while others did not. Second, how the opportunity-finders interpreted the event led to markedly different opportunity concepts.

Bonney et al. (2016) ran a market simulation testing both what participants noticed and their ability to sense or predict where the market was going. In this study, not all participants noticed information that provided clues to where the market was going, some did not perceive it accurately but of equal interest is that among those who did notice the information accurately, not all developed useful predictions.

The research design incorporating a market simulation is very useful for the study of alertness because it requires participants to engage their cognitive processes in a forward-looking way. The use of think-aloud protocols in which participants verbalize their thinking while doing the task could provide significant insights into the interplay of noticing and interpreting.

This particular study also used teams, which is an important approach to include in the study of alertness. Origin stories about the Digital Revolution's disruptive opportunities include both those about solo individuals (e.g., Bezos of Amazon, Dorsey of Twitter, Meister of AOL, Zuckerberg of Facebook) and those about two- or three-person teams (e.g., Brin & Page of Google, Fanning & Parks of Napster, Gates & Allen of Microsoft, Jobs & Wozniak of Apple).

The Data-Environment of the Next Generation

The empirical record on entrepreneurial alertness is intriguing but far from conclusive or complete. As with the start of the investigation of any theory, assumptions were made but scholarship requires that these be challenged.

The impoverished data environment placed constraints on inquiry at the time of the original Gaglio and Katz article. The sampling frame of small business owners and new venture founders historically used is of serious concern. It is intuitively appealing to think that the cognitive processing (e.g., means-end framework) that led to the iPhone and its first app would be different than the cognitive processing that led to the thousands of apps that followed. Certainly, the level of risk and uncertainty differs but cognitive processes may differ in other important ways. Or not. What is certain is that in the data-impoverished environment, it was virtually impossible to find or create a large enough sample to allow stratification based on characteristics of interest without introducing other threats to validity.

Along these same lines, grouping businesses aged 10 years with new ventures, as has been done, would similarly threaten the validity of the findings because of the variation in history. It is highly unlikely that everyone has encountered the same market/economic events over the course of a decade which, if the findings on munificence and environmental turbulence are true, would affect whether alertness was prompted.

Schumpeter and Kirzner are interested in opportunities on a different scale although Kirzner would argue that alertness is still the catalyst for opportunities that result in creative destruction. Several scholars have called for making distinctions based on the scale of opportunity: ordinary vs. extraordinary (Yu, 2001); small scale vs. large scale (Shane, 2004); existing vs. newly created (Endres & Woods, 2007); new to the world vs. underexploited (Plummer et al., 2007).

As noted earlier, using samples of small business owners and new venture founders conflates the opportunity to introduce a new product or service with the opportunity to start a business. Are these equally conflated in the minds of entrepreneurs? What if they are not? Kirzner (1979) argues that the moment of insight about the opportunity is driven by alertness whereas anything that follows (e.g., the business) is driven by the traditional allocative reasoning described in traditional Economic theory. He may be wrong. Or not.

Finally, using samples of small business owners and new venture founders conflates the opportunity and the success of the opportunity. So, essentially, we may only know something about successful business opportunities. No doubt failed business opportunities existed but in a data-poor environment made it was very difficult to locate those business people and convince them to discuss their thinking and decision-making. It is worth noting that Katz and Gartner (1988) suggested a conceptual model for organizational emergence which identifies some of the very earliest stage evidence of emerging businesses, including those that do not reach the level of formal, recognized creation.

We have found that of the schemas we share and have found most useful in our own professional and conceptual development, counterfactual thinking holds a special place. With that in mind, we would like to offer one radical and potentially disruptive idea that might seem at odds with many of the arguments we've put forth in this paper: Let's put aside our theories, assumptions, and findings and start from scratch using this newfound wealth of data. Let's take one step back in order to make significant theoretical and empirical advances. Let's assume we really don't know anything but we now have mountains of data. Let's go digging.

Entrepreneurial Archeology. We hope that the title of this section piques your interest and you are curious about what it may mean for entrepreneurship. *The International Encyclopedia of the Social Sciences* defines archeology as:

> *a set of specialized techniques for obtaining cultural data from the past,data that may be used by anthropologists, historians, art critics, economists or any others interested in man and his activities.* (Sills, 1968, p. 378)

If we accept the challenge to start from scratch and examine opportunity perception without *any* preconceptions, we will need to put aside questionnaires, scales, experiments, etc., and, for the time being, carefully study the artifacts of the Digital Revolution.

This is not an entirely unfamiliar research strategy; generations of researchers in data-poor environments, recall-based narratives by entrepreneurs, historical records, or combinations of the two have been the mainstays of understanding the identification and pursuit of opportunity. For example, Skarbek (2009) painstakingly builds a historical record tracing the opportunity perception, shaping, and implementation process that John Chapman (aka Johnny Appleseed) used to facilitate European settlement of the American frontier. Using artifacts such as land deeds, bills of sale, advertising; newspaper articles, letters and diaries revealing cultural norms and biographical sources about Chapman, Skarbek provides evidence of Chapman's upbringing (including strong spiritual ties to nature) and the existing context of the American frontier (e.g., few courts and squatter rights). From this, Skarbek develops an explanation of how these two components blended into the opportunity Chapman tested and ultimately exploited.

Alternatively, narration can be done consciously, creating a record in real time, as the founders of The Republic of Tea did when they created and then sold their company (Ziegler et al., 1992), which itself became the basis for multiple analyses by entrepreneurship researchers (Gartner, 2010).

These efforts have been limited because of the relative paucity of data sources, data points, and the time between action, recording, and analysis. The Digital Revolution has produced an unprecedented data-rich environment. There are multiple types of data, with large numbers of datapoints, many of which show great recency (Schwab & Zhang, 2019). Examples in entrepreneurship have included personality-based entrepreneurial culture mapping (Obschonka, 2017) and entrepreneurial network analysis (Wang et al., 2017). There are now thousands of opportunities of varying scales and degrees of success to be found within a very short timeframe (which limits the "history" threat to validity). To be sure, some of these data approaches will require new learning for entrepreneurship researchers and students (Sedkaoui, 2018). But the new data analytic opportunities could well be worth it. Consider the following potential avenues for contemporary entrepreneurial archeology:

1. Enlisting a fraction of individuals online who have expressed an interest in startup companies (5 million per month on Facebook[6]), invention (15 million), problem-solving (3.5 million), or self-employment (1 million). With permission to employ social media and search tracking, researchers could explore a significant portion of the exposure (e.g., sites visited) and concept development (e.g., search terms used, specific products/services viewed) processes for people who might be becoming aware of and exploring potential opportunities they see (Acar et al., 2015). If in addition to computer-based tracking efforts, people permit tracking of their smartphone, additional areas of information related to location, calls, SMS messages, and other forms of data become available for analysis (Hutchinson, 2019; Kaltheuner & Weatherhead, 2018).

[6] These numbers were taken from Facebook Audience Insights in October 2019 using the terms given.

2. Leveraging naturally occurring efforts such as Startup Weekend (https://startupweekend.org/), ProductCamp (http://www.productcamp.org/), hackathons, or their online equivalents where people come together to invent solutions to problems, and where ideas and inventions outnumber business possibilities. Alertness researchers could follow samples of participants using conventional survey and self-report techniques, cognitive-mapping techniques (Brännback & Carsrud, 2009, 2017), social media tracking techniques, or a combination of these.
3. Creating online competitions, games, or quizzes inviting the public to explore topics or problems and offer suggestions and solutions. Participants could be followed to explore if any have demonstrated behaviors or mindsets associated with entrepreneurial alertness and compare those with and without signs of alertness.

Why might people do this? Some may volunteer just to do something (like Wikipedians). Some might agree to volunteer in order to be part of a university study or to advance science (like Citizen Scientists). Others might be enticed by access to materials curated or created by the researchers to help prospective entrepreneurs. These observational and incentivizing opportunities are merely the tip of the proverbial iceberg. The point is that as peoples' online lives grow in breadth, depth, and complexity, and as much of our lives are visible or potentially accessible, future researchers' abilities to explore the opportunity alertness process will largely be limited by the researchers own alertness to the research opportunities available in the next generation digital environment. Entrepreneurship has truly the potential to become a data-rich discipline.

Reconstructing narratives of opportunity perception is necessary but not sufficient in developing a new and better understanding of entrepreneurial alertness. For example, Skarbek's reconstruction based on artifacts can be seen as support for Gaglio and Katz's model of alertness as well as Valliere's model of situation attention. Effectuation and bricolage theorists can interpret this story as an example of how Chapman created an opportunity based on what was around him. What is missing—and must be added—is a critical inspection of what parts of the account do *not* fit existing theoretical explanations and hypothesizing why.

Presumably, there will be a lot of data that will *not* fit existing theories. Comparing and contrasting these accounts; conducting meta-analysis across them; debating the findings through journal special issues and/or conferences should reveal one or more patterns. Hopefully, these findings stimulate better questions which can guide theoretical development and research using more traditional empirical methods.

We believe that the future exploration of entrepreneurial alertness is best accomplished when it is based in rigorous theory, tested using the most complete, direct, and current data available, and discussed and dissected to improve the theory, methods, and resulting practices. Seeing how much was accomplished in data-poor environments, the future of research in the field given the advent of big data and data-rich environments seems one of promise.

The opportunity exists. The benefit can be significant. Excavation can be fun. As scholars, can we afford to miss this opportunity until it ceases to be one?

References

Acar, G., Alsenoy, B. V., Piessens, F., Diaz, C., & Preneel, B. (2015). *Facebook tracking through social plug-ins: Technical report prepared for the Belgian Privacy Commission.* Retrieved from KU Leuven website: https://www.esat.kuleuven.be/cosic/publications/article-2555.pdf

Ardichvili, A., Cardozo, R., & Ray, S. (2003). A theory of entrepreneurial opportunity identification and development. *Journal of Business Venturing, 18*(1), 105–123.

Arnetz, J., Sautet, F., & Storr, V. (2013). Prior knowledge and opportunity identification. *Small Business Economics, 41*, 461–478.

Baker, T., & Nelson, R. (2005). Creating something from nothing: Resource construction through entrepreneurial bricolage. *Administrative Science Quarterly, 50*, 329–366.

Baron, R. (2006). Opportunity recognition as pattern recognition: How entrepreneurs "connect the dots" to identify new business opportunities. *The Academy of Management Perspectives, 20*(1), 104–119.

Barron, R., & Ensley, M. (2006). Opportunity recognition as the detection of meaningful patterns: Evidence from comparisons of novice and experienced entrepreneurs. *Management Science, 52*(9), 1331–1344.

Berglund, H. (2007). Opportunities as existing and created: A study of entrepreneurs in the Swedish mobile internet industry. *Journal of Enterprising Culture, 15*(3), 243–273.

Betta, M., Jones, R., & Latham, J. (2010). Entrepreneurship and the innovative self: A Schumpeterian reflection. *International Journal of Entrepreneurial Behavior and Research, 16*, 229–244.

Bonney, L., Davis-Sramek, B., & Cadotte, E. (2016). “Thinking” about business markets: A cognitive assessment of market awareness. *Journal of Business Research, 69*, 2641–2648.
Borgman, C. L. (2010). *Scholarship in the digital age: Information, infrastructure, and the Internet*. MIT Press.
Brännback, M., & Carsrud, A. (Eds.). (2009). *Understanding the entrepreneurial mind: Opening the black box*. International Studies in Entrepreneurship. Springer.
Brännback, M., & Carsrud, A. (Eds.). (2017). *Revisitng the entrepreneurial mind*. International Studies in Entrepreneurship. Springer.
Busenitz, L., Plummer, L., Klotz, A., Shahzad, A., & Rhoads, K. (2014). Entrepreneurship research (1985–2009) and the emergence of opportunities. *Entrepreneurship Theory and Practice, 38*, 1–20.
Casson, M., & Wadeson, N. (2007). The discovery of opportunities: Extending the economic theory of the entrepreneur. *Small Business Economics, 28*, 285–300.
Chandra, Y. (2018). Mapping the evolution of entrepreneurship as a field of research (1990–2013): A scientometric analysis. *PLoS ONE 13*(1): e0190228. https://dpi.org/10.13.1371/journal.pone.0190228
Chen, M., Chang, Y. Y., & Pan, J. Y. (2018). Typology of creative entrepreneurs and entrepreneurial success. *Journal of Enterprising Communities, 5*, 632–656.
Crump, M., Singh, R., & Abbey, A. (2011). Examining opportunity recognition research output: 1995–2006. *Journal of Marketing Development and Competitiveness, 5*, 64–79.
Davidsson, P. (2015). Entrepreneurial opportunities and the entrepreneurship nexus: A reconceptualization. *Journal of Business Venturing, 30*(5), 675–695.
Demmert, H., & Klein, D. (2003). Experiment on entrepreneurial discovery: An attempt to demonstrate the conjecture of Hayek and Kirzner. *Journal of Economic and Behavior Organization, 50*, 295–310.
Dew, N., Read, S., & Sarasvathy, S. (2011). On the entrepreneurial genesis of new markets: Effectual transformations versus causal search and selection. *Journal of Evolutionary Economics, 21*, 231–253.
Dimov, D. (2007). From opportunity insight to opportunity intention: The importance of person-situation learning match. *Entrepreneurship Theory and Practice, 31*, 561–583.
Dimov, D. (2011). Grappling with the unbearable elusiveness of entrepreneurial opportunities. *Entrepreneurship Theory and Practice, 35*, 57–81.
Dyer, J. H., Gregersen, H. B., & Christensen, C. (2008). Entrepreneur behaviors, opportunity recognition, and the origins of innovative ventures. *Strategic Entrepreneurship Journal, 2*(4), 317–338.

Endres, A., & Woods, C. (2007). The case for more "subjectivist research on how entrepreneurs create opportunities. *International Journal of Entrepreneurial Behavior and Research, 13*(4), 222–234.

Endres, A., & Woods, C. (2010). Schumpeter's conduct model of the dynamic entrepreneur: Scope and distinctiveness. *Journal of Evolutionary Economics, 20*, 583–607.

Fiet, J. (2002). *The systematic search for entrepreneurial discoveries*. Quorum Books.

Fiske, S., & Taylor, S. (1991). *Social cognition*. McGraw Hill.

Gaglio, C. M. (1997a). Opportunity identification: Review, critique and suggested research directions. In J. Katz & R. Brockhaus (Eds.), *Advances in entrepreneurship, firm emergence and growth, 3*, 139–202.

Gaglio, C. M. (1997b). *The entrepreneurial opportunity identification process*. PhD thesis, University of Chicago.

Gaglio, C. M. (2004). The role of mental simulations and counterfactual thinking in the opportunity identification process. *Entrepreneurship Theory & Practice, 28*, 533–552.

Gaglio, C. M., & Dimov, D. (2019). Opportunity identification redux. In Katz, J. & Corbett, A. (Eds.) *Advances in entrepreneurship, firm emergence and growth, 20*, 49–69.

Gaglio, C. M., & Katz, J. A. (2001). The psychological basis of opportunity identification: Entrepreneurial alertness. *Journal of Small Business Economics, 16*, 95–111.

Gaglio, C. M., & Winter, S. (2009). Entrepreneurial alertness and opportunity identification: Where are we now? In M. Brännback & A. Carsrud (Eds.), *Understanding the entrepreneurial mind* (pp. 305–325). Springer.

Gaglio, C. M., & Winter, S. (2017). Entrepreneurial alertness and opportunity identification 3.0: Yes, we can talk empirical! In M. Brännback & A. Carsrud (Eds.), *Revisitng the entrepreneurial mind* (pp. 359–377). International Studies in Entrepreneurship, *35*.

Gartner, W. (2010, January). ENTER: Entrepreneurial narrative theory ethnomethodology and reflexivity: An issue about the republic of tea. *Entrepreneurial Studies*. https://tigerprints.clemson.edu/cudp_entrepreneur/5

Gerschlager, C. (2012). Agents of change. *Journal of Evolutionary Economics, 2*, 413–441.

Grégoire, D., Barr, P. & Shepherd, D. (2010). Cognitive processes of opportunity recognition: The role of structural alignment. *Organization Science, 21*(2), 413–431. 587–588, 590.

Grégoire, D., Shepherd, D., & Lambert, L. (2010). Measuring opportunity recognition beliefs: Illustrating and validating an experimental approach. *Organizational Research Methods, 13*, 114–145.

Hansen, D. J., Lumpkin, G. T., & Hills, G. T. (2011). A multidimensional examination of a creativity-based opportunity recognition model. *Journal of Entrepreneurial Behaviour & Research, 17*(5), 515–533.

Hansen, D., Monllor, J., & Shrader, R. (2016). Identifying the elements of entrepreneurial opportunity constructs: Recognizing what scholars are really examining. *International Journal of Entrepreneurship and Innovation, 17*, 240–255.

Haynie, M., Shepherd, D., & McMullen, J. (2009). An opportunity for me? The role of resources in opportunity evaluation decisions. *Journal of Management Studies, 46*, 337–361.

Hsieh, C., Nickerson, J. A., & Zenger, T. R. (2007). Opportunity discovery, problem solving and a theory of the entrepreneurial firm. *Journal of Management Studies, 44*(4), 1255–1277.

Hutchinson, A. (2019). What does Facebook know about you really? Retrieved October 20, 2019, from Social Media Today website. https://www.socialmediatoday.com/news/what-does-facebook-know-about-you-really/546502/

Kahneman, D., & Tversky, A. (1979). Prospect theory: An analysis of decision under risk. *Econometrica, 47*(2), 263–291.

Kaltheuner, F., & Weatherhead, C. (2018). *How Facebook tracks you on Android*. Retrieved from https://media.ccc.de/v/35c3-9941how_facebook_tracks_you_on_android

Katz, J., & Gartner, W. B. (1988). Properties of emerging organizations. *Academy of Management Review, 13*(3), 429–441.

Kirzner, I. (1979). *Perception, opportunity, and profit*. University of Chicago Press.

Kirzner, I. (1985). *Discovery and the capitalist process*. University of Chicago Press.

Kitzmann, J., & Schiereck, D. (2005). Entrepreneurial discovery and the Demmert/Klein experiment: Another attempt at creating proper context. *Review of Austrian Economics, 18*, 169–178.

Ko, S., & Butler, J. (2007). Creativity: A key link to entrepreneurial behavior. *Business Horizons, 50*, 365–372.

MacMillian, I., & Katz, J. (1992). Idiosyncratic milieus of entrepreneurial research: The need for comprehensive theory. *Journal of Business Venturing, 7*, 1–8.

Maine, E., & P. & Dos Santos, N. (2015). The role of entrepreneurial decision-making in opportunity creation and recognition. *Technovation, 39*, 53–72.

Manne, H. (2014). Resurrecting the ghostly entrepreneur. *Review of Austrian Economics, 27*, 249–258.

Minniti, M. (2004). Entrepreneurial alertness and asymmetric information in a spin-glass model. *Journal of Business Venturing, 19*(5), 637–658.

Minniti, M., & Lévesque, M. (2008). Recent developments in the economics of entrepreneurship. *Journal of Business Venturing, 23*, 603–612.

Newell, G., & Holian, M. (2017). An agent-based model of entrepreneurship: Examining the role of alertness and transaction costs. *Journal of Entrepreneurship and Public Policy, 6*, 259–270.

Obschonka, M. (2017). The quest for the entrepreneurial culture: Psychological big data in entrepreneurship research. *Current Opinion in Behavioral Sciences, 18*, 69–74.

Pelly, R. (2017). Entrepreneurial opportunity—A perspective from the theory of forms. *American Journal of Management, 17*(5), 87–102.

Plummer, L. A., Haynie, J. M., & Godesiabois, J. (2007). An essay on the origins of entrepreneurial opportunity. *Small Business Economics, 28*(4), 363–379.

Roundy, P., Harrison, D., Khavul, S., Perez-Nordtvedt, L., & McGee, J. (2018). Entrepreneurial alertness as a pathway to strategic decisions and organizational performance. *Strategic Organization, 16*(2), 192–226.

Sarasvathy, S. (2001). Causation and effectuation: Toward a theoretical shift from economic inevitability to entrepreneurial contingency. *Academy of Management Review, 26*, 243–263.

Sautet, F. (2018). The battle for the essence of entrepreneurship: A review essay on Nicolai Foss and Peter Klein's Organizing entrepreneurial judgment: A new approach to the firm. *Review of Austrian Economics, 31*, 123–139.

Schumpeter, J. A. (1950). *Capitalism, socialism, and democracy*. 3rd ed. Harper and Brothers.

Schwab, A., & Zhang, Z. (2019). A new methodological frontier in entrepreneurship research: Big data studies. *Entrepreneurship Theory and Practice, 43*(5), 843–854. https://doi.org/10.1177/1042258718760841

Sedkaoui, S. (2018). How data analytics is changing entrepreneurial opportunities? *International Journal of Innovation Science, 10*(2), 274–294. https://doi.org/10.1108/IJIS-09-2017-0092

Shane, S. (2000). Prior knowledge and the discovery of entrepreneurial opportunities. *Organizational Science, 11*(4), 448–469.

Shane, S. (2004). *A general theory of entrepreneurship: The individual-opportunity nexus*. Edward Elgar.

Shane, S., & Venkataman, S. (2000). The promise of entrepreneurship as a field of research. *The Academy of Management Review, 25*(1), 217–226.

Shepherd, D., & DeTienne, D. (2005). Prior knowledge, potential financial reward and opportunity identification. *Entrepreneurship Theory & Practice, 29*, 91–112.

Short, J., Ketchen, D., Shook, C., & Ireland, D. (2010). The concept of 'opportunity' in entrepreneurship research: Past accomplishments and future challenges. *Journal of Management, 36*, 40–65.

Sills, D. L. (Ed.). (1968). *International encyclopedia of the social sciences* (Vol. 1, p. 1968). Macmillan Company & The Free Press.

Skarbek, D. (2009). Alertness, local knowledge and Johnny Appleseed. *Review of Austrian Economics, 22*(4), 415–424.

Tang, J. (2008). Environmental munificence for entrepreneurs: Entrepreneurial alertness and commitment. *International Journal of Entrepreneurial Behaviour and Research, 14*(3), 128–151.

Tang, J., Kacmar, M., & Busenitz, L. (2012). Entrepreneurial alertness in the pursuit of new opportunities. *Journal of Business Venturing, 27*, 77–94.

Tang, J., & Khan, S. (2007). Dynamic interactions between alertness and systematic search: A yin and yang perspective on opportunity recognition and innovation. *International Journal of Entrepreneurship and Innovation, 8*(3), 175–187.

Valliere, D. (2013). Towards a schematic theory of entrepreneurial alertness. *Journal of Business Venturing, 28*, 430–442.

Wang, F., Mack, E. A., & Maciewjewski, R. (2017). Analyzing entrepreneurial social networks with big data. *Annals of the American Association of Geographers, 107*(1), 130–150. https://doi.org/10.1080/24694452.2016.1222263

Welter, C., & Alvarez, S. (2015). The state of opportunities: Clarifying the transitions between opportunity types. *Management Decisions, 53*, 1398–1411.

Yu, T. F.-L. (2001). Entrepreneurial alertness and discovery. *Review of Austrian Economics, 14*(I), 47–63.

Ziegler, M., Rosenzweig, B., & Ziegler, P. (1992). *The republic of tea: Letters to a Young Zentrep[r]eneur*. Doubleday.

CHAPTER 6

The Emergence of Entrepreneurship Education

Mary K. Foster

In 2005, Donald Kuratko's *The Emergence of Entrepreneurship Education: Development, Trends, and Challenges* was published by *Entrepreneurship: Theory and Practice*. The article presents an evidence-based case for the extent and importance of entrepreneurial activity, entrepreneurial perspective, and entrepreneurial education; a compendium of sources of entrepreneurship information; a list of the most significant themes in entrepreneurship research and education; a discussion of the historical context of entrepreneurship education; a description of the state of entrepreneurship education; ten future challenges for entrepreneurship education; and a call to action. The article is packed with information, ideas, and opinions. And the author makes several important, quotable declarations:

M. K. Foster (✉)
Morgan State University, Baltimore, MD, USA
e-mail: mary.foster@morgan.edu

A. E. Osorio et al. (eds.), *Modern Classics in Entrepreneurship Studies*,
https://doi.org/10.1007/978-3-030-61029-6_6

> ...the question of whether entrepreneurship can be taught is obsolete. (p. 580)
>
> It is becoming increasingly clear that entrepreneurship, or certain facets of it, *can* be taught. (p. 580)
>
> In the midst of this huge expansion of courses [in entrepreneurship,] remains the challenge of entrepreneurship's complete academic legitimacy. (p. 579)

The author also suggests that the field should focus on what should be taught and how it could best be taught while working to achieve "complete respectability and leadership" (p. 587) within academia.

Summary of a Modern Classic

The Extent and Importance of Entrepreneurial Activity, Entrepreneurial Perspective, and Entrepreneurial Education

Entrepreneurial Activity. Kuratko (2005) marshals a dense assemblage of facts and factoids about entrepreneurial activity—new businesses incorporated, new small businesses, fastest-growing new firms, job creation, small business job creation, small business employment, businesses open less than a year, percent of new inventions created by small firms, percent of people by age trying to start a business, and percent of people by age wanting to start a business—drawn from the 1999 and 2004 *Global Entrepreneurship Monitor Executive Reports*, predominately the 1999 report. The key message from the 1999 report was that: "...the conjunction of intense entrepreneurial dynamism and rapid economic growth—coupled with low employment and low inflation [as exemplified by the United States]—seemingly points to only one conclusion: entrepreneurship fuels economic growth, creating employment and prosperity" (Reynolds et al., 1999, p. 7). Specifically, "entrepreneurship and innovation are central to the creative process in the economy and to promoting growth, increasing productivity, and creating jobs" (Reynolds et al., 1999, p. 7).

Entrepreneurial Perspective. Kuratko (2005) declares that "an 'entrepreneurial perspective' can be developed in individuals" (p. 578). He defines entrepreneurial perspective as "seeking opportunities, taking risks beyond security, and having the tenacity to push an idea through to reality" (p. 578). Further, he argues that an entrepreneurial perspective could be exercised in any type of organizational setting (e.g., non-profit, for profit, etc.), and implies that it is a good thing—revolutionizing "the way business is conducted at every level in every country" (p. 578).

Entrepreneurial Education. Citing Katz (2003), Kuratko (2005) notes that the number of colleges and universities offering entrepreneurship courses has grown to 1600 (p. 579). Katz (2003) defined entrepreneurship education as courses, infrastructure elements, and publications. Entrepreneurship courses include the following subjects: "entrepreneurship, new venture creation, entrepreneurial finance, small business, family business, free enterprise, private enterprise, high-technology business, new product development, microenterprise development, applied economic development, professional practice studies, women's entrepreneurship, minority entrepreneurship and ethnic entrepreneurship" (Katz, 2003, p. 284). Kuratko cautions that the key challenge for entrepreneurship education is "complete academic legitimacy" (2005, p. 579).

Compendium of Sources of Entrepreneurship Information

Kuratko (2005) notes three major sources of information about entrepreneurship: publications, direct observation, and speeches/presentations. He elaborates on publications identifying specific examples of academic journals, textbooks, books, periodicals, newsletters, proceedings, and government publications.

Significant Themes as Entrepreneurship Research and Education Emerge

Kuratko (2005) declares that entrepreneurship "*can* be taught" (p. 580) and that the question of whether it can be taught is "*obsolete*" (p. 580). He turns his attention to "what should be taught and how it should be taught" (p. 581) and briefly describes ten significant themes in entrepreneurship research and education:

- The intersection of entrepreneurship and management
- Venture financing
- Corporate entrepreneurship
- The intersection of entrepreneurship and strategy (entrepreneurial strategies)
- Psychological predictors of entrepreneurial success

- Risks and trade-offs of an entrepreneurial career
- Women and minority entrepreneurship
- Ubiquity of the entrepreneurial spirit; international/global entrepreneurship
- Economic and social contributions of entrepreneurship
- Ethics in entrepreneurship.

The Historical Context of Entrepreneurship Education

Kuratko (2005) argues that entrepreneurship education became a presence in business education in the 1970s when the University of Southern California launched the first MBA with a concentration in entrepreneurship, yet the real growth in entrepreneurship education came in the 1980s. He references Katz (2003), who notes there were 16 higher education organizations offering entrepreneurship courses in 1970. He also cites Solomon et al. (1994), who established via surveys that there were 263 higher education institutions offering small business management and entrepreneurship courses in 1979. By 1992, that number had grown to 1060.

Kuratko (2005) references three studies from the late 1980s–early 1990s, two of which included surveys of entrepreneurship education activities at universities, to describe how entrepreneurship education was evolving or should evolve. He reports on Zeithaml and Rice's (1987) recommendations for the future of entrepreneurship education and research: (1) evolve course offerings to include more recent conceptualizations of entrepreneurship including intrapreneurs and corporate venturing; (2) focus on entrepreneurship research; (3) focus on entrepreneurship pedagogy research; or (4) investigate ways to make entrepreneurship courses/programs/centers sources of funds for institutions through participation in government-funded partnerships like the Small Business Development Center program or partnerships with private entities like local entrepreneurs and foundations.

Kuratko (2005) reports that Zeithaml and Rice (1987) argue that institutions which offer "a broad, integrative, pragmatic, rational approach to business" (p. 582) will be more appealing to aspiring entrepreneurs, managers, and CEOs than programs that focus on specialization and take a more narrow or fragmented view of management.

Kuratko (2005) describes Ronstadt's (1987) recommendation that entrepreneurial programs be designed to help potential entrepreneurs become aware of the barriers they are likely to encounter and provide them with the skills and networks to overcome those barriers. Ronstadt developed these recommendations after defining and critiquing the old school and new school approaches to entrepreneurship education. The old school approach (~1940s to mid-1980s) focused on new venture creation: "go out and do it now" all you need is a business plan and the "right stuff" (Ronstadt, 1987, p. 41). Ronstadt argues that a new school approach is needed and emerging in response to new insights about how entrepreneurship really works and the dissonance of the old school emphasis on action *and* a business plan that often required "75 to 150 hours of analysis and writing" (1987, p. 41). The new school approach focuses on entrepreneurship as a career, at any age, involving several ventures over time, where people, business model, and environment influence success. Ronstadt calls for entrepreneurship education to support the new school approach with structured and unstructured offerings which develop both "knowhow" and "knowwho" (1987, p. 43).

Kuratko (2005) also reports on the findings from Robinson and Haynes' (1991) survey of universities with over 10,000 students, which found that 18% of surveyed universities had no entrepreneurship courses and 32% had one course. Kuratko (2005) summarized Robinson and Haynes (1991) concern that the primary weakness of entrepreneurship education is the lack of depth of most programs. They argue that programs and personnel must be developed to improve the quality of the field, despite: the lack of theoretical bases for building pedagogical models and methods, the lack of formal academic development and training programs, and the need to maintain student interest in academic programs.

The State of Entrepreneurship Education

Kuratko (2005) draws on Katz's (2003) history of entrepreneurship education to quantify entrepreneurship education in the late 1990s–early 2000s:

- 2200 courses in more than 1600 higher education institutions
- 100 funded entrepreneurship centers at higher education institutions
- 277 endowed chairs/professors
- $440 million in endowments for entrepreneurship
- 44 refereed entrepreneurship journals

Quoting extensively from Solomon et al.'s (2002) comprehensive empirical analysis of entrepreneurship education, Kuratko (2005) summarizes the objectives, content, and pedagogical approaches of entrepreneurship education.

Objectives. Entrepreneurship education has a different objective than other types of business education (i.e., starting versus managing a business).

Content. Given the different educational objectives of entrepreneurship education, the content must be different as well, focusing on skill building (e.g., negotiation, leadership, new product development, creative thinking, technology innovation, and tolerance of ambiguity) and expertise development (e.g., sources of venture capital, idea protection, stages of venture development, and entrepreneurial career options).

Pedagogical Approach. Experiential learning is widely used and executed in many different ways. Business plans, cases, and small business consulting are widely used. Entrepreneurship education is being expanded to target non-business majors (e.g., art, engineering, and science majors) and people who support (e.g., accountants, lawyers) or manage entrepreneurs (e.g., top management). Research that focuses on the scholarship of teaching and learning in entrepreneurship education is emerging. For example, Babson started an annual symposium entitled *Frontiers in Entrepreneurship Research* in 1981 and the National Consortium of Entrepreneurship Centers (NCEC) was founded in 1998. The United States Association for Small Business and Entrepreneurship (USASBE) started the National Model Programs awards.

Kuratko (2005) suggests: "...legitimacy has been attained in the current state of entrepreneurship education" (p. 586), yet other challenges remain.

Challenges for Entrepreneurship Education

After assessing the state of entrepreneurship education, Kuratko (2005) identifies ten challenges for the field:

1. The Maturity/Complacency/Stagnation Trap—Kuratko (2005) argues that the field may be legitimized but is not yet mature. He makes an impassioned argument for the zealous pioneers of entrepreneurship education to continue to wage war for complete respectability and leadership within business schools.

2. The Research/Publications Dilemma—Kuratko (2005) notes the publication glut (many journals chasing too few articles) and the push for leading entrepreneurship researchers to publish in top-ranked management journals (versus entrepreneurship journals) and calls for a focus on getting more entrepreneurship journals accepted by more academic institutions for tenure and promotion purposes.
3. The Faculty Pipeline Shortage—Kuratko (2005) laments the shortage of entrepreneurship faculty at every academic rank and the lack of entrepreneurship doctoral programs. He calls on NCEC, USASBE, the Academy of Management's Entrepreneurship division, the Coleman Foundation, and the Ewing Marion Kauffman Foundation to address these shortcomings. Further, Kuratko urges entrepreneurship faculty to develop the education they need for themselves.
4. The Technology Challenge—Kuratko (2005) notes the need to embrace technology (i.e., distance learning technologies). A field associated with innovation must not stagnate but should expand the use of online learning for entrepreneurship education.
5. The "Dot-Com" Legacy—Kuratko (2005) cites the 1999 dot-com bust as a cautionary example and urges entrepreneurship educators to remain focused on teaching students how to create enduring enterprises. He enjoins faculty not to get caught up in the infatuation with fast cash, quick exits, and no real commitments, which he calls the investment mentality.
6. The Academia vs. Business Incongruence—Kuratko (2005) highlights what roles academics and practitioners should play in entrepreneurship education. He notes that practitioners must do more than tell interesting stories. They must help illuminate the real problems and issues faced in launching and growing a venture. He calls on entrepreneurship educators to address this issue by identifying the "lessons learned" or "make a difference" ideas (p. 589).
7. The "Dilution Effect"—As entrepreneurship becomes more legitimized and more popular on campuses, Kuratko (2005) notes there is a risk that the entrepreneurship label will be co-opted or adopted as a means of garnering attention or resources. He urges entrepreneurship educators to guard the true meaning and intent of the word.

8. The Security-Risk Dilemma—Kuratko (2005) characterizes entrepreneurs as calculated risk-takers and worries that risk is not adequately represented in entrepreneurship curricula and that faculty do not model risk-taking adequately—pursuing tenure rather than taking risks developing entrepreneurship programs and curricula. He calls on all entrepreneurship educators, particularly senior faculty, to sponsor and support younger, aggressive entrepreneurship professors.
9. The Administrative Leadership Revolving Door Problem—Kuratko (2005) laments the short tenure of administrative leaders (e.g., chairs, deans, provosts, and presidents), which leads to sporadic support for entrepreneurship education. His solution is to change the power base to include entrepreneurship educators in all those roles.
10. The "Power of One" Challenge—Kuratko (2005) observes, as others have, that many entrepreneurship programs have been driven by the drive and determination of a single individual. Some see this as a weakness of the field; he chooses to see it as a strength suggesting that the field models the power of one for other academic fields.

Call to Action

Kuratko (2005) closes the article with a motivational call to action. He emphasizes the contribution each person can make and calls on entrepreneurship educators to be open to new ideas, to remember the importance of innovation and creativity, and to be a leader who defines and creates the future of entrepreneurship education.

Is *The Emergence of Entrepreneurship Education: Development, Trends, and Challenges* a Classic?

The Emergence of Entrepreneurship Education: Development, Trends, and Challenges was published in *Entrepreneurship Theory and Practice* in 2005. In a search of "entrepreneurship education" using Google Scholar (on April 25, 2021), this article had the highest citation rate by a significant margin with 3007 citations. According to PlumX Metrics[1] (April 9, 2021), this article has 1014 citations (98th percentile), 3549 full text views, and 1119 readers. Per Altmetric[2] (September 22, 2019), this article has 658 citations, is among the top 10% of all research articles in terms of research outputs (quality and quantity of online attention), and is ranked #33 in terms of all research outputs from *Entrepreneurship Theory and Practice*. So, by the numbers, this article is certainly an influential article in the field of entrepreneurship education. And it is a relative newcomer by academic standards, having been published within the last 16 years.

So, what made this article so popular or useful within the field? Both contextual factors and content factors probably had an impact on the utility of this article.

Contextual Factors

Timing. In 2005, when the article was published, the United States was in the middle of a moderate economic expansion (2001–2007, +2.8% annual GPD growth), following a long period of economic expansion (1991–2001, +3.6% annual GDP growth), at the time, the second-longest period of economic expansion in the country's history, even though it did include the dot-com bubble (Amadeo, 2020). During the 1980s and 1990s, after the post-World War II expansion driven by large firms, there was a new appreciation for the role of small and medium enterprises (SMEs) in driving economic growth—during this period in the US, more than 80% of all new jobs were created by small enterprises, that is firms with less than 500 employees (Conte & Karr, 1981). During this period, entrepreneurship education also experienced rapid growth (Solomon et al., 1994). One could argue that 2005 was a perfect time to recap the enormous interest in and growth of entrepreneurship education during the prior two decades. After a period of rapid expansion and growth, a field is ripe for review, reflection, and focus on new challenges.

[1] PlumX Metrics provides insights about how people use scholarly research. For more detail about the definitions and meaning of their metrics go to: https://plumanalytics.com/learn/about-metrics/.

[2] Altmetric assesses the impact of research. For more detail about the definitions and meaning of their measures go to: https://www.altmetric.com/about-our-data/.

Journal Ranking. The paper was published in *Entrepreneurship Theory and Practice*, a journal that was at the time and continues to be very highly ranked and respected as a top entrepreneurship journal. According to *Cabells' Journalytics*, in 2005, the journal had a cite index of 0.916 with a median mention of 129 instances per article; those same figures for 2020 are 0.901 and 129, respectively. Since the article was published, the journal has grown in stature and is now cited as the second-highest impact entrepreneurship and innovation journal by Google Scholar and continues to be highly rated by *Journal Citation Reports* and *Financial Times*. Being published in an accessible, respected journal has probably contributed to awareness and use of the article.

Relative Paucity of Entrepreneurship Education Articles. In 2005, when this article was published, there were approximately 7078 peer-reviewed journal articles related to entrepreneurship education in the 71 databases included in EBSCOHost searches; this compares with 6949 for accounting education, 65,245 for management education, and 49,086 for business education. See Fig. 6.1 for a summary of the cumulative number of peer-reviewed entrepreneurship education journal articles available by

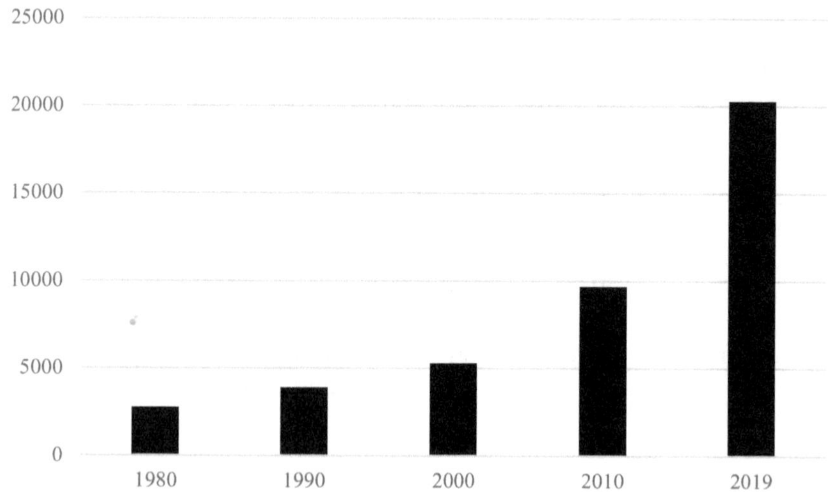

Fig. 6.1 Cumulative number of "entrepreneurship education" peer-reviewed journal articles

year, which illustrates the explosive growth in entrepreneurship education research in the 2000s. Whether one attributes it to timing, stage of field development, or the number of competing articles, Kuratko's (2005) work likely benefited from being published when the pool of entrepreneurship education articles to cite was much smaller.

Content Factors

Key Messages. Kuratko's (2005) article includes some great soundbites for which the field of entrepreneurship was likely ready after a decade of rapid growth with an increasing number of practitioners and educators. Some of the key quotes include: "…the question of whether entrepreneurship can be taught is obsolete" (p. 580); "It is becoming increasingly clear that entrepreneurship, or certain facets of it, ***can*** be taught" (p. 580); "In the midst of this huge expansion of courses [in entrepreneurship,] remains the challenge of entrepreneurship's complete academic legitimacy" (p. 579); "…the more relevant question regarding entrepreneurial education: What should be taught and how should it be taught?" (pp. 580–591); and "…the 'real war' continues to wage for [entrepreneurship's] complete respectability and leadership" (p. 587). This paper captured the shift from a fledgling field working to establish its legitimacy to an established and growing field focusing on the quality and utility of its ideas and research, thus providing the justification for researchers to explore new and exciting directions within the field.

In addition to the pithy quotes, this article covered a very broad and somewhat unusual array of topics: the importance of the field, sources of information about the field, a history of the field, current research themes, the state of the field, and future challenges for the field. Thus, it became a "go to" source for entrepreneurship educators, a rich compendium of facts, information, opinions, and references.

Kuratko (2005) writes in a collegial, positive, inspirational/ motivational tone, especially about the future. At this point in his career, he had been working in this no-longer nascent field for about 20 years. He generously quotes peers and comes across as a true believer, one of the passionate pioneers who made a difference through individual effort and perseverance. This tone was likely attractive to scholars writing in the field.

Accessible Language. Kuratko (2005) writes in an accessible, easy-to-read style, and even his densest sections convey valuable information. The accessibility of the language in the article likely has contributed to the popularity of this work.

Reference Value. This fifteen-page paper references 111 articles, so it provides a deep pool of references and helps the reader see the influence various authors have had on the field. This makes it a useful resource for authors digging into the topic and increases the odds of being cited in their work.

Does This Article Stand the Test of Time?

Then and Now: The Extent and Importance of Entrepreneurial Activity, Entrepreneurial Perspective, and Entrepreneurial Education

Entrepreneurial Activity. Per the U.S. Census Bureau's Business Dynamics Report (2018), in the ten years before the publication of the article, the average number of establishments launched each year was 721,921 and the average number of establishments that closed per year was 626,278 for an average net growth in establishments of 95,643. In the 13 years since 2005, the average number of establishments launched each year was 691,548, and the average number of establishments that closed per year was 644,270 for an average net growth in establishments of 47,278. As you can see in Fig. 6.2, prior to the article being published, new business startups were generally growing and well above business exits. Since the article was published, firm births spiked, declined, recovered, and declined again. Since the article was published, net growth rates for establishments have declined, and the birth rate for new firms has declined (see Fig. 6.3).

In 2020, per the Small Business Administration (SBA) Advocacy Office's *Profile of Small Businesses*, small business employees accounted for 47.1% of the private workforce in the country (SBA, 2020). This is down from 53% at the time the Kuratko article was published. Per the SBA definition, a small business is a firm with less than 500,000 employees. Small businesses accounted for 43.5% of the non-farm U.S. economy in 2014 (Kobe & Schwinn, 2018). The share of GDP attributable to small businesses declined from 48% in 1998 to 43.5% in 2014; small business GDP has been growing at about 1.4% (real annual growth rate from 1998 to 2014), while large businesses have been growing at a real annual rate of

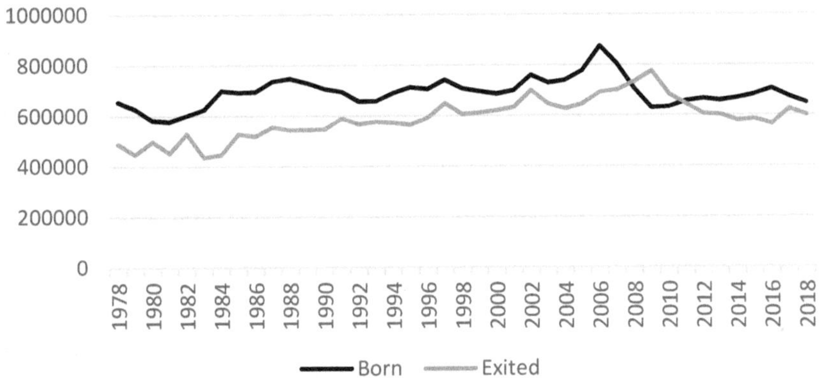

Fig. 6.2 Trends in firm births and exits by year (*Source* U.S. Census Bureau, Business Dynamics Statistics: Geography: 1978–2018)

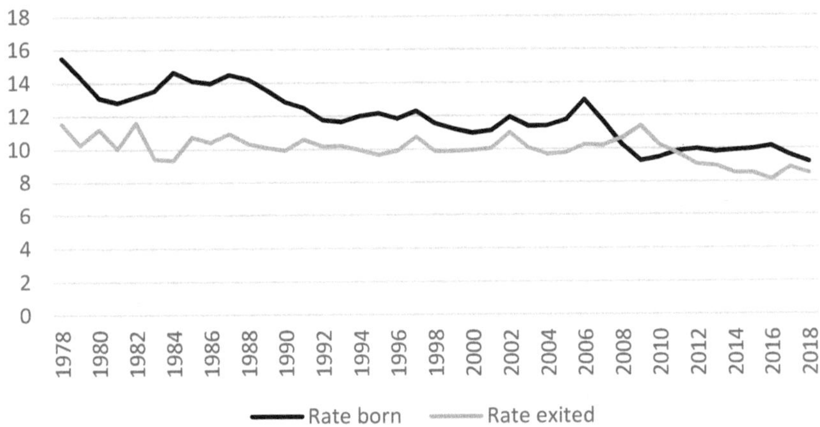

Fig. 6.3 Trends in firm birth and exit rates (*Source* U.S. Census Bureau, Business Dynamics Statistics: Geography: 1978–2018)

2.5% during the same period (Kobe & Schwinn, 2018). Kuratko reported small businesses accounted for 51% of private-sector GDP, but it was not clear what year he was referring to or the source of the information.

Kuratko's description of entrepreneurial activity was positive and upbeat; he presented a dense assemblage of facts and figures with few sources and limited precision about definitions, timing, or terminology. So, it is difficult to make direct comparisons between his analysis of entrepreneurial activity and entrepreneurial activity today. Despite these difficulties, the data today indicates that entrepreneurial activity was growing more rapidly and was more important to the economy in the period Kuratko analyzed than today.

Entrepreneurial Perspective. Using select facts and hypotheticals, Kuratko built the case that small businesses have an important positive impact on the economy via jobs, innovation, and contribution to the gross domestic product (GDP). He argued that entrepreneurial firms play two important roles in the economy: (1) they contribute to economic renewal—innovation, improvements in productivity and thus competitive changes in the market structure; and (2) they provide a pathway to the American dream of economic growth, equal opportunities, and upward mobility, especially for women, minorities, and immigrants. He claimed that the entrepreneurial perspective is the force creating a positive economic revolution. His optimistic message about entrepreneurial activity as a key driver of economic growth was consistent with political and economic thinking at the time and was likely not critically challenged.

Today, arguments about the importance and contributions of entrepreneurship are more nuanced and contested as we seek to understand the complex conditions driving long-term downward trends in new business births and the lower real annual growth rates for small businesses versus larger ones. In the last 15 years, there has been more interest in understanding how different types of small businesses contribute to economic and social life. Researchers strive to understand how differences in firm size, age, reasons for starting a business, and type of business affect job creation, innovation, the standard of living, and economic growth. Further, researchers want to know if there are differences in interest, obstacles, experiences, and success for women, minorities, and immigrants when starting a business. All of these factors may have an impact on the importance and contribution of entrepreneurship to society.

For example, in the 2020 Bureau of Economic Analysis Report: *Measuring the Small Business Economy*, the authors report on their work to better understand growth trends and the relative contributions of small businesses in the U.S. economy by using more refined definitions of business size (Highfill et al. 2020). They note that in the United States, the literature on small business output defines small businesses as businesses employing fewer than 500 employees. In other countries and organizations, the definition of small businesses varies (see Highfill et al., 2020, p. 15), although many definitions use employment as a size indicator. For their analysis, they used the following definitions:

- Very small = 0–19 employees
- Small = 20–49 employees
- Medium small = 50–99 employees
- Medium = 100–499 employees
- Large = 500 or more employees

Using this more fine-grained approach to analyzing the contributions of small businesses, they found that wage and employment growth from 2012 to 2016 was slowest for very small enterprises (those with less than 20 employees) and fastest for large enterprises (those with 500 or more employees), although this relationship differed across industries. Additionally, enterprises with 0–99 employees saw wages increase at a slower rate than medium and large enterprises (those employing 100 or more employees), lagging by 1.5% (Highfill et al., 2020).

The Kauffman Indicators of Entrepreneurship examines the reasons people start a business in an effort to better understand the influence of economic conditions on business creation (Fairlie & Desai, 2021). They track trends in the percentage of new entrepreneurs who create a business out of choice instead of necessity (i.e., because they have lost their job). Their findings indicate that during times of economic crises such as recessions, depressions, and pandemics, the rate of new entrepreneurs (all new business owners regardless of size or origin) rises, as does the percent who are doing so out of necessity, not opportunity.

Work by the Kauffman Foundation and the Brookings Institution examines the economic contributions of small firms by type of firm. Wiens and Jackson of the Kauffman Foundation found that between 1988 and 2012, new and young firms (0–5 years old) were the primary source of job creation in the American economy, not small businesses generally (2015). They note that firms with less than 50 employees make up 95% of all U.S. firms and are an important part of the economy. And the few large firms with millions of employees are also important to the economy. However, neither group (small or large) contributes to new job creation like young entrepreneurial firms do (Wiens & Jackson, 2015).

New businesses account for nearly all new job creation and almost 20% of gross job creation; firms less than one year old have created an average of 1.5 million jobs per year over the last three decades (Wiens & Jackson, 2015). Many young firms exhibit an "up or out" dynamic where innovative successful firms grow rapidly, create jobs, and contribute to economic growth or quickly fail and exit the market (Wiens & Jackson, 2015). Unfortunately, new businesses represent a declining share of the business community; new firms represented 16% of all firms in the late 1970s and by 2011 represented only 8% (Wiens & Jackson, 2015). Further, the gross number of jobs created by new firms fell by more than 2 million between 2005 and 2010 (Wiens & Jackson, 2015). New firm entry rates are declining, and the jobs being created by new firms are declining.

Hathaway and Litan (2014), researchers at the Brookings Institution, confirm the decline in new firm formations and job reallocation rates between 1989 and 2011. They note that these declines are universal across states, metro areas, industries, and by firm size (Hathaway & Litan, 2014). These declines are associated with deficits in jobs, slow productivity growth, stagnant wages, and rising inequality (Hwang, 2019). Hathaway and Litan (2014) illustrate that a very small percentage of firms account for a substantial majority of new job growth in any given year, yet it is hard to know at the time of founding which firms are likely to survive and produce large numbers of jobs. Thus, they argue that increasing new firm startups is the path to creating more rapid growth firms that contribute more job growth (Hathaway & Litan, 2014).

In addition to the decades-long decline in entrepreneurial activity outlined in the 2017 *Kauffman Index of Startup Activity* (Fairlie et al., 2017) and other reports mentioned above, certain groups face more significant and more persistent barriers to starting a firm, specifically, women and people of color (Hwang, 2019). Women are half as likely as men to own employer businesses (Morelix et al., 2017), and the gender gap has increased from 1996 to 2016 with women now representing less than 40% of new entrepreneurs (Fairlie et al., 2017). Minorities own half as many businesses as non-minorities do, and minority businesses tend to start and stay smaller (Morelix et al., 2017). Between 1996 and 2016, Latinos and Asians have grown significantly as a percentage of total new entrepreneurs, while Blacks have grown by one percentage point (Fairlie et al., 2017). Adults without formal education (e.g., a high school or college degree) are much less likely to start a new venture (Morelix et al., 2017). College graduates now account for the largest percentage of new entrepreneurs (Fairlie et al., 2017). The lack of education, experience, and access to capital are significant barriers to entrepreneurial endeavors for women and people of color (Fairlie & Robb, 2008; Fairlie et al., 2017; Robb & Fairlie, 2006).

In 2005, Kuratko touted the rise of young entrepreneurs (people less than 34 years old) as a force driving entrepreneurship education (p. 578). From 1996 to 2016, people 20–24 years old had the lowest rate of new entrepreneurs and the rate has declined over that time period (Fairlie et al., 2017). The 55–64 year-old age group has grown as a share of new entrepreneurs, at the expense of 20–24 year olds, over the last 20 years (Fairlie et al., 2017).

In summary, today, we have a more nuanced understanding of the contributions entrepreneurial firms make to the economy; contributions vary by age and size of the firm. More detailed, fine-grained data and analyses have helped us better understand long-term trends in startups and small business contributions to job growth and productivity, and the trends are not generally favorable (i.e., declines in startups are associated with deficits in jobs, slow productivity growth, stagnant wages, and rising inequality). Similarly, the expectation that entrepreneurial activity will spur equal opportunities and upward mobility for all have been challenged as barriers to entry for women and minorities have become apparent and as growth in new entrepreneurs has come from college-educated and older age groups.

Kuratko states:

> An 'entrepreneurial perspective' can be developed in individuals. This perspective can be exhibited inside or outside an organization, in profit or not-for-profit enterprises, and in business or non-business activities for the purpose of bringing forth creative ideas. Thus, entrepreneurship is an integrated concept that permeates an individual's business in an innovative manner. It is a perspective that has revolutionized the way business is conducted at every level and in every country. The revolution has begun in an economic sense, and the entrepreneurial perspective is a dominant force! (2005, p. 578)

Perhaps with a bit of hyperbole, this statement suggests that an entrepreneurial perspective might be a simple, homogeneous, monolithic idea, one powerful enough to fuel a successful economic revolution. Today, there is growing appreciation for the idea that entrepreneurship is not a monolithic phenomenon, but instead includes many diverse and moving parts (Fairlie et al., 2017). The skills and resources required to successfully create a new venture (startups), operate a small business (main street, local small businesses), or grow a business (growth entrepreneurship) are different, and their contributions to the economy are different (Fairlie et al., 2017). All are important and have a role to play in a robust economy, but each has unique needs and challenges.

Today people encourage, cultivate, and assess entrepreneurial mindset,[3] entrepreneurial intentions,[4] and entrepreneurial self-efficacy,[5] an updated interpretation of Kuratko's entrepreneurial perspective might go something like this: An entrepreneurial mindset can be learned and it contributes to desirable outcomes, individually and organizationally. This mindset can be exhibited inside or outside an organization, in profit or not-for-profit enterprises, and in business or non-business activities for the purpose of solving problems, innovating, and creating value. It is a perspective that should be encouraged; it is a perspective that is increasingly valued in a highly competitive global economy facing many complex problems, economically, socially, and environmentally.

[3] Entrepreneurial mindset is a set of skills that enable people to identify and make the most of opportunities, overcome and learn from setbacks, and succeed in a variety of settings. Gold, T., & Rodriquez, S. (2018). *Measuring entrepreneurial mindset in youth: Learnings from NFTE's entrepreneurial mindset index*. https://www.nfte.com/wp-content/uploads/2020/04/NFTE-Whitepaper-Measuring-Entrepreneurial-Mindset-in-Youth-November-2018.pdf.

[4] Intentions are the single best predictor of any planned behavior, including entrepreneurship. Understanding the antecedents of intentions increases our understanding of the intended behavior. Attitudes influence behavior by their impact on intentions. Intentions and attitudes depend on the situation and person. Accordingly, intentions models will predict behavior better than either individual (for example, personality) or situational (for example, employment status) variables. Predictive power is critical to better post hoc explanations of entrepreneurial behavior; intentions models provide superior predictive validity. Krueger, N. F., Jr., Reilly, M. D., & Carsrud, A. L. (2000). Competing models of entrepreneurial intentions. *Journal of Business Venturing, 15*(5–6), 411–432.

[5] Entrepreneurial self-efficacy (ESE) "is a construct that measures a person's belief in their ability to successfully launch an entrepreneurial venture. ESE is particularly useful since it incorporates personality as well as environmental factors, and is thought to be a strong predictor of entrepreneurial intentions and ultimately action (Bird, 1988; Boyd & Vozikis). Moreover, recent research suggests that an individual's ESE may be elevated through training and education; thus, potentially improving the rate of entrepreneurial activities (Florin, Karri, & Rossiter, 2007; Mueller & Goic, 2003; Zhao et al.)." McGee, J. E., Peterson, M., Mueller, S. L., & Sequeira, J. M. (2009). Entrepreneurial self-efficacy: Refining the measure. *Entrepreneurship Theory and Practice, 33*(4), 965–988.

Entrepreneurial Education. It is difficult to compare growth in entrepreneurial education then and now because of differences in terminology and lack of census counts. Kurtko cited Katz (2003) when he noted that the number of institutions offering entrepreneurship courses had grown from a handful to 1600. Four recent reports on entrepreneurship education note continued enthusiasm for entrepreneurship education and the desire for entrepreneurship education to be pervasive or widespread (Brooks et al., 2008; Lackeus, 2015; Morris & Liguori, 2016; Solomon, 2014). The Kauffman Foundation's report on *Entrepreneurship in American Higher Education* (Brooks et al., 2008) attempts to quantify the size or growth of entrepreneurship education. They note that entrepreneurship is one of the fastest-growing subjects in U.S. undergraduate curricula and that formal entrepreneurship programs (i.e., majors, minors, and certificates) have grown from 104 in 1975 to more than 500 in 2006; more than 5000 entrepreneurship courses are offered in two- and four-year higher education institutions (Brooks et al., 2008). Solomon (2014), in an update of his survey of entrepreneurship education, compares the results from 2004, where over 1600 institutions had courses in entrepreneurship or small business management, with his 2014 survey results, where most institutions list not only courses but minors or majors in entrepreneurship or small business management. In the *2016 Annals of Entrepreneurship Education and Pedagogy*, Morris and Liguori say: "From a handful of programs three decades ago, today there are more than 3,000 institutions offering entrepreneurship programs" (p. xiv).

Then and Now: Sources of Entrepreneurship Information

Kuratko comprehensively highlights the sources of information about entrepreneurship in 2005: academic journals, textbooks, books, biographies and autobiographies, compendiums, news periodicals, venture periodicals, newsletters, proceedings of conferences, government publications, direct observation, and speeches/presentations by practitioners. He provides examples for each of the first ten sources and notes that all these sources provide the context for entrepreneurship education. One notable addition since 2005 to academic journals is USASBE's introduction of Entrepreneurship Education and Pedagogy in 2018.

In 1999, Babson and the London School of Business launched the Global Entrepreneurship Monitor (Radicioni, 2015); in 2004, Mark Zuckerberg launched Facebook (World wide web timeline, 2014); and in 2005, 68% of all adult Americans used the internet (Perrin & Duggan, 2015). The internet and innovations related to the internet have transformed the availability and accessibility of information today. Databases and internet-based media, like podcasts, blogs, electronic newsletters, and videos, have become significant sources of entrepreneurship information. Further, non-profits/non-governmental organizations, educational institutions, and partnerships of government agencies/non-profits/educational institutions have become leading sources of entrepreneurship information.

Databases. See the Kauffman Foundation's *Data Resources* web page for almost 100 databases with information about entrepreneurship (*Data resources*). See for example, The Annual Survey of Entrepreneurs (ASE) by the U.S. Census Bureau; the Business R&D and Innovation Survey (BRDIS) by the Census Bureau Research Data Centers; the Kauffman Firm Survey (KFS); the Connecting Outcome Measures in Entrepreneurship, Technology, and Science (COMETS) database created by a community of scholars; the Panel Study of Entrepreneurial Dynamics II (PSED II) database at the University of Michigan; the Global Entrepreneurship Monitor (GEM) run by a non-governmental entity that manages a consortium of national teams, where each national team is led by a local academic institution; and the Kauffman Index of Entrepreneurial Activity/Kauffman Indicators of Entrepreneurship.

Internet-Based Media. In 2021, there were 1.9 million podcasts with 47 million episodes; 56% of the people in the United States had listened to at least one podcast, 37% listen to at least one podcast monthly, and 24% listen to at least one podcast weekly; podcast usage rates are higher among 12–34 year olds (*2021 global podcast statistics, demographics, and habits*, 2021). Conventional media like *Inc.*, *Entrepreneur*, and others publish lists of recommended and popular podcasts about entrepreneurship and innovation (see for example, Fortune magazine's recommendations: https://www.forbes.com/sites/forbescoachescouncil/2021/03/31/top-10-most-recommended-entrepreneurship-podcasts/?sh=50b26815791d). *The Tim Ferris Show* hosted by the author of *The 4-Hour Workweek*, *How I Built This with Guy Raz* of National Public Radio, *Startup Stories—Mixergy* hosted by Andrew Warner a young entrepreneur who wants to help others learn to become successful entrepreneurs, and *HBR IdeaCast* from the Harvard Business Review are examples of some popular podcasts about entrepreneurship.

Entrepreneurship enthusiasts, thought leaders, and/or institutions are also creating websites filled with resources like videos, web links, blogs, and/or podcasts often combined with periodic email newsletters and social media posts (e.g., Twitter, LinkedIn, etc.) to create branded, trusted sources of entrepreneurship information. See for example:

- Steve Blank: https://steveblank.com/
- Disciplined entrepreneurship from Bill Aulet of MIT's entrepreneurship center: https://www.d-eship.com/
- Michael Seibel of Y Combinator: https://www.michaelseibel.com/.

All of the sources of entrepreneurship information Kuratko described in 2005 remain relevant today, and many have exploded in terms of the number of resources available (see for example, the growth in entrepreneurship education peer-reviewed journal articles in Fig. 6.1). In addition, new sources such as databases, internet-based media, organizations (i.e., non-profit/non-governmental, higher education institutions, governmental agencies), and partnerships/alliances have become important sources of entrepreneurship information. Entrepreneurship information is more available and more accessible than ever.

Then and Now: Themes in Entrepreneurship Education

Perhaps the most important contribution of Kuratko's article, or at least one of the most quotable statements, is "...the question of whether entrepreneurship can be taught is obsolete" (2005, p. 581). This is a message entrepreneurship educators were likely eager to hear and happy to embrace. Accepting this message allowed academe to focus on the next question: What to teach? Kuratko identified ten topics or themes as the domain of entrepreneurship research and education: differentiating entrepreneurship from management, venture financing, intrapreneurship/corporate entrepreneurship, predictors of entrepreneurial success, risk management, women and minority entrepreneurship, the contributions of entrepreneurs, new ventures, family businesses versus large corporations, and ethics.

Today, the field remains focused on what to teach and how to teach it more effectively (Bacigalupo et al., 2016; Brooks et al., 2008; Matthews et al., 2021; Morris & Liguori, 2016; Neck & Greene, 2011; Penaluna, 2018; Solomon, 2014). Differentiating and defining entrepreneurship education has received significant attention. A number of approaches to defining/differentiating entrepreneurship have emerged:

- Entrepreneurship involves the creation of a new venture, a startup, which involves a different skillset (e.g., exploratory or search mode) than the skillset required to manage or grow an existing firm (e.g., exploitative mode) (see for example, Blank, 2013a, 2013b; Blank & Dorf, 2012)
- Entrepreneurship involves value creation which is relevant and useful in many contexts (not just startups); entrepreneurship education should focus on the knowledge, skills, and attitudes required to create value (see for example, Lackeus, 2015)
- Entrepreneurship involves two different types of activity: creation and management of small and medium enterprises (main street entrepreneurship) and creation and growth of innovation-driven ventures (growth or innovation entrepreneurship); each requires unique competencies—competencies that are not the same as those required to manage a large or established firm (see for example, Aulet, 2013; Fairlie et al., 2017)
- Entrepreneurship is a life skill and should be taught from pre-k through higher education and continue through careers and vocational education; using a progression model competencies are defined, and learning outcomes are identified as learners progress from foundation to intermediate to advanced to expert levels of competence (see for example, Bacigalupo et al., 2016).

Ideas about the contributions that entrepreneurship makes to society have also evolved. As Kuratko emphasized, entrepreneurship education is valued because entrepreneurship is widely viewed as a major engine of economic growth and job creation. As discussed previously, these beliefs are still strongly held, although now there are more nuanced understandings of how, when, and where these benefits are achieved. Today, entrepreneurship education is also valued for:

- Equipping people and organizations with the competencies to be successful in an increasingly competitive and complex global world
- Increasing engagement and motivation in school and the workplace
- Empowering people and organizations to create social value for the public good (Lackeus, 2015).

Kuratko notes the emergence of women and minority entrepreneurs and that "they appear to face obstacles and difficulties different from those that other entrepreneurs face" (2005, p. 581). As discussed above, the rate of new entrepreneurs by gender and race indicates that women and minority entrepreneurs do indeed face obstacles to engaging in entrepreneurship (Fairlie & Robb, 2008; Fairlie et al., 2017; Robb & Fairlie, 2006). Today, scholars and practitioner's talk about the myths of entrepreneurship, one being the perception of entrepreneurs as predominantly heroic, young, white male figures with special traits who work independently against adversity to achieve great success (Lackeus, 2015; Neck et al., 2018; Reich, 1987). This mythical conception is counterproductive in entrepreneurship education and alienating to women and minorities, and flies in the face of evidence about the effectiveness of teams versus individuals as founders (Aulet, 2013; Lackeus, 2015). A more contemporary, inclusive conceptualization of entrepreneurship that better serves entrepreneurship education is that it is a generic method for human action, composed of principles and techniques that anyone can learn through education (Lackeus, 2015).

The other themes of entrepreneurship education that Kuratko identified (i.e., venture financing, intrapreneurship/corporate entrepreneurship, predictors of entrepreneurial success, risk management, and ethics) continue to be relevant themes in entrepreneurship education and research and each of these fields has evolved significantly. For example, consider evolutions in bootstrapping and peer-to-peer or marketplace lending and the emergence of crowd funding in venture financing (Neck et al., 2018; Peek, 2020).

One important theme in entrepreneurship education not mentioned in Kuratko's (2005) article is social entrepreneurship. Social entrepreneurship is a field, a movement, and a mechanism for organizing social problem-solving; it is a process where individuals "build or transform institutions to advance solutions to social problems" (Bornstein & Davis, 2010, p. 1). It is a growing field (Bornstein, 2007; Chaaban, 2015; *The emergence of social entrepreneurship*, 2014); per Solomon (2014) 40%

of schools in the United States offer a social entrepreneurship course, and 61% teach the concept of social entrepreneurship in their core entrepreneurship course. For perspective, social entrepreneurship is the second largest special interest group for USASBE members[6] (*USASBE interest groups*).

Then and Now: Entrepreneurship Education Historical Context and Content

Kuratko references Katz's (2003) *The chronology and intellectual trajectory of American entrepreneurship education: 1876–1999* and highlights a few reviews of entrepreneurship education from the late 1980s and early 1990s (2005). He (Kuratko, 2005) briefly summarizes proposed ways that entrepreneurship could or should evolve per the reviews (i.e., in a manner consistent with new conceptualizations of entrepreneurship; as a broad, integrative, pragmatic approach to business, or as an approach to skill building and network building, etc.).

In 2015, Brush, Neck, and Greene described how entrepreneurship education and pedagogy evolved from the late 1940s/early 1950s to today in three phases: "the Genesis Phase, the Apprentice Phase, and the Academic Phase" (p. 37). During the ***Genesis Phase*** (~1947 to ~1984), there were few courses/programs, courses featured speakers sharing real-world experiences with students, and there was little connection to theory (Brush et al., 2015). During the ***Apprentice Phase*** (~1989 to late 1990s), courses and programs grew, the case method was widely adopted, and students were put in the role of the decision-maker or entrepreneur—the apprentice (Brush et al., 2015). During the ***Academic Phase*** (~late 1990s to ~2010), a more analytical approach was adopted (i.e., analyze markets, identify gaps, create financial plans, estimate returns, etc.) with an emphasis on creating business plans and business plan competitions (Brush et al., 2015). Brush et al. (2015) indicate that many entrepreneurship education programs are still in the Academic Phase. They argue that taking a more open view of entrepreneurship, a creative approach versus a predictive approach will be better for entrepreneurship education and entrepreneurs—the ***Method or Practice Phase***.

[6] The largest USASBE special interest group is: corporate entrepreneurship and innovation.

Engel et al. (2016) share another perspective on the historical evolution of entrepreneurship education; he identifies three phases: the small business, the startup, and the lean startup phases. In the 1980s, in the ***small business phase***, he says: "… when we thought of entrepreneurship education, if we thought about it at all, we thought of 'Small Business'—SMEs" (Engel et al., 2016, p. 4). Entrepreneurship was often a stand-alone capstone course where students built business plans, case studies were the new pedagogical innovation, and experiential learning was very limited (Engel et al., 2016). In the 1990s, during the ***startup phase***, "we discovered the startup" (Engel, 1980, p. 5), the internet made it possible for anyone to start a business, business plan competitions flourished, startups were just smaller versions of big businesses with the possibility of explosive growth, and business plans were the tool to plan and manage that growth. In the 2000s, the ***lean launchpad phase*** began after reflection on the dot.com bubble burst, there was a realization that startups have special attributes, they are not established firms, they are a means of experimenting to discover and validate a business model, and thus, the lean startup or lean launchpad approach to entrepreneurship was born (Engel et al., 2016).

Today, I suggest that we are in the ***Branded Ecosystem Phase*** of entrepreneurship education (~2010 to the present). In this new phase, various entrepreneurship and entrepreneurship education schools of thought have been espoused (see Then and Now: Themes...above). Individuals and organizations have developed branded ecosystems of books, websites, social media, training programs, software platforms, and other teaching and learning resources to increase awareness and use of their approach to entrepreneurship education. Further, some of these ecosystems have developed ways to monetize the use of their system by developing proprietary web-based platforms which allow individuals, teams, and organizations access to resources or tools in the system for a fee. The major branded entrepreneurship education ecosystems which have emerged in this phase are:

The Lean Startup or the Lean LaunchPad. Associated with Steve Blank, Eric Ries, Bob Dorf, and the University of California, Berkeley, this approach to entrepreneurship education distinguishes between a startup and a going concern. The lean approach focuses on customer discovery and validation using a rapid, build-measure-learn method, turning to customer creation and company building only after customer validation is successful. This approach has been integrated into the National Science

Foundation's (NSF) Innovation Corps (I-Corps), a 10-week experiential immersion in the Lean LaunchPad method for NSF-funded scientists pursuing technology commercialization; it is also being incorporated into the technology commercialization efforts of the National Institutes of Health (NIH), the Department of Energy, and other federal agencies (e.g., Department of Defense: Hacking for Defense Program, State Department: Hacking for Diplomacy Program). Solomon (2014) notes that the lean startup method is increasingly integrated into entrepreneurship programs and courses in higher education. See Table 6.1: *Overview of Branded Ecosystems Influencing Entrepreneurship Education* for a comparison of key elements of each branded ecosystem.

Disciplined Entrepreneurship. Associated with Bill Aulet and MIT, this approach to entrepreneurship education distinguishes between small and medium enterprises and innovation-driven enterprises and guides students through six themes and 24 steps for creating an innovation-driven venture (see Table 6.1 for more details).

The Method or Practice Approach. Associated with Candida Brush, Heidi Neck, Patricia Greene, and Babson College, this approach to entrepreneurship education views entrepreneurship as a creative process that requires practice to develop the mindsets and skills to be effective at entrepreneurship (see Table 6.1 for more details).

The Value Creation Approach. Developed by the European Commission, this comprehensive progression approach to entrepreneurship education is based on the belief that entrepreneurship, value creation, is one of the eight essential competencies every person should have. The approach includes three competency areas: creativity, working with others, and mobilizing resources; 15 specific competencies (five for each competency area) have been identified and mapped to learning outcomes, practical outcomes, learning activities, and resources for foundational, intermediate, advanced, and expert learners. This approach is more widely accepted in Europe and the UK than in the United States. See Table 6.1 for more details.

Business Model Canvas. Created by Alexander Osterwalder and Yves Pigneur using an online, open, iterative process to engage practitioners in reviewing, providing feedback, and contributing to the development of *Business Model Generation*, this approach emphasizes the importance of business model innovation. A simple tool, the business model canvas, provides a means to describe, visualize, assess, and evolve or innovate business models. Solomon (2014) notes that the use of the business model

Table 6.1 Overview of branded ecosystems influencing entrepreneurship education

Characteristics/ approach	*Lean Startup or Lean LaunchPad*	*Disciplined entrepreneurship*	*Practice or method*	*Value creation*	*Business model canvas*	*Design thinking*
Leaders/key figures	Steve Blank	Bill Aulet	Candida Brush, Heidi Neck, Patricia Greene		Alexander Osterwalder, Yves Pigneur	IDEO
Institutions associated with	University of California, Berkeley	MIT	Babson	European Commission		Stanford
Books associated with	Blank, S. (2013). *The four steps to the epiphany*. K&S Ranch Blank, S., & Dorf, B. (2012). *The startup owner's manual*. K&S Ranch Ries, E. (2011). *The lean startup*. Crown Business	Aulet, B. (2013). *Disciplined entrepreneurship*. Wiley	Brush, C., Neck, H., & Greene, P. (2015). A practice-based approach to entrepreneurship education. In V. L. Crittenden, K. Esper, N. Karst, & R. Slegers (Eds.), *Evolving entrepreneurial education: Innovation in the Babson classroom* (pp. 35–53). Emerald Neck, H. M., Greene, P. G., & Brush, C. G. (2014). *Teaching entrepreneurship: A practice-based approach*. Edward Elgar	*EntreComp: The European Entrepreneurship Competence Framework*. (2018). Publications Office of the European Union, European Commission, Directorate-General for Employment, Social Affairs and Inclusion: https://books.google.com/books?id=D8IzywEACAAJ	Osterwalder, A., & Pigneur, Y. (2010). *Business model generation*. Wiley	Kelley, T., & Kelley, D. (2013). *Creative confidence: Unleashing the creative potential within us all*. Currency Brown, T. (2009). *Change by design*. Harper Business

(continued)

Table 6.1 (continued)

Characteristics/ approach	*Lean Startup or Lean LaunchPad*	*Disciplined entrepreneurship*	*Practice or method*	*Value creation*	*Business model canvas*	*Design thinking*
Key ideas	Startups are different from established firms; a startup is a temporary organization in search of a scalable business model; the startup process should focus on search (customer discovery and customer validation), then execution (customer creation and company building); the startup process should be agile or lean, embracing a fast, iterative build-measure-learn approach	There are two types of entrepreneurship: small and medium enterprise (SME) and innovation-driven (IDE); each requires different mindsets and skills; disciplined entrepreneurship is the process for IDE: this process includes six themes and 24 steps (steps for each theme are in parentheses below): (1) Who is your customer? (market segments, beachhead market, end user profile, market size estimates, persona profile, next 10 customers); (2) What can you do for your customer? (full life cycle use case, high-level product specification, quantified value proposition, core competencies, competitive position); (3) How does your customer acquire your product? (customer decision making unit, process to acquire a paying customer, sales process); (4) How do you make money off your product? (business model, pricing, lifetime value of a customer, cost of customer acquisition); (5) How do you design and build your product? (key assumptions, testing, minimum viable business product, show demand); and (6) How do you scale your business? (market size estimates, product plan)	Entrepreneurship is a method of creation; creation requires action, collaboration, and iteration; there are tools and skills which can be learned through practice; the key practices to be developed are: play, empathy, creation, and experimentation	Everyone should have a key set of competencies for personal development, social inclusion, citizenship, and employment; entrepreneurship is one of the eight essential competencies everyone should have; entrepreneurship is defined as creation of cultural, social, or economic value; the entrepreneurship competencies include: (1) Creativity—ideas and opportunities (spotting opportunities, creativity, vision, valuing ideas, ethical and sustainable thinking); (2) Mobilizing resources (self-awareness and self-efficacy, motivation and perseverance, mobilizing resources, financial and economic literacy, mobilizing others); and (3) Working with others—into action (taking the initiative, planning and management, coping with uncertainty, ambiguity, and risk, working with others, learning through experience); these competencies can be developed over a lifetime from pre-k forward	A shared language for describing, visualizing, assessing, and changing business models; business models are composed of nine basic building blocks: customer segments, value propositions, channels, customer relationships, revenue streams, key resources, key activities, key partnerships, and cost structure	An empathetic or human-centered approach to solving problems; per the Stanford d. school the key steps in the process are: empathize, define, ideate, prototype, test; per IDEO the key steps are: discovery, interpretation, ideation, experimentation, and iteration

Characteristics/ approach	*Lean Startup or Lean LaunchPad*	*Disciplined entrepreneurship*	*Practice or method*	*Value creation*	*Business model canvas*	*Design thinking*
Educator resources	Videos, slides workshops: https://steveblank.com/slides/ Educators Summit: https://steveblank.com/category/lean-launchpad/	Videos, slides, and other resources for authorized educators: https://www.d-eship.com/resources-2/for-educators/	Typical educator resources for textbook, including Vantage e-book and learning platform Neck, H. M., Neck, C. P., & Murray, E. L. (2018). *Entrepreneurship: The practice and mindset* (2nd ed.). Sage	User guide and support material: https://ec.europa.eu/jrc/en/entrecomp/support-material EntreComp Playbook: Videos, classroom activities, other resources	Free templates (with email)—business model canvas with explanation video, value proposition canvas, business portfolio map, team alignment map, etc.: https://www.strategyzer.com/canvas	IDEO: courses, books, articles, tools, videos, and other resources: https://designthinking.ideo.com/resources https://www.ideo.com/post/design-thinking-for-educators https://www.ideo.org/tools Stanford d.school: Activities, tools, how-tos: https://dschool.stanford.edu/resources/getting-started-with-design-thinking https://dschool.stanford.edu/resources
Ecosystem resources	Website, videos, e-newsletter, social media, educator training, courses	Website, book, workbook, videos, blog, social media, e-newsletter	Website, faculty training programs, webinars	EntreComp Teacher Cards: https://issuu.com/bantaniedu/docs/entrecomp_cards EntreComp Playbook	App (innovation management software), training, enterprise solutions, blog, canvas templates, books, e-newsletter, social media	Websites, guides, kits, free training courses

(continued)

Table 6.1 (continued)

Characteristics/ approach	*Lean Startup or Lean LaunchPad*	*Disciplined entrepreneurship*	*Practice or method*	*Value creation*	*Business model canvas*	*Design thinking*
Monetized resources	Launchpad central: https://launchpadcentral.com/	DE Toolbox: https://www.detoolbox.com/	Babson educator professional development workshops, symposium, and Collaborative: https://www.babson.edu/academics/babson-academy/entrepreneurship-educator-resources-and-tips/ VentureBlocks simulation: https://ventureblocks.com/		https://www.strategyzer.com/	IDEO method cards: https://www.ideo.com/post/method-cards IDEO travel cards: https://www.designkit.org/resources/9

canvas is growing in U.S. entrepreneurship education. See Table 6.1 for more details.

Design Thinking. This human-centered approach to problem-solving is associated with IDEO and the d.school at Stanford University and key figures in those organizations (for example, Tim Brown, David Kelley, and Tom Kelley). The design thinking approach focuses on teaching an iterative, design approach to innovation including discovery, interpretation, ideation, experimentation, and iteration. IDEO has created a non-profit, ideo.org, that provides design thinking tools and training for educators. SAP, a leading enterprise software firm, has developed extensive resources, courses, and programs to encourage educators, students, and employees to integrate design thinking into their work. See Table 6.1 for more details.

There are numerous other branded ecosystems influencing entrepreneurship education today. See, for example, the Goldman Sachs 10,000 Small Businesses Program, Venture for America, TeachingE ntrepreneurship.org, Where to play—The Market Opportunity Navigator.

Then and Now: Entrepreneurship Education Challenges

Kuratko outlines ten key challenges facing entrepreneurship education in 2005. Today, some of those challenges seem less relevant while some seem less entrepreneurship specific and more applicable to higher education in general. Some of the challenges seem as important or more important than ever. And, of course, there are new challenges facing the field.

The "Dot-Com" legacy challenge, which is about having an enduring enterprise mentality versus an investment mentality, seems less relevant; since the article was published, the world has had a major global recession (2007–2009) and a coronavirus pandemic (2020–202?). Entrepreneurship, with all its varying definitions and approaches, is widely viewed as a positive force that can contribute to economic prosperity, job creation, and other social benefits. With the growing emphasis on entrepreneurship as value creation, in all its forms—cultural, social, and economic—the field appears to be embracing what Kuratko described as an enduring enterprise mentality, which might be described today as a value creation mentality.

The research/publication dilemma, the faculty pipeline shortage, the academic vs. practitioner dilemma, the administrative leadership revolving door, and the "power of one" dilemma with hindsight seem less unique to entrepreneurship education and applicable to many fields in higher education. The combination of tenure requirements and technology, that is innovations in online publishing, has resulted in the proliferation of academic journals and papers across all academic fields (Seigel & Baveye, 2010; Trimble et al., 2010). Faculty pipeline shortages in higher education have been forecast for decades; the anticipated shortages are attributed to declines in the production of doctorates, increased retirements among baby boomers, and increased student enrollments (Owen, 2009). However, there is some evidence that the assumptions underlying these forecasts may not be valid or may not have actually happened (Owen, 2009). Nonetheless, the impact of the coronavirus pandemic on student enrollment, teaching and learning modes, and disruption of the higher education experience for both students and faculty remains to be seen and may well pose challenges in higher education for years to come (Flaherty, 2020). The tension between academics and practitioners is an ongoing dilemma in most fields and seems likely to remain so (Johnson, 2015; McNatt et al., 2010). Turnover in academic administrators, like Presidents, Provosts, and Deans, continues to be an issue within academia ("College administrator data/turnover rates: 2016–Present," 2018; McGlynn, 2018).

The challenge of institutionalizing important initiatives and programs in higher education continues and is exacerbated by turnover in administrators, the shifting priorities that ensue, and the decentralized, siloed structure of higher education institutions where faculty have significant degrees of autonomy regarding what work they do and how they do it.

The technology challenge is more relevant than ever. In the United States the number of students taking at least one online course has grown 151% from 21 to 48% in the ten years between 2009 and 2019 (Bouchrika, 2020). The number of students taking *only* online courses has more than doubled, growing from 6 to 14% in the same time period. In Solomon's (2014) survey of entrepreneurship education, only 27% of respondents indicated they offered online courses. Further, many respondents focus on delivering experiential learning to achieve a competitive advantage (Solomon, 2014). The focus on experiential learning, the slow adoption of online modes of teaching, and a lack of focus on effectively delivering experiential learning online, have resulted in entrepreneurship educators being unprepared for the rapid conversion to online learning caused by the coronavirus pandemic (Matthews et al., 2021).

With hindsight, the issues of the maturity/complacency/stagnation trap (and the associated call to battle for legitimacy and leadership within business schools), the security-risk dilemma, and the dilution effect seem to have been framed in an insular manner especially in light of contributions to the field from practitioners and others (see discussion above) and the integration of entrepreneurship in many disciplines (see for example, Kauffman Campus Initiatives and the profiles of innovative entrepreneurship education programs in Kauffman's *Entrepreneurship in Higher Education* [Brooks et al., 2008]). As Matthews notes, the field still struggles "with the core definition of entrepreneurship and the hijacking of the discipline by just about everyone" (Matthews et al., 2021, p. xviii). Today the challenge is not to focus on business schools, but to globally examine all the different aspects and approaches to entrepreneurship (e.g., main street, innovation-driven, value creation; lean, disciplined; practice/method, etc.) and determine if, how, and when they contribute to the goals of entrepreneurship (i.e., economic growth, job creation, value creation, equity and social inclusion, etc.). With this evidence, plus evidence about what, how, and when to effectively teach the various aspects and approaches, entrepreneurship education could help train people globally to achieve the goals of entrepreneurship.

Comparing the perspectives of recent authors on the challenges facing the field with Kuratko's perspectives provides additional insights. Of the ten challenges Kuratko (2005) identified, only technology seems salient to current authors (Cohen et al., 2021; Matthews et al., 2021). Recent works about entrepreneurship education (Bacigalupo et al., 2016; Brooks et al., 2008; Brush et al., 2015; Cohen et al., 2021; Lackeus, 2015; Matthews et al., 2021; Morris et al., 2014; Neck & Greene, 2011; Penaluna, 2018) consistently identify what to teach, how to teach, and where to teach as the most significant challenges facing the discipline. If you define entrepreneurship as new venture creation, you are inclined to teach about startups. If you define entrepreneurship as value creation, you are inclined to teach the skills required to create value. If you believe entrepreneurship is a business skill set, you are inclined to teach in business schools. If you believe entrepreneurship is a life skill applicable in many settings, you are inclined to incorporate entrepreneurship training in many disciplines and make it accessible across the curriculum and throughout education and training systems (i.e., pre-school to continuing education). As more nuanced and varied understandings of the field have emerged, so have calls to define the field's content, substance, and boundaries. As the field has grown, there is also increased attention on the challenges of quality and accountability. More rigorous research on entrepreneurship teaching and learning methods and practices is needed—What pedagogy works? How? When? How can/should effectiveness be measured? Assessed? Are unique teaching quality standards needed (i.e., are higher education quality standards like Quality Matters Rubric Standards: https://www.qualitymatters.org/qa-resources/rubric-standards or SUNY Online Course Quality Review Rubric: https://oscqr.suny.edu/ sufficient or does the field have unique aspects requiring different standards)? Are unique ethical standards needed?

Another challenge emerging in the field is who will create, critique/evaluate, and disseminate knowledge in the discipline in a brand agnostic manner? Who will do the fundamental research and theory building that helps us know what works and in what conditions it works? As the branded ecosystems of entrepreneurship education grow; who will help us understand the relative merits and disadvantages of each brand? Who will develop integrating theories and help identify substantive differences versus "packaging" differences? Can we rely on brand leaders or brand proponents to do so (see for example, these critiques: Sadler, 2019; Ursache, 2019)?

How Did This Article Contribute to the Field?

Since 2005, Kuratko's article has been cited more than 1000 times (Scopus, 2021). Per SciVal, this article is part of the Entrepreneurial Intention/Effectuation/Opportunity Recognition topic, a cluster of articles with a common focus or theme. This topic falls in the 99.849th percentile in topic prominence, a measure of citation counts, Scopus views, and average CiteScore. The authors who most frequently cited Kuratko's article are: A. Fayolie, P. Jones, A. Bagheri, D.F. Kuratko, M.H. Morris, Z.A.L. Pihie, A. Kakouris, K. Kasemsap, K. Fellnhofer, and J. Heinonen. Most citing authors were from the United States, followed by authors from the UK. Citing authors came from institutions around the world, the institutions with the highest concentrations of citing authors are: Emlyon Business School in France, the University of Florida in the United States, and Indiana University Bloomington, Kuratko's institution.

Kuratko's (2005) article covers a wide range of topics and provides an excellent summary of thinking about entrepreneurship education at the time. Filled with quotable facts and some highly quotable statements, the article has been referenced significantly in the entrepreneurship literature. This article deserves to be called a modern classic because of its impact on the field in a relatively short time span. It is a modern classic because of its high citation rate, comprehensive review of sources of entrepreneurship understanding, the declaration that entrepreneurship can be taught, a summary of themes central to entrepreneurship research and education, review of the state of entrepreneurship education, enumeration of ten challenges to entrepreneurship education, call to action, and accessible, readable language.

Conclusions

Kuratko's (2005) *The Emergence of Entrepreneurship Education: Development, Trends, and Challenges* has been referenced in over 1000 publications in 16 years. The broad scope of the content, the interesting quotes, and the large reference list make the article a useful resource for those interested in entrepreneurship education.

When Kuratko's (2005) work is compared with work in the field today, it highlights changes in the discipline of entrepreneurship education. Kuratko's perspective on the value of entrepreneurship—it drives economic growth, creating employment and prosperity for all—holds up well. This perspective is still widely held today. However, today more nuanced understandings of how and when ventures contribute to economic growth are evolving (e.g., young firms contribute more new jobs). Today, there is a greater understanding of the obstacles faced by women and minorities pursuing entrepreneurship (e.g., lack of access to education, experience, and capital). And today there is a broader conceptualization of the benefits entrepreneurship can contribute to society (e.g., increasing engagement and motivation in school and in the workplace, equipping people and organizations to be successful in a competitive global economy, empowering people and organizations to create social value for the public good, etc.).

Kuratko (2005) painted a positive picture of growth in entrepreneurship and entrepreneurship education. He was writing the article just as firm births were peaking in the United States and entrepreneurship education had grown rapidly. Today, long-term declines in entrepreneurship as measured by trends in firm birth and exit rates, lower job growth rates from new firms, and a growing appreciation of the roles of different types of firms (e.g., small vs. new vs. large) result in a more complex picture of entrepreneurship. Today, entrepreneurship education is described as widespread, ubiquitous. Kuratko was excited about the rise of young entrepreneurs; today, there is concern that younger, less educated people are less likely to pursue entrepreneurial endeavors. Kuratko saw entrepreneurship as something that had value for anyone in many contexts. Today this theme is expressed through an emphasis on entrepreneurial mindset and value creation skills which can be taught to anyone and used in many settings.

Kuratko (2005) provided an extensive and still relevant listing of sources of entrepreneurship information. Notable new sources of information in the field include *Entrepreneurship Education and Pedagogy*, databases, and internet-based media.

Kuratko (2005) declared that entrepreneurship could be taught and encouraged the field to focus on what to teach. He identified ten broad topics as the domain of entrepreneurship research and education: differentiating entrepreneurship from management, venture financing, intrapreneurship/corporate entrepreneurship, predictors of entrepreneurial success, risk management, women and minority entrepreneurship, the contributions of entrepreneurs, new ventures, family businesses versus large corporations, and ethics. Since his work was published, social entrepreneurship has emerged as an important and growing topic within the discipline. And, the barriers women and minorities face in entrepreneurship have received increased attention. New schools of thought about entrepreneurship and entrepreneurship education have emerged: the lean startup or lean launchpad approach, the disciplined entrepreneurship approach, the method/practice approach, the value creation approach, the business model canvas, and design thinking. Branded ecosystems of advocates, books, websites, videos, social media, training programs, software platforms, and educator resources have developed around these new schools of thought. Some of these ecosystems are free and open to the public, some have fees for access and/or restrict access to registered users.

Kuratko (2005) identified ten challenges facing the field. Some of those challenges seem less relevant today, some seem relevant to higher education generally, including entrepreneurship, and some seem more important than ever. The technology challenge is more important than ever since entrepreneurship educators have been slow to embrace online learning, instead focusing on in-person experiential learning. In light of the growth in online learning and the rapid shift to online learning due to the coronavirus pandemic, finding effective ways to deliver experiential entrepreneurship learning online should be a priority for the field. The most salient challenges facing entrepreneurship educators today include: what to teach, how to teach, and where to teach. Defining the field's content and boundaries and finding ways to effectively teach and assess effectiveness is even more top of mind and urgent today. The rise of branded ecosystems around entrepreneurship schools of thought, concepts, and tools creates a need for brand agnostic research to assess the relative merits, uses, and effectiveness of each approach. Brand agnostic perspectives will be crucial to developing integrative theories and evidence-based best practices.

Kuratko (2005) made a significant contribution to the field. He painted a vivid picture of entrepreneurship education after a period of robust growth. Many of the ideas and resources shared in the article remain relevant today. His work provides an important benchmark against which we can compare where entrepreneurship education is today—a maturing discipline with many important challenges ahead.

References

2021 global podcast statistics, demographics, and habits. (2021). Retrieved April 3 from https://podcasthosting.org/podcast-statistics/?gclid=CjwKCAjwpKCDBhBPEiwAFgBzj-GmDdBOdeW0WcjWRUOUD1P5A1dKg8Zo5cQOsrolpyFkQI4FB0M8GxoCeWIQAvD_BwE.

Amadeo, K. (2020). U.S. GDP by year compared to recessions and events. https://www.thebalance.com/us-gdp-by-year-3305543.

Aulet, B. (2013). *Disciplined entrepreneurship*. Wiley.

Bacigalupo, M., Kampylis, P., Punie, Y., & VandenBrande, G. (2016). *EntreComp: The entrepreneurship competency framework*. https://ec.europa.eu/jrc/en/publication/eur-scientific-and-technical-research-reports/entrecomp-entrepreneurship-competence-framework.

Blank, S. (2013a). *The four steps to the epiphany*. K&S Ranch.

Blank, S. (2013b). Why the lean start-up changes everything. *Harvard Business Review, 91*(5), 63–72.

Blank, S., & Dorf, B. (2012). *The startup owner's manual*. K&S Ranch.

Bornstein, D. (2007). *How to change the world: Social entrepreneurs and the power of new ideas*. Penguin Books.

Bornstein, D., & Davis, S. (2010). *Social entrepreneurship: What everyone needs to know*. Oxford University Press.

Bouchrika, I. (2020). 50 online education statistics: 2020 data on higher learning and corporate training. *Guide2Research*. https://www.guide2research.com/research/online-education-statistics.

Brooks, R., Green, W. S., Hubbard, R. G., Jain, D., Katehi, L., McLendon, G., Plummer, J., & Roomkin, M. (2008). *Entrepreneurship in American higher education*. https://www.kauffman.org/wp-content/uploads/2019/12/entrep_high_ed_report.pdf.

Brush, C., Neck, H., & Greene, P. (2015). A practice-based approach to entrepreneurship education. In V. L. Crittenden, K. Esper, N. Karst, & R. Slegers (Eds.), *Evolving entrepreneurial education: Innovation in the Babson classroom* (pp. 35–53). Emerald.

Business Dynamics Statistics: Geography: 1978–2018. (2018). Unites States Census Bureau. https://data.census.gov/cedsci/table?q=business%20dynamics&tid=BDSTIMESERIES.BDSGEO&hidePreview=false.

Chaaban, F. (2015). *Social entrepreneurship is on the rise: Soushiant Zanganehpour's advice for 'treps acting as agents of change*. Retrieved April 4 from https://www.entrepreneur.com/article/251981.

Cohen, D., Jones, P., Katz, J., Pollack, J., & White, R. (2021). What I have learned about teaching entrepreneurship: Perspectives of five master educators. In C. H. Matthews & E. W. Liguori (Eds.), *Annals of entrepreneurship education and pedagogy—2021*. Edward Elgar.

College administrator data/turnover rates: 2016–Present. (2018). *Higher Ed Direct*. https://hepinc.com/newsroom/college-administrator-data-turnover-rates-2016-present/.

Conte, C., & Karr, A. R. (1981). Small business and the corporation. *United States Economy*. http://countrystudies.us/united-states/economy-4.htm.

Data resources. Ewing Marion Kauffman Foundation. Retrieved April 3 from https://www.kauffman.org/entrepreneurship/research/data-resources/.

The emergence of social entrepreneurship. (2014). Retrieved April 4 from https://www.hult.edu/blog/the-emergence-of-social-entrepreneurship/.

Engel, G. L. (1980). The clinical application of the biopsychosocial approach. *American Journal of Psychiatry, 137*(5), 535–544. <Go to ISI>://WOS:A1980JQ76400001.

Engel, J. S., Schindehutte, M., Neck, H. M., Smilor, R., & Rossi, B. (2016). What I have learned about teaching entrepreneurship: Perspectives of five master educators. In M. H. Morris & E. Liguori (Eds.), *Annals of entrepreneurship education and pedagogy—2016*. Edward Elgar.

Fairlie, R., & Desai, S. (2021). *National report on early-stage entrepreneurship in the United States: 2020* (Kauffman Indicators of Entrepreneurship, Issue). https://indicators.kauffman.org/wp-content/uploads/sites/2/2021/03/2020_Early-Stage-Entrepreneurship-National-Report.pdf.

Fairlie, R., Morelix, A., & Tareque, I. (2017). *2017 Kauffman index of startup activity*. https://www.kauffman.org/wp-content/uploads/2020/04/2017_Kauffman_Index_Startup_Activity_National_Report_Final.pdf.

Fairlie, R. W., & Robb, A. M. (2008). *Race and entrepreneurial success*. MIT Press.

Flaherty, C. (2020). Faculty pandemic stress is now chronic. *Inside Higher Ed*. https://www.insidehighered.com/news/2020/11/19/faculty-pandemic-stress-now-chronic.

Gold, T., & Rodriquez, S. (2018). *Measuring entrepreneurial mindset in youth: Learnings from NFTE's entrepreneurial mindset index*. https://www.nfte.com/wp-content/uploads/2020/04/NFTE-Whitepaper-Measuring-Entrepreneurial-Mindset-in-Youth-November-2018.pdf.

Hathaway, I., & Litan, R. (2014). *Declining business dynamism: It's for real* (Economic Studies at Brookings, Issue). https://www.brookings.edu/research/declining-business-dynamism-its-for-real/.

Highfill, T., Cao, R., Schwinn, R., Prisinzano, R., & Leung, S. (2020). *Measuring the small business economy*. https://www.bea.gov/system/files/papers/BEA-WP2020-4_0.pdf.

Hwang, V. (2019). *Entrepreneurial ecosystem building playbook 3.0*. Kauffman Foundation. Retrieved April 1 from https://www.kauffman.org/ecosystem-playbook-draft-3/entrepreneurs/.

Johnson, T. (2015). *Why is there a divide between academics and practitioners in tech comm?* https://idratherbewriting.com/2015/08/05/acadmic-and-practitioner-divide/.

Katz, J. A. (2003, 2003/03/01). The chronology and intellectual trajectory of American entrepreneurship education: 1876–1999. *Journal of Business Venturing, 18*(2), 283–300. https://doi.org/10.1016/S0883-9026(02)00098-8.

Kobe, K., & Schwinn, R. (2018). *Small business GDP 1998–2014*. https://cdn.advocacy.sba.gov/wp-content/uploads/2018/12/21060437/Small-Business-GDP-1998-2014.pdf.

Krueger, N. F., Jr., Reilly, M. D., & Carsrud, A. L. (2000). Competing models of entrepreneurial intentions. *Journal of Business Venturing, 15*(5–6), 411–432.

Kuratko, D. F. (2005). The emergence of entrepreneurship education: Development, trends, and challenges. *Entrepreneurship: Theory & Practice, 29*(5), 577–597. https://doi.org/10.1111/j.1540-6520.2005.00099.x.

Lackeus, M. (2015). *Entrepreneurship education: What, why, when, how*. https://www.oecd.org/cfe/leed/BGP_Entrepreneurship-in-Education.pdf.

Matthews, C. H., Liguori, E. W., & Santos, S. C. (2021). Preface: Entrepreneurship education—What is it we need to know? In C. H. Matthews & E. W. Liguori (Eds.), *Annals of entrepreneurship education and pedagogy—2021*. Edward Elgar.

McGee, J. E., Peterson, M., Mueller, S. L., & Sequeira, J. M. (2009). Entrepreneurial self-efficacy: Refining the measure. *Entrepreneurship Theory and Practice, 33*(4), 965–988.
McGlynn, T. (2018). Why relentless administrative turnover makes it hard for us to do our jobs. *The Chronicle of Higher Education*. https://www.chronicle.com/article/why-relentless-administrative-turnover-makes-it-hard-for-us-to-do-our-jobs/?cid=gen_sign_in.
McNatt, D. B., Glassman, M., & Glassman, A. (2010). The great academic-practitioner divide: A tale of two paradigms. *Global Education Journal*.
Morelix, A., Hwang, V., & Tareque, I. S. (2017). *Zero barriers: Three mega trends shaping the future of entrepreneurship* (State of Entrepreneurship 2017, Issue). https://www.kauffman.org/wp-content/uploads/2020/04/state_of_entrepreneurship_address_report_2017.pdf.
Morris, L., Ma, M., & Wu, P. (2014). *Agile innovation*. Wiley.
Morris, M. H., & Liguori, E. (2016). Preface: Teaching reason and the unreasonable. In M. H. Morris & E. Liguori (Eds.), *Annals of entrepreneurship education and pedagogy—2016*. Edward Elgar.
Neck, H. M., & Greene, P. G. (2011). Entrepreneurship education: Known worlds and new frontiers. *Journal of Small Business Management, 49*(1), 55–70. https://doi.org/10.1111/j.1540-627X.2010.00314.x.
Neck, H. M., Neck, C. P., & Murray, E. L. (2018). *Entrepreneurship: The practice and mindset* (2nd ed.). Sage.
Owen, R. S. (2009). Managing a U.S. business school professor shortage. *Research in Higher Education Journal, 2*, 1.
Peek, S. (2020). Small business financing options that bypass traditional banks. *Business News Daily*. Retrieved April 4 from https://www.businessnewsdaily.com/1733-small-business-financing-options-.html.
Penaluna, A. (2018). *Enterprise and entrepreneurship education: Guidance for UK higher education providers*. https://www.qaa.ac.uk/docs/qaas/enhancement-and-development/enterprise-and-entrpreneurship-education-2018.pdf?sfvrsn=15f1f981_8.
Perrin, A., & Duggan, M. (2015). *Americans' internet access: 2000–2015*. https://www.pewresearch.org/internet/2015/06/26/americans-internet-access-2000-2015/.
Radicioni, B. (2015). *More than half of all entrepreneurs expect to create jobs in the next five years*. https://www.babson.edu/about/news-events/babson-announcements/global-entrepreneurship-monitor-report/#:~:text=The%20Global%20Entrepreneurship%20Monitor%20(GEM)%20was%20initiated%20in%201999%20as,latest%20survey%20spans%2062%20economies.
Reich, R. (1987). Entrepreneurship reconsidered: The team as hero. *Harvard Business Review, 65*(May), 77–83.

Reynolds, P. D., Hay, M., & Camp, S. M. (1999). *Global entrepreneurship monitor 1999 executive report*.

Robb, A. M., & Fairlie, R. W. (2006). Access to financial capital among U.S. businesses: The case of African-American firms. *The Annals of the American Academy of Political and Social Science, 613*(1), 47–72.

Robinson, P., & Haynes, M. (1991, Spring91). Entrepreneurship education in America's major universities. *Entrepreneurship: Theory & Practice, 15*(3), 41–52. https://doi.org/10.1177/104225879101500304.

Ronstadt, R. (1987, Spring87). The educated entrepreneurs: A new era of entrepreneurial education is beginning. *American Journal of Small Business, 11*(4), 37–53. https://doi.org/10.1177/104225878701100403.

Sadler, H. (2019). *Disciplined entrepreneurship vs. lean startup vs. design thinking for startups: An analysis*. https://www.linkedin.com/pulse/disciplined-entrepreneurship-vs-lean-startup-design-thinking-sadler/.

SBA. (2020). 2020 small business profile. https://cdn.advocacy.sba.gov/wp-content/uploads/2020/06/04144224/2020-Small-Business-Economic-Profile-US.pdf https://cdn.advocacy.sba.gov/wp-content/uploads/2020/06/04144224/2020-Small-Business-Economic-Profile-US.pdf.

Scopus. (2021). *Cite score metrics*. Elsevier B.V.

Seigel, D., & Baveye, P. (2010). Battling the paper glut. *Science, 329*(5998). https://doi.org/10.1126/science.329.5998.1466-a.

Solomon, G. T. (2014). *The national survey of entrepreneurship education: An overview of 2012–2014 survey data*. http://www.nationalsurvey.org/files/2014KauffmanReport_Clean.pdf.

Solomon, G. T., Duffy, S., & Tarabishy, A. (2002). The state of entrepreneurship education in the United States: A nationwide survey and analysis. *International Journal of Entrepreneurship Education, 1*(1), 65–86.

Solomon, G. T., Weaver, K. M., & Fernald, L. W. (1994). A historical examination of small business management and entrepreneurship pedagogy. *Simulation and Gaming, 25*(3), 338–352.

Trimble, S. W., Grody, W. W., McKelvey, B., & Gad-el-Hak, M. (2010). The glut of academic publishing: A call for a new culture. *Academic Questions, 23*(3), 276–286.

Ursache, M. (2019). Building a bulletproof startup: Business model canvas vs. lean startup vs. disciplined entrepreneurship. *Disciplined Entrepreneurship*. https://medium.com/disciplined-entrepreneurship/building-a-bulletproof-startup-business-model-canvas-vs-lean-startup-vs-disciplined-464b317c927b.

USASBE interest groups. Retrieved April 4 from https://www.usasbe.org/members/group_select.asp?type=10257.

Wiens, J., & Jackson, C. (2015). *The importance of young firms for economic growth* (Entrepreneurship Policy Digest, Issue). https://www.kauffman.org/wp-content/uploads/2019/12/entrepreneurship_policy_digest_september 2014.pdf.

World wide web timeline. (2014). https://www.pewresearch.org/internet/2014/03/11/world-wide-web-timeline/.

Zeithaml, C. P., & Rice, G. H. (1987). Entrepreneurship/small business in American universities. *Journal of Small Business Management, 25*(1), 44–50. http://search.ebscohost.com/login.aspx?direct=true&db=bth&AN=5266729&site=ehost-live.

CHAPTER 7

The Path Beyond the Opportunity Wars: Exploring the Continued Relevance of McMullen and Shepherd (2006) for the Future of Entrepreneurial Action Theory

David Townsend, Rick Hunt, and Parul Manocha

Introduction

Over the past decade, entrepreneurial action theory (EAT) has emerged as one of the foundational, multi-level theories of entrepreneurship (Townsend et al., 2018). Among the many pieces of scholarship on EAT to pour forth in this period, McMullen and Shepherd's (2006)

D. Townsend (✉) · R. Hunt · P. Manocha
Department of Management, Pamplin College of Business, Virginia Tech, Blacksburg, VA, USA
e-mail: dtown@vt.edu

R. Hunt
e-mail: rickhunt@vt.edu

A. E. Osorio et al. (eds.), *Modern Classics in Entrepreneurship Studies*,
https://doi.org/10.1007/978-3-030-61029-6_7

Academy of Management Review article (hereafter: "M&S (2006)")—"*Entrepreneurial Action and the Role of Uncertainty in the Theory of the Entrepreneur*"—was uniquely conceived in order to establish a much-needed bridge between system-level and individual-level perspectives of why entrepreneurs vary in their willingness to pursue possible opportunities. Towards this end, the foundational contribution of M&S (2006) is the introduction of a two-stage model of entrepreneurial action under conditions of uncertainty (McMullen, 2015) whereby entrepreneurs "bring agency to opportunities" (Alvarez & Barney, 2007) by translating "third-person opportunities" (i.e., an opportunity for someone) into "first-person opportunities" (i.e., an opportunity for me). As the basis for this approach, McMullen and Shepherd (2006) draw upon a rich vein of work spanning decades of work, across multiple fields in economics, philosophy, and social theory (e.g., James, 1884; Poincaré, 1914; Popper, 1977; Searle, 2007) to place the entangled mutuality of knowledge and motivation at the center of a meso-level theory of human action.

At the same time, despite receiving well-deserved accolades reflecting the central importance of M&S (2006) for entrepreneurship theory,[1] our review of the follow-on research points to misunderstandings, misuse, and disuse, as evidenced by problematic patterns in the articles citing M&S (2006). First, although their work addresses the early debates between subjectivist and objectivist positions on the ontology of opportunities, much of the nuance of their model has been lost in a cacophony of voices which advocate for an increasingly hardened position on one side or the other in the "opportunity wars" (Davidsson, 2015; Wood, 2017; Wood & Mckinley, 2017). But now, as scholars question the continued relevance and importance of this ontological debate for entrepreneurship theory (Ramoglou & Tsang, 2016), the two-stage model in M&S (2006) offers the means to bridge the ontological "divide" with a robust, meso-level model of human action.

Second, our analysis of the citation patterns reveals a reversion away from the nuanced theory of uncertainty they incorporate within the two-stage model back to a problematic assumption of the universality of uncertainty in the entrepreneurial context (Townsend & Hunt, 2019; Townsend et al., 2018). Instead of viewing uncertainty as something

[1] Among its various distinctions, McMullen and Shepherd (2006) received the 2018 Foundational Award from the Entrepreneurship Division of the Academy of Management.

that varies across both actors and situational contexts throughout the entrepreneurial process, many articles which purport to build on M&S (2006) adopt the view that uncertainty is universally absolute, resulting in a completely unstructured decision environment (e.g., Alvarez & Barney, 2007). Yet, consistent with emerging work which calls into question the validity of the universalistic applicability of the uncertainty assumption in entrepreneurship research (Townsend et al., 2018), there is much to be gained through the re-adoption of the more nuanced theorizing of uncertainty in M&S (2006).

Third, our review of the citation patterns for M&S (2006) indicates that many of the citing works focus on the mutuality of knowledge and motivation as key antecedents of entrepreneurial action and judgment. Emerging work, however, broadens this conversation by pointing to the prevalence of impulsivity (Wiklund et al., 2017), sensation-seeking behaviors (Lerner & Hunt, 2012), and other less-deliberative motivations as precursors to entrepreneurial action (Lerner et al., 2018; Wiklund et al., 2018). In these situations, the door is opened for a revitalized "theory of mind" to augment the two-stage model in M&S (2006) with "alternative rationalities" that influence both the perceived desirability and feasibility assessments in shaping entrepreneurial action.

In summary, our review of the burgeoning literature which builds upon M&S (2006) confirms that while all of the accolades the article has garnered over the past decade are well-deserved, numerous opportunities remain for future researchers to build on this contemporary classic in order to advance entrepreneurship theory. Consistent with this view, we conclude the chapter with a robust discussion of future research opportunities in entrepreneurial action theory. In many cases, these opportunities consist of re-focusing attention on the depth and nuance of the original two-stage model developed in M&S (2006). But at the same time, we also discuss how important trends shaping the practice of entrepreneurship (e.g., the emergence of artificial intelligence—Townsend & Hunt, 2019) raise important new questions for entrepreneurial action theory, pointing to new possibilities of augmented forms of entrepreneurial action where machine intelligences complement the actions of human entrepreneurs in pursuit of new opportunities.

McMullen and Shepherd's Two-Stage Model of Entrepreneurial Action

As noted above, in developing an elemental theory of entrepreneurial action, M&S (2006) sets forth a two-stage model based on the premise that uncertainty acts as a barrier to entrepreneurial action, thereby establishing a basis for differentiating those who take entrepreneurial action from those who do not. The model simultaneously extends and amends the most influential theories of entrepreneurship, deriving much of its inspiration from economics (Kirzner, 1979; Knight, 1921; Schumpeter, 1934), and the relative failure of these theories to provide a comprehensive, integrated model of the entrepreneurial process. In particular, M&S (2006) takes into account the epistemological and motivational drivers of entrepreneurial action, which they conceptualize as a sequential process, consisting of two stages: attention and action. The crux of their model, as Zott and Huy (2007, p. 100) describe, "centers on entrepreneurial action, rather than firm-level or industry characteristics, following the belief that theories of the entrepreneur require theories of action." By necessity, this involves agentic individuals "overcoming ignorance, reducing doubt, and expressing the willingness to bear perceived uncertainty" (Shepherd et al., 2007, p. 76).

In addition, M&S (2006) contends that entrepreneurship is a meso-level phenomenon, wherein prospective entrepreneurs operate in a wider system-level approach that leads to entrepreneurial action despite the inescapable reality that environmental uncertainty is central and pervasive. As such, M&S (2006) constitutes the first fully integrated, multi-level expression of the entrepreneurial process, one that simultaneously contemplates the essentiality of macro-environmental context and micro-level, cognitive drivers. This distinguishes M&S (2006) from preceding and contemporaneous theories of entrepreneurial action, which fail to provide a complete view of the individual-level foundations of entrepreneurial action. At stake was the veridicality of entrepreneurship scholarship, which McMullen and Dimov (2013, p. 1481) would later refer to as "the growing disconnect between the process-oriented conception of entrepreneurship taught in the classroom and theorized about in premier journals and the variance-oriented conception of entrepreneurship that characterizes empirical studies of the phenomenon." In addressing this disconnect, the elemental process model proffered in

M&S (2006) resolved existing errors and charted the future course of scholarship regarding the entrepreneurial process.

The lynchpin of M&S's approach involved contextualizing the role of uncertainty in a more constructive fashion than had existing theories of entrepreneurship, particularly those heavily influenced by economics, where the inhibiting role of uncertainty is captured through perceived uncertainty and an individual's willingness to bear uncertainty. Prominent theories typically differentiated between individuals who take entrepreneurial action and those who do not based on epistemological and motivational differences. In the first case, uncertainty acts as a barrier to entrepreneurial action owing to differential access to and comprehension of knowledge. In the second case, the willingness to bear uncertainty acts as a differentiating force owing to cognitive and motivational differences.

By disentangling these two stages, M&S addresses several notable flaws in existing theories that collapse entrepreneurial action into a single step of action under conditions of uncertainty. First, in much of the prior research, entrepreneurial action was not conceived as a process at all, but rather as a discrete decision, which lacks veridicality (McMullen & Dimov, 2013). Second, existing theories were missing the multi-step nature of the entrepreneurial process, which makes it impossible to differentiate those who willingly bear uncertainty from those who do not. In essence, M&S (2006) aims to address the absence of the entrepreneur in existing theories of entrepreneurial action, particularly in the field of economics (Casson, 1982). The sequential two-stage conceptualization developed by M&S (2006) remedies both of these shortcomings by modeling agentic and environmental features simultaneously and stipulating that there is no entrepreneurship without action. The two-stage process developed by M&S (2006) requires that both knowledge and motivation are needed in each stage by the actor to achieve entrepreneurial action.

Stage 1: Attention Stage and Third-Person Opportunities

In Stage 1, an individual—contingent upon his or her knowledge, acumen, insight, or alertness—identifies a third-person opportunity (i.e., an opportunity for someone in the marketplace). This "escape from ignorance" is the precursor to opportunity assessment, without which there is no action, since an unconceived opportunity remains under the shroud of an actor's ignorance. For this reason, the power of information and the presence of prior domain-specific knowledge is important to identify a third-person opportunity since both knowledge and information enable prospective entrepreneurs to form beliefs that they have recognized a third-person opportunity, and allows the prospective entrepreneur "to overcome belief-related doubt" as to whether or not the technological change represents a third-person opportunity.

Stage 2: Evaluation and First-Person Opportunities

Stage 2 applies only to those who have identified a third-person opportunity, wherein the willingness to bear uncertainty takes center stage in an actor's decision to potentially undertake entrepreneurial action. While Stage 1 underscores the importance of knowledge and motivation in dealing with the perceived uncertainty, Stage 2 focuses attention on how the actor takes into consideration whether the identified third-person opportunity represents a first-person opportunity for himself/herself, based on his/her knowledge and motivation. In this fashion, the actor weighs the potential costs of undertaking an action in light of the potential rewards. If the actor believes that the payoff is justified, and if there exists ample, idiosyncratic motivation, then s/he is expected to act. Since an individual determines the payoffs subjectively, the lack of tolerance for uncertainty can be compensated by the knowledge that leads the actor believe in the opportunity, and vice-versa. Therefore, as in Stage 1, the roles of knowledge and motivation are indispensable to this stage, as well. Knowledge is needed for the assessment of whether the third-person opportunity is uniquely feasible for the attentive actor, and motivation is needed to gauge the desirability of undertaking the third-person opportunity.

In these respects, M&S's two-stage model bridges the actor-environment divide by integrating action, opportunity, and uncertainty. While existing conceptualizations—largely grounded in facets of the neoclassical microeconomic model of perfect information, rational actors, and general equilibrium—sought to define away one or more of these critical components of an elemental model, M&S (2006) demonstrated the essentiality and integration of all three. In the following section, we turn towards assessing the scholarly impact of M&S (2006) in entrepreneurship theory.

Assessing the Impact of Mcmullen and Shepherd (2006)

Despite several unexpected delays, the publication of M&S (2006) came at a propitious time, marked by mounting efforts among entrepreneurship scholars to take into account both actors and the environment. As Ramoglou and Tsang (2016) observed, "One of the greatest advances in contemporary entrepreneurship scholarship comes from metatheoretical studies into the fundamental conceptual blocks of entrepreneurial discourse, as demonstrated by the influence of Shane and Venkataraman's (2000), Sarasvathy's (2001), McMullen and Shepherd's (2006), and Alvarez and Barney's (2007) contributions." Fundamentally, each of these articles sought to ask and answer the question: What is the distinctive nature of entrepreneurial action? In this sense, these foundational articles, published in the first decade of the new millennium, reflect the growing momentum of entrepreneurship's efforts to self-identify as a field of its own.

Writing in 2016, Ramoglou and Tsang were more prescient than perhaps they imagined in identifying the publication of these EAT classics as a watershed period in entrepreneurship scholarship. Beginning in 2017, three consecutive EATs were recognized by the Academy of Management's Entrepreneurship Division as recipients of the Division's "Foundational Paper Award": Sarasvathy's (2001) "*Causation and Effectuation: Toward a Theoretical Shift from Economic Inevitability to Entrepreneurial Contingency*" won in 2017; McMullen and Shepherd's (2006) "*Entrepreneurial Action and the Role of Uncertainty in the Theory of the Entrepreneur*" won in 2018; and Alvarez and Barney's (2007) "*The Discovery-Creation: Alternative Theories of Entrepreneurial Action*" won in 2019. For their part, Shane and Venkataraman's (2000) distinctive domain piece was recognized in 2010 as the *Academy of Management Review*'s conceptual contribution of the decade. As these successive accolades demonstrate, the concerted focus on developing EAT was indispensable to the process of shaping entrepreneurship's emerging identity as a distinctive field of inquiry.

Yet, even among these foundational works, M&S (2006) provides the most comprehensive, well-integrated, and elemental conception of entrepreneurial action. And yet, in the vibrant, often chaotic, intellectual marketplace for theories of entrepreneurial action since 1997, M&S (2006) is also more difficult to situate than other major treatments of

EAT. Though M&S (2006) is heavily cited, as we will discuss below, our analysis indicates that most citing articles fail to engage the article's most important insights. And despite the authors' aim of quelling looming battles among entrepreneurship scholars over issues such as opportunity discovery or creation, and even the existence of opportunities themselves, the rich insights proffered by M&S (2006) remain largely unexplored opportunities to advance entrepreneurship theory. As is the fate of many foundational theories, the social construction of academic literatures creates cascades of "ceremonial citations" while obfuscating more meaningful engagement with the conceptual nuance and richness of a theory (DiMaggio, 1995).

Nonetheless, new debates are emerging—many involving disruptive technologies such as artificial intelligence (AI) and machine learning (ML) (Townsend & Hunt, 2019)—that elevate the central importance of addressing the epistemological assumptions undergirding EAT. Emerging work also suggests that a more refined and nuanced theory of the mind is needed to account for a broader set of individual-level factors underpinning EAT, such as impulsivity (Lerner et al., 2018; Wiklund et al., 2017), neurobiological drivers (Krueger & Day, 2010), genetic predispositions (e.g., Nicolaou & Shane, 2009; Nicolaou et al., 2008; Zhang et al., 2009), and alternative modalities of entrepreneurial action (Hunt & Lerner, 2018). Overall, the long-term durability of M&S (2006) mirrors questions regarding the long-term impact of entrepreneurial action theories more generally. Will the EAT classics of last decade quell the "civil wars" or exacerbate them?

A Complex Classic with an Uncertain Legacy

The legacy of M&S (2006) is a work-in-progress. As with all well-cited scholarship, the article's strengths and weaknesses, its hidden treasures, and its glaring omissions, each becomes more apparent through the passage of time as scholarly communities debate, reflect, and construct the contribution of an article (DiMaggio, 1995). Indeed, although published pieces fix in time and space all the arguments, logics, and perspectives comprising the architecture of an article, often reflecting the zeitgeist of the era in which the article was written. Meanwhile, authors and scholarly communities, move forward, evolving, elaborating, and self-correcting the original insights. "Classics," then, are pieces that rise above the forces that tend to corrode relevance through the march of time by offering each new reader a sense of "discovery" and fresh awareness. R.J. Smith, a renowned scholar of Chinese history, noted that the essence of a "classic" text rests upon four premises (Popova, 2012), which can be paraphrased as:

1. The work must focus on matters of great importance and provide some sort of guidance for dealing with them.
2. It must address these issues in memorable ways, with stimulating and inviting images.
3. It must be complex, nuanced, comprehensive, and profound, requiring careful and repeated study.
4. It must possess great staying power across both time and space.

Smith's criteria offer an intriguing basis for adjudicating the long-term influence of written work. In applying the spirit of these high standards to M&S (2006), we have sought to summarize and assess the article's past, present, and future impact by examining the extent to which it is substantive and transformational, memorable and illuminating, profound and thorough, and spatially and temporally durable.

Substantive and Transformational

Given the ambitious elemental nature of M&S's (2006) conceptual model, there is little doubt that their contribution is substantive; however, the extent to which it may or may not be transformational is subject to debate and will ultimately be a function of its temporal durability in entrepreneurship theory, which is discussed below. Substantively, M&S drew together in novel fashion the vital facets of entrepreneurship—actor, environment, opportunity, uncertainty, and action—in a unitary integrative model designed to express when, how, and why actors emerge from a state of ignorance and exercise agency through the pursuit of a perceived opportunity. Doing so requires sufficient motivation to act despite the need to bear uncertainty regarding the opportunity's ultimate prospects. Although prior scholarship (e.g., Alvarez, 2005; Venkataraman, 1997) had hinted at the importance of action, M&S (2006) succeeded in demonstrating the necessity of action to theories of entrepreneurship. As Heavey and colleagues (2009, p. 138) noted, "McMullen and Shepherd (2006) place special emphasis on motivation, which, at its core, concerns individuals' willingness to bear uncertainty, in explaining the propensity of individuals to act entrepreneurially. Entrepreneurial action, therefore, is a product of the conjoint influence of knowledge and motivation." By postulating a two-stage theory of entrepreneurial action—one that differentiated third-person from first-person opportunities, yet integrated action and environment—M&S (2006) prophetically pointed the field to a path forward past the early skirmishes of the soon-to-be civil war over the ontology of entrepreneurial opportunities through acknowledging the necessity of actor agency and environmental realities.

Ironically, the subsequent eclipse of M&S (2006) by the opportunity discovery versus creation "civil wars" was presaged by DiMaggio (1995) who argued that the process of socially constructing the contribution and legacy of a theory often falls prey to the siren song of "primordial antinomies" (i.e., binary oppositions, A versus B). Whereas M&S (2006) faithfully weaves Kirzner's (1979) theory of alert entrepreneurs and opportunity discovery into a complex analytical integration of entrepreneurial action theory that negated neither discovery nor creation, its harmonization of these perspectives was largely ignored. Instead, much of the research within the "opportunity wars" has been sparing in its reference to M&S (2006), amplifying the tribal allegiances of scholars situated on various sides of the divide. Yet, several exceptions do exist. Klein (2008), for example, takes important strides to correct course by referring to creation and discovery as "purely metaphorical concepts." He shifts the discussion away from the *ex ante* ontology of opportunities to a focus on decision-making and judgment in light of individual beliefs regarding an opportunity's prospects.

In the end, M&S (2006) and Klein (2008) could not prevent entrepreneurship from diving headlong into an unnecessary civil war over the ontology of opportunities. On one side stands Davidsson's (2015, p. 674) oft-cited indictment of what he calls the "inherent and inescapable problems" of the opportunity construct, especially in applying the construct to individual, micro-level enactments of the entrepreneurial process. On the other side, scholars have expressed serious misgivings regarding abandonment of opportunity as an "umbrella" construct in entrepreneurship (e.g., Wood, 2017), particularly related to the potential peril of definitional fragmentation that would accompany a pivot away from opportunities. In an important way, M&S (2006) addresses this debate through the first- and third-person model. Greater care incorporating M&S (2006) into the core of EAT might have forestalled civil wars over the opportunity construct, but this has not occurred.

Instead, it appears that M&S (2006) is a substantive theory but the full transformational potential has not yet been fully realized.

Memorable and Illuminating

There is an old adage that people do not remember events as much as they remember their own memories of events. The same could be said about the citation patterns of classic articles from scholarly journals. This is because the process of social construction of a contribution of a theory (DiMaggio, 1995) often involves "memories of memories" rather than direct intellectual connections. Citation patterns for M&S (2006) bear this out and are cause for arguing that facets of their conceptualization have been under-appreciated.

While it is difficult to refer to any article that has generated nearly 2200 citations (as of September 2019) over a span of thirteen years, as being "under-appreciated," our analysis of the citations reveals several problematic findings. First, an enormous number of these citations are what authors have taken to calling "ceremonial citations" (DiMaggio, 1995); that is, references that superficially take note of an article's general relevance to a topic as signal of relevance and often as an attempt to build legitimacy with readers by invoking well-known pieces. It is more than a little closely akin to scholarly "name-dropping." Interestingly, the vast majority of M&S's (2006) ceremonial citations occur in its home field of entrepreneurship while scholars completely outside of the field (e.g., economics, sociology, social psychology, and public policy) generally offer more substantive citations of the work. In fact, slightly less than half of the citations (47%) of M&S (2006) are in entrepreneurship journals, about one-third of which appear in the two most prominent entrepreneurship journals, the *Journal of Business Venturing* and *Entrepreneurship Theory and Practice*. Of these, 82% invoke M&S (2006) as what would be regarded as a ceremonial citation, typically cued without elaboration by a single word or phrase, such as uncertainty, entrepreneurial action, or opportunity. Approximately one-fifth engage M&S's elemental model and a small sub-set of these critically assess the conceptual model. Just under one-third of all citations appear in management journals falling outside entrepreneurship (31%) and 60% of these appear to be ceremonial citations of M&S (2006).

At the same time, although only 22% of the M&S's (2006) citations appear in journals whose fields lie outside organizational and management studies altogether, fewer than one-quarter (24%) are ceremonial citations. Instead, the overwhelming majority of the citations from these non-management articles critically engage the substance and structure of M&S's conceptual model. One explanation of this, of course, could be that scholars more proximal to the purpose and heritage of M&S (2006) have the least reason to elaborate on the model for readers of entrepreneurship journals. In our review of these citations, however, the more likely explanation for the tendency towards ceremonial citations is the fact that entrepreneurship scholars are more heavily invested in perpetuating the "tribal debates" that sparked civil wars among entrepreneurship scholars. In this sense, M&S is memorable to the extent that it provides "signaling value" for authors seeking the legitimacy of their own published works, but not to the extent that M&S (2006) can provide an rmistice for ongoing discord.

In comparison, the issue of whether or not M&S (2006) is illuminating can be swiftly and resolutely addressed. As a novel elemental model of entrepreneurial action, M&S (2006) offered a fresh perspective that effectively integrated actors and environments. Each new reader can see in M&S (2006) a framework that demonstrates how and why entrepreneurship is a distinctive domain; not through definitions, as Shane and Venkataraman (2000) provide, but rather as an evolving interactive process that is differentiable from all other activities. The illumination of M&S (2006) is also born out through a considerable body of work generated by both Shepherd and McMullen since 2006. Reading these subsequent lines of inquiry (e.g., McMullen, 2015; McMullen & Dimov, 2013; Shepherd et al., 2007) broadens and deepens the illuminating impact of the original 2006 article. For example, McMullen (2015, p. 657) offers the following insights:

> McMullen and Shepherd (2006) responded to this emphasis on opportunity recognition by pointing out that individuals can only believe (not know) that they have recognized entrepreneurial opportunities under uncertainty and that subsequent action is therefore required to prove that this belief is justified (see also Gregoire et al., 2010; Shepherd et al., 2007). Consequently, they proposed that entrepreneurial action, as opposed to opportunity recognition, should be the focus of the emerging field because, in order to become an entrepreneur, an individual must form, evaluate, and act on an opportunity belief.

This, in turn, provides a compelling bridge to entrepreneurial cognition and through it, many of the most vital aspects of the business venturing process. As Shepherd (2015) noted:

> …following the lead of research on nascent entrepreneurship that focuses less on the single act of exploiting an opportunity and more on the series of activities involved in the emergence of a new firm (Delmar & Shane, 2004; Gartner, 1985; Lichtenstein et al., 2007), future research can focus on activity as the key unit of analysis. This research will help break down entrepreneurial action into its constituent activities and explore the inter-relationships between activities, the inter-relationship between an activity (or sequence of activities) and the motivation to form an opportunity belief, and the inter-relationship between an activity (or sequence of activities) and the knowledge to form an opportunity belief. In doing so, such research will begin to build a theory of the micro-foundations of entrepreneurial action.

The springboard for this thinking traces back to the illuminating aspects of M&S (2006). For those who return to the original work armed with the succession of papers that Shepherd, McMullen, and their various co-authors have produced, the experience reawakens and enriches the forcefulness of the original contribution. M&S (2006) is illuminating and is, therefore, worthy of being remembered. The question—as befalls the judgment accorded all classics—is whether it will literally be remembered, or simply remembered for being memorable?

Profound and Thorough

The question of whether M&S (2006) is both profound and thorough is virtually self-apparent. As an elemental theory of entrepreneurial action, M&S (2006) staked out unique ground among the various attempts to construct an EAT. To be profound, a work must be novel, insightful, and surprising—even improbable, to an extent. That is a high bar. Yet, elements of each are revealed in the article. Perhaps most importantly, M&S (2006) rights a lot of wrongs, consisting of mistakes and oversights that trace back to Schumpeter (1934), Kirzner (1979), and Knight (1921). In this sense, M&S (2006) is profound precisely because it is thorough. The erudition required to link together two and a half centuries of scholarly meandering on what precisely constitutes entrepreneurial action under conditions of uncertainty is a tall order and M&S (2006) offers a compelling framework for correcting these issues.

In one fell swoop, wrongs are largely righted in M&S (2006), allowing the study of entrepreneurship to legitimately claim that it had become the "field" of entrepreneurship because a description of entrepreneurial action's unique qualities was articulated in a holistic fashion that could not be subsumed by existing theory from other fields.

Spatially and Temporally Durable

Of all Smith's criteria governing the declaration of a "classic," none is more foreboding than the issue of spatial and temporal durability. Much to its credit, M&S (2006) has transcended the study of entrepreneurship and even management, evidenced by its infiltration into diverse fields and influence exerted in multi-disciplinary lines of inquiry. Aside from this intellectual boundary spanning, M&S (2006) has enjoyed success in traversing varied academic enclaves and even across national borders. Over half of M&S's (2006) citations appeared in articles authored by scholars affiliated with non-U.S. institutions. Of these, a higher proportion of internationally authored articles move beyond mere ceremonial citation of the work. In essence, the article appears to have resonated with scholars from varied backgrounds and who possess varied perspectives.

Temporal durability is more difficult to judge since far too little time has elapsed since 2006 to credibly determine whether or not M&S (2006) has withstood the test of time. By any measure, entrepreneurship is a young field and EAT is very much a work-in-progress. In the coming decades, M&S (2006) will be subjected to numerous challenges, some of which are certain to stress-test the first- and third-person conceptualization of opportunities and entrepreneurial action. But the signs are encouraging that in striving to move beyond the "opportunity wars," more constructive EAT conversations are emerging. In the following section, we explore conversations that will benefit from and challenge the insights of M&S (2006).

Issues and Opportunities Attendant to the Legacy of M&S (2006)

As the foregoing discussion makes clear, M&S (2006) has emerged as one of the foundational theories of entrepreneurship (Townsend et al., 2018), bridging system-level with individual-level factors in a meso-level theory of entrepreneurial action. Yet, despite all of the well-deserved accolades and attention the article has received to date in the field of entrepreneurship, numerous opportunities remain to apply the two-stage model to explore both the antecedents and consequences of entrepreneurial action. In this section, we explore these opportunities with an eye towards identifying promising, new directions for future research.

Implications for Entrepreneurial Action Theory

The foundational contribution of M&S (2006) centers on the introduction of a two-stage model of entrepreneurial action under conditions of uncertainty (McMullen, 2015), whereby entrepreneurs translate "third-person opportunities" (i.e., an opportunity for someone) into "first-person opportunities" (i.e., an opportunity for me). Despite the power of this model to integrate emerging, conflicting perspectives regarding the ontology of entrepreneurial opportunities, as we noted above, these insights were not heeded sufficiently to avoid the escalation of these skirmishes into the opportunity civil wars. While others have discussed and debated the complicated legacy of the opportunity wars (e.g., Alvarez & Barney, 2019; Alvarez et al., 2013), on this point we simply note that the two-stage model presented in M&S (2006) is perfectly consistent with fundamental work across numerous fields including economics, philosophy, and even social theory (e.g., James, 1884; Poincaré, 1914; Popper, 1977; Searle, 2007) which utilizes two-stage models to transcend similar ontological debates. And, as entrepreneurship scholars increasingly look for models to build upon to move past the opportunity wars, the work of M&S (2006) and others provide useful framework to support these aims.

Two-stage models offer a powerful framework for transcending ontological debates by bridging the conceptual separation of sensory processes whereby individual actors perceive the external world with willful choice to act or not to act in response to these sensory inputs (James, 1884). At the same time, however, two-stage models have also been criticized by scholars embedded within naturalistic or realist camps who criticize the emphasis on the central role of "free will" in human action. Many contemporary cognitive neuroscientists dispute the role of "free will" in human action and decision-making (Libet, 1999a). Instead, these scholars point to a growing volume of empirical evidence gathered from fMRI scans and other non-invasive methods which appears to demonstrate that what humans typically experience as "free will" is largely epiphenomenal (Gallagher, 2006), and anchored in subconscious mental processes

(Libet, 1999b). Under these conditions, the phenomenological experience of "free will" in a two-stage rational choice model simply reflects the sequencing of neurological inputs that originate in the subconscious before being filtered through the conscious part of the brain where actors appear to exercise "agentic choice" (Haggard & Libet, 2001). Yet, because these "choices" are anchored in and determined by the automaticity of the subconscious mind, free will is thought to be a useful mirage (Caruso, 2012).

In contrast, recent work by McMullen and colleagues (2014) discusses the implications of social cognitive approaches to neuroscience and highlights the problems of selective inference in thwarting the confirmation of a deterministic link between brain regions and cognitive functioning. This view argues that, at best, contemporary neuroscientists can only identify which brain regions are activated during specific cognitive processes, not whether activation of specific brain regions determines specific cognitive functions (McMullen et al., 2014). In as far as the phenomenological experience of two-stage agentic choice is a natural byproduct of the emergent complexity of brain function, judgments, decisions, and actions are informed by—but not determined by—single neurological inputs (Chalmers, 1996). Instead, what actors experience in the second stage of this model reflects the processes through which agentic choices are infused with the higher-level cognitive functions, wherein human values, motivations, and other intentional cognitive processes, enrich subconscious sensory inputs to shape subsequent human action (McMullen et al., 2014).

Consistent with this view, future research building on the M&S (2006) model may employ contemporary neuroscience research to provide robust means for incorporating emerging work on the neurological processes of impulsivity (Wiklund et al., 2017), sensation-seeking behaviors (Lerner & Hunt, 2012), and other less-deliberative, neurological processes as precursors to entrepreneurial action (Lerner et al., 2018; Wiklund et al., 2018). By building on the two-stage model, scholars can account more effectively for the diverse range of lower-level sensory inputs that are infused with higher order human values and motivation through an emergent process. Such theorizing invites more robust conceptions of the mind within EAT (e.g., Clark, 2015), revealing how entrepreneurial actors navigate uncertain environments.

The final opportunity we address in this chapter for building on M&S (2006) involves the implications of artificial intelligence and machine learning (Townsend & Hunt, 2019). New dimensions of AI allow managers to deploy systems and new solutions for navigating environments characterized by uncertainty. In many important ways, the emergence of AI will pose unavoidable challenges to canonical theories of entrepreneurial action. By rendering moot many of the persistent biases and heuristics that plague forecasting, judgment, and decision-making attendant to the processes comprising entrepreneurial action, machine-based systems appear poised to improve the consistency and quality of outcomes even under dynamic complexity, while driving the marginal costs of forecasting towards zero (Agrawal et al., 2018). Given the unique abilities of AI systems, the crucial question for entrepreneurial action theorists to ask is: What is the role of entrepreneurs in the emerging age of AI?

In a sense, the capabilities of AI systems to navigate entrepreneurial environments and address problems of modal uncertainty (Townsend & Hunt, 2019) suggest that AI systems will provide powerful tools for augmenting the process of identifying third-person opportunities as described in M&S (2006). Yet, these systems do not provide a full solution for solving the problems of first-person opportunities, or whether the opportunity is an opportunity for me (the entrepreneur)? In some cases, because AI systems lack allegiances to self-regard, self-reflection, and impression management, these systems would not be susceptible to inflated self-appraisals, and unrealistic expectations of success lack a computational equivalent to the human ego. However, at the same time, these systems lack the full range of human values, empathy, and ethical reasoning that might constrain some of the unintended but problematic issues surrounding intelligence software enacting "rational choices" under conditions of uncertainty. In these cases, the pause before the action, where the human agent reflects upon and chooses to act based on moral reasoning, ethics, and other human motives, likely remains an important feature of designing AI systems. The stakes of which continued to be raised as more and more automation is built into these systems. In this sense, the coupling of humans and AI in augmented two-stage models of entrepreneurial action points to an alternative system to fully automated AI systems.

Concluding Thoughts

M&S (2006) possesses many of the markings of a contemporary classic. Throughout this critical assessment of the work, we have sought to make the case that the article is substantive, illuminating, profound, thorough, and spatially durable. Despite its many merits, it is not clear whether M&S (2006) constitutes scholarship that will ultimately prove to be transformative, memorable, and temporally durable. It is, by any measure, an important work, whose most important insights have been underappreciated, courtesy of a *zeitgeist* of a young field that often seems to favor civil war as the preferred form of discourse. The petulant teenager phase of entrepreneurship's evolution is both appropriate to its age and far from complete. As with all new fields, the constructive churning of provisional theories and tools is equal parts chaotic and useful. On the positive side, through the rapid-fire sifting and sorting of perspectives, unwanted and unneeded artifacts are more quickly discarded. On the negative side, battle lines draw scholars into choosing sides prematurely and artificially. Concurrently, attempts to harmonize conflicting perspectives fall on deaf ears because they are offered before the masses are prepared to listen. Such is the fate of M&S (2006). For all of its many attributes and insights, it may have simply been written ahead of its time. Clear thinking rarely gets its due in the middle of a revolution.

What is, however, unmistakable, is the extent to which M&S (2006) directly led to the recognition of entrepreneurship as a distinctive domain. Even at the time of its publication, the stakes attendant to this work were high. Despite the immediate influence of work by Shane and Venkataraman (2000) to demarcate the distinctive domain of entrepreneurship, acclamation on entrepreneurship's distinctiveness was far from universal, evidenced by works such as Sorenson and Stuart's *Annals* piece (2008), which argued that the aims of entrepreneurship scholarship are most faithfully served by considering it as a phenomenon to be studied and co-owned by more established, associated fields.

> ….we neither place high odds on the prospects of success for the study of entrepreneurship as a field, nor do we believe that those interested in the subject should seek such an outcome. In contrast to the increasingly prevalent view within the community of self-identified entrepreneurship scholars, we believe that this area of research will witness the greatest progress if interest in a related set of phenomena rather than a common theoretical cannon forms the basis for scholarly interaction. Instead of

> attempting to establish an independent field, we see the creation of a multi-disciplinary "invisible college" of discipline-based scholars with an interest in entrepreneurship as a better path along which to push forward our understanding of the subject. (2008, p. 519)

Yet, independent fields are rarely established through raw intentionality and brute force. Instead, they tend to emerge when research questions are posed that produce incomplete or inadequate answers from incumbent frameworks. In some sense, then, by 2008, the Sorenson and Stuart argument was addressing a debate that no longer existed. Scholars in the field had moved on. Contrast the Sorenson and Stuart (2008) quote above with McMullen's observation (2019, p. 3) regarding the state of entrepreneurship scholarship ten years later:

> ...just as technologies, companies, and even entire industries rise and fall over time in the business world, so do journals and entire fields of research...Perhaps, entrepreneurship is not a sub-field of management whatsoever...Entrepreneurship scholars study multiple contexts and entrepreneurial phenomena, including but, not limited to, new value creation, new venture creation, opportunity identification, evaluation, and exploitation, ideation and innovation, emergence, new organizing and entry, innovation in established firms, and firm growth and exit, to name only a few. Moreover, we do so through both original and borrowed theoretical lenses from psychology, economics, sociology, political science, anthropology, and most functional areas. Therefore, it is difficult to imagine a field of entrepreneurship that can be understood as anything but interdisciplinary.

McMullen's reasoning echoes Sorenson and Stuart's emphasis on entrepreneurship's multi-disciplinary core, but arrives at a dramatically different conclusion, one that heralds an independence amidst cross-fertilization in recognition that there are research questions attendant to the entrepreneurial process that require the development of new theories and frameworks, forming the bulwark of a distinctive domain. For reasons substantively apprehended in M&S (2006), the research questions requiring the consideration of entrepreneurship as a distinctive domain have become settled science. The scholarly challenges that lie ahead will only make it more so.

References

Agrawal, A., Gans, J., & Goldfarb, A. (2018). *Prediction machines: The simple economics of artificial intelligence*. Harvard Business Press.

Alvarez, S. A. (2005). Theories of entrepreneurship: Alternative assumptions and the study of entrepreneurial action. *Foundations and Trends® in Entrepreneurship*, *1*(3), 105–148.

Alvarez, S. A., & Barney, J. B. (2007). Discovery and creation: Alternative theories of entrepreneurial action. *Strategic Entrepreneurship Journal, 1*(1–2), 11–26.

Alvarez, S. A., & Barney, J. (2019). Has the concept of opportunities been fruitful in the field of entrepreneurship? *Academy of Management Perspectives*, (ja).

Alvarez, S. A., Barney, J. B., & Anderson, P. (2013). Forming and exploiting opportunities: The implications of discovery and creation processes for entrepreneurial and organizational research. *Organization Science, 24*(1), 301–317.

Brown, L., Packard, M., & Bylund, P. (2018). Judgment, fast and slow: Toward a judgment view of entrepreneurs' impulsivity. *Journal of Business Venturing Insights*, *10*, e00095.

Caruso, G. D. (2012). *Free will and consciousness: A determinist account of the illusion of free will*. Lexington Books.

Casson, M. (1982). *The entrepreneur: An economic theory*. Rowman & Littlefield.

Chalmers, D. J. (1996). *The conscious mind: In search of a fundamental theory*. Oxford University Press.

Chandler, G. N., DeTienne, D. R., McKelvie, A., & Mumford, T. V. (2011). Causation and effectuation processes: A validation study. *Journal of Business Venturing, 26*(3), 375–390.

Clark, A. (2015). *Surfing uncertainty: Prediction, action, and the embodied mind*. Oxford University Press.

Coleman, J. S. (1994). *Foundations of social theory*. Harvard University Press.

Davidsson, P. (2015). Entrepreneurial opportunities and the entrepreneurship nexus: A re-conceptualization. *Journal of Business Venturing, 30*(5), 674–695.

Delmar, F., & Shane, S. (2004). Legitimating first: Organizing activities and the survival of new ventures. *Journal of Business Venturing, 19*(3), 385–410.

DiMaggio, P. J. (1995). Comments on "What theory is not. *Administrative Science Quarterly, 40*(3), 391–397.

Gallagher, S. (2006). Where's the action? Epiphenomenalism and the problem of free will. *Does consciousness cause behavior*, 109–124.

Gartner, W. B. (1985). A conceptual framework for describing the phenomenon of new venture creation. *Academy of Management Review, 10*(4), 696–706.

Grégoire, D. A., Barr, P. S., & Shepherd, D. A. (2010). Cognitive processes of opportunity recognition: The role of structural alignment. *Organization Science, 21*(2), 413–431.

Haggard, P., & Libet, B. (2001). Conscious intention and brain activity. *Journal of Consciousness Studies, 8*(11), 47–64.

Heavey, C., Simsek, Z., Roche, F., & Kelly, A. (2009). Decision comprehensiveness and corporate entrepreneurship: The moderating role of managerial uncertainty preferences and environmental dynamism. *Journal of Management Studies, 46*(8), 1289–1314.

Hunt, R. A., & Lerner, D. A. (2018). Entrepreneurial action as human action: Sometimes judgment-driven, sometimes not. *Journal of Business Venturing Insights, 10*, e00102.

James, W. (1884). *The dilemma of determinism* (pp. 114–140). Kessinger Publishing.

Kirzner, I. M. (1979). *Perception, opportunity, and profit: Studies in the theory of entrepreneurship*. University of Chicago Press.

Klein, P. G. (2008). Opportunity discovery, entrepreneurial action, and economic organization. *Strategic Entrepreneurship Journal, 2*(3), 175–190.

Knight, F. H. (1921). *Risk, Uncertainty and Profit*. University of Chicago Press.

Krueger Jr, N. F., & Day, M. (2010). Looking forward, looking backward: From entrepreneurial cognition to neuro-entrepreneurship. In *Handbook of entrepreneurship research* (pp. 321–357). Springer.

Lerner, D., & Hunt, R. (2012, July). Sensation seeking and entrepreneurial behavior in the formal and informal economy. In *Academy of management proceedings* (Vol. 2012, No. 1, p. 10057). Briarcliff Manor, NY: Academy of Management.

Lerner, Hunt, & Dimov. (2018). Action! Moving beyond the intendedly-rational logics of entrepreneurship. *Journal of Business Venturing, 33*, 52–69.

Libet, B. (1999a). Do we have free will? *Journal of Consciousness Studies, 6*(8–9), 47–57.

Libet, B. (1999b). How does conscious experience arise? The neural time factor. *Brain Research Bulletin, 50*(5–6), 339–340.

Lichtenstein, B. B., Carter, N. M., Dooley, K. J., & Gartner, W. B. (2007). Complexity dynamics of nascent entrepreneurship. *Journal of Business Venturing, 22*(2), 236–261.

McMullen, J. S. (2015). Entrepreneurial judgment as empathic accuracy: A sequential decision-making approach to entrepreneurial action. *Journal of Institutional Economics, 11*(3), 651–681.

McMullen, J. S. (2019). A wakeup call for the field of entrepreneurship and its evaluators. *Journal of Business Venturing, 34*(3), 413–417.

McMullen, J. S., & Dimov, D. (2013). Time and the entrepreneurial journey: The problems and promise of studying entrepreneurship as a process. *Journal of Management Studies, 50*(8), 1481–1512.

McMullen, J. S., & Shepherd, D. A. (2006). Entrepreneurial action and the role of uncertainty in the theory of the entrepreneur. *Academy of Management Review, 31*, 132–152.

McMullen, J. S., Wood, M. S., & Palich, L. E. (2014). Entrepreneurial cognition and social cognitive neuroscience. In *Handbook of entrepreneurial cognition*. Edward Elgar Publishing.

Nicolaou, N., & Shane, S. (2009). Can genetic factors influence the likelihood of engaging in entrepreneurial activity? *Journal of Business Venturing, 24*(1), 1–22.

Nicolaou, N., Shane, S., Cherkas, L., Hunkin, J., & Spector, T. D. (2008). Is the tendency to engage in entrepreneurship genetic? *Management Science, 54*(1), 167–179.

Poincaré, H. (1914). Science and method, trans. Maitland, London: Thomas Nelson.

Popper, K. R., & Eccles, J. C. (1977[2012]). *The self and its brain*. Springer Science & Business Media.

Popova, M. (2012). What makes a classic? Lessons from the Chinese book of changes. *Brainpickings*. Accessed August 28, 2019: https://www.brainpickings.org/2012/06/13/what-makes-a-classic-i-ching/

Ramoglou, S., & Tsang, E. W. (2016). A realist perspective of entrepreneurship: Opportunities as propensities. *Academy of Management Review, 41*(3), 410–434.

Sarasvathy, S. (2001). Causation and effectuation: Toward a theoretical shift from economic inevitability to entrepreneurial contingency. *Academy of Management Review, 26*(2), 243–263.

Schumpeter, J. A. [2017(1934)]. *Theory of economic development*. Routledge.

Searle, J. R. (2007). Freedom and neurobiology: Reflections on free will. *Language, and political power*. Columbia University Press.

Shane, S., & Venkataraman, S. (2000). The promise of entrepreneurship as a field of research. *Academy of Management Review, 25*(1), 217–226.

Shepherd, D. A. (2015). Party on! A call for entrepreneurship research that is more interactive, activity based, cognitively hot, compassionate, and prosocial. *Journal of Business Venturing, 30*(4), 489–507.

Shepherd, D. A., McMullen, J. S., & Jennings, P. (2007). The formation of opportunity beliefs: Overcoming ignorance and reducing doubt. *Strategic Entrepreneurship Journal, 1*, 75–95.

Sorenson, O., & Stuart, T. E. (2008). 12 Entrepreneurship: A field of dreams? *Academy of Management Annals, 2*(1), 517–543.

Townsend, D. M., & Hunt, R. A. (2019). Entrepreneurial action, creativity, & judgment in the age of artificial intelligence. *Journal of Business Venturing Insights, 11*, e00126.

Townsend, D. M., Hunt, R. A., McMullen, J. S., & Sarasvathy, S. D. (2018). Uncertainty, knowledge problems, and entrepreneurial action. *Academy of Management Annals, 12*(2), 659–687.

Venkataraman, S. (1997). The distinctive domain of entrepreneurship research. *Advances in Entrepreneurship, Firm Emergence and Growth, 3*(1), 119–138.

Wiklund, J., Yu, W., & Patzelt, H. (2018). Impulsivity and entrepreneurial action. *Academy of Management Perspectives, 32*(3), 379–403.

Wiklund, J., Yu, W., Tucker, R., & Marino, L. D. (2017). ADHD, impulsivity and entrepreneurship. *Journal of Business Venturing, 32*(6), 627–656.

Wood, M. S. (2017). Misgivings about dismantling the opportunity construct. *Journal of Business Venturing Insights, 7*, 21–25.

Wood, M. S., & Mckinley, W. (2017). After the venture: The reproduction and destruction of entrepreneurial opportunity. *Strategic Entrepreneurship Journal, 11*(1), 18–35.

Zhang, Z., et al. (2009). The genetic basis of entrepreneurship: Effects of gender and personality. *Organizational Behavior and Human Decision Processes, 110*(2), 93–107.

Zott, C., & Huy, Q. N. (2007). How entrepreneurs use symbolic management to acquire resources. *Administrative Science Quarterly, 52*(1), 70–105.

CHAPTER 8

Entrepreneur Is so Much More Than Just Money Making: Reclaiming the Space of Entrepreneurship in Society

Arturo E. Osorio and Alexander Settles

Introduction

Can we understand entrepreneurship beyond narrow economic views of wealth transfer?

Steyaert and Katz (2004) article asks this question to frame their article, the introduction to a special issue on the journal of *Entrepreneurship & Regional Development*. Their goal is deceivingly simple: to reclaim the space of entrepreneurship beyond its restricted depiction as an economic instrument to present it, instead, as a dynamic multi-discursive space. As they acknowledge, entrepreneurship scholars have

A. E. Osorio (✉)
Rutgers Business School Newark & New Brunswick, Newark, NJ, USA
e-mail: Osorio@business.rutgers.edu

A. Settles
Warrington College of Business, University of Florida, Gainesville, FL, USA
e-mail: Alex.Settles@warrington.ufl.edu

A. E. Osorio et al. (eds.), *Modern Classics in Entrepreneurship Studies*,
https://doi.org/10.1007/978-3-030-61029-6_8

already embraced a multidisciplinary basis (Landström, 1999), yet this might be needed to reconsider if we want to conceive a new "language" to rewrite entrepreneurship (Hjorth, 2003) to be understood beyond economics. Reaching beyond the economic transactional nature of entrepreneurship opens up the narrative regarding the value of entrepreneurship to include social development, cultural growth, mental health improvements, geographic impact, and the development of the life of communities.

Anchored by the journal's focus on entrepreneurship as an instrument for regional development, Steyaert and Katz (2004) explore the role of entrepreneurship as a tool of societal transformation and invite others to join in this conversation. To encourage the dialog, Steyaert and Katz (2004) present several non-economic examples of entrepreneurial impact, including:

> - *National governments demonstrating entrepreneurship through efforts such as privatization of nationalized businesses, the revitalization of existing government services, and even concepts such as public entrepreneurship, which embody a more innovative and citizen-oriented (in comparison to a customer or consumer) focus* (Laurent, 2000);
> - *Local governments creating new entities such as free trade zones* (Hitt & Bartkus, 1997), *innovative funding opportunities* (Perlmutter & Cnaan, 1995), *or even whole cities created to compete with established cities for new firms and settlers* (Dobers, 2003);
> - *Therapists who have seen in the process of entrepreneurship the opportunity to create new societies in which value and institutional systems can be built-in from the start to result in more humane and even therapeutic environments* (Sarason, 1972);
> - *Ethnic groups who have embraced entrepreneurship as a means of social and economic betterment for the community as well as a means of entry to the mainstream of their societies* (Bonacich & Modell, 1980; Waldinger & Aldrich, 1990);
> - *Artists and artisans who have embraced entrepreneurship as part of their work* (Caplin, 1983), *or even as a model for thinking about the creative process* (Halprin, 1970).
>
> (Steyaert & Katz, 2004, pp. 181–182)

This broader understanding of entrepreneurial enactments as a tool of societal transformation has become an important inquiry among researchers, policymakers, and community leaders alike. Researching this broader notion of entrepreneurial actions can provide much-needed insights and new directions regarding the underscoring challenges and opportunities faced by communities addressing social inequality, including the inadequate local access to products and services for marginalized groups (e.g., women, refugees, minorities). This broader understanding allows for the exploration of the actions individuals take when tackling everyday life situations in transformative ways that may disrupt the social status quo. Further, this lens may also bring about a focus on how communities may become co-created, regulated, and/or transformed by its members.

Focusing on what the Steyaert and Katz (2004) article has meant to scholars, this chapter highlights the extent of entrepreneurial possibilities outside the economic realm (e.g., Calás et al., 2009; Daskalaki et al., 2015; Hjorth, 2003), and opens the door for the emergence of a far-reaching conceptualization of entrepreneurship. This broad remit for the extent of entrepreneurship opens up a broad dialogue to better understand the role entrepreneurship plays in society beyond the economic impact. This chapter is divided into four areas. First, we examine Steyaert and Katz's (2004) article that reclaimed the space of entrepreneurship in society. Second, we explore the impact that Steyaert and Katz's (2004) work has had to highlight why their article should be considered a seminal article in the field of entrepreneurship. Third, we discuss the current research that is anchored on the contribution that Steyaert and Katz (2004) have made. Finally, we explore some possibilities for future research based on the framework Steyaert and Katz (2004) created.

Steyaert and Katz (2004): Reclaiming the Space of Entrepreneurship in Society

In 2004, Steyaert and Katz (2004) were one of the first to call attention to the occurrence of socially innovative actions taking place within communities. By exploring these dynamics, they noticed a shared pattern, a common aim to change the societal arrangements within the community. Key to their observations, Steyaert and Katz (2004) identified that these innovative changes fulfilled all the elements of an entrepreneurial undertaking with the exception of holding the ultimate goal of achieving economic gains, even if wealth transfer was part of this socially innovative action. This highlight of the social aspects of entrepreneurial actions enriches the discourse of the phenomena.

Informed by these observations, Steyaert and Katz (2004) strive to reclaim the space where entrepreneurship takes place, in a geographic and social sense. Thus, Steyaert and Katz (2004) open the door to an intriguing set of possibilities where entrepreneurship is outlined and reframed within three distinct yet interrelated dimensions; geographical, discursive, and social. To foster the conversation, they further develop each one of these three dimensions into a unique proposition endowed with its own research path.

Geographical Dimension

Exploring sites (i.e., locations) and spaces (i.e., geographies, spatial) concurrently focuses attention on how societies occupy and reterritorialize spaces (geographies) across the earth to create (co-create and recreate) sites (locations). Looking into the resulting geospatial and geopolitical occupation patterns, the geographical dimension considers the preferential connections between entrepreneurial enactments and the choices of development that place some regions over others. This highlights how entrepreneuring shapes local geography by creating value (beyond economic) in specific places and leaving other geographies undeveloped with the subsequent implications for (local) society. Thus, this dimension brings forward a critical lens emphasizing that entrepreneurial location choices are not "spatial" neutral but rather informed by the prevailing uneven geoconditions across the earth.

Moving through the different levels of geospatial clustering, the geographical dimension articulates that site selection choices reterritorialize entrepreneurship into a series of spatial categories that are independent yet nested within each other. Accordingly, Steyaert and Katz (2004) place nations and regions on one hand, while on the other one neighborhoods and circles of individuals (i.e., networks) are considered. This conceptual structuring of spatial arrangements of individuals allows to explore the geosocial dynamics within and across communities.

Framed by these geospatial conceptualizations, Steyaert and Katz (2004) developed their first proposition. This *first proposition* states that entrepreneurship (and entrepreneuring) takes place at the intersection of spaces (i.e., geographies) and sites (i.e., locations). Thus, acknowledging the concurrent physical and social embeddedness of the phenomenon. The subsequent two propositions, discursive and social, are anchored on the ideas of this first proposition describing entrepreneurship as embedded within an uneven, purpose-driven geospatial condition.

Discursive Dimension

This dimension sets a geopolitical framework considering entrepreneurship as a multidimensional phenomenon rather than a limited transactional economic discourse. This dimension advances the understanding of the entrepreneurial processes as complex political dynamics realized (and conceptualized) through (local) social narratives. As a social construction, Steyaert and Katz (2004) argue entrepreneurial narratives need to be released from dominant economic discourses to be better understood. Under this discursive dimension, where entrepreneurial action occurs at local geography level matters for the full understanding of the phenomena. Thus, the discursive dimension attempts to explore entrepreneurial actions beyond the constraints of monolithic economic frameworks looking for economic-driven intentionality.

Exploring non-economic discourses as frameworks for entrepreneurial narratives can help illuminate current (and emerging) non-economic societal understandings of value. Social discourses are collectively constructed agreements of social norms, including what is valuable (acceptable) or not within a group (Berger & Luckman, 1967). As part of societal dynamics, the social discourses are constantly emerging from (and recreated by) geospatially localized community relations and hierarchies of power. Thus, social discourses establish (and sustain) the value hierarchies that include dominant (i.e., mainstream) and marginalized (i.e., periphery, stigmatize) narratives of value within communities. As such, the discursive dimension presented by Steyaert and Katz (2004) recognized the local value of non-economic narratives as enacting geographical spaces of entrepreneurship. Further, these non-economic narratives are understood as voicing the actions disrupting the dynamics of marginalization and/or recognizing (or creating) the emergence of new objects of value within communities.

Examining these non-economic power narratives furthers the understanding of entrepreneurship and serves to highlight the ever-evolving nature of entrepreneurship as a socially acceptable and collectively constructed practice of value creation, identification, extraction, and transfer. In terms of the (extant) dominant discourses on entrepreneurship, the framing of non-economic entrepreneurial values is seen as deviant.

By overcoming the dominant (i.e., restricting) economic definition of entrepreneurship, the *second proposition* aims to advance two interrelated goals. First, to make explicit the tacitly understood discourses in entrepreneurship that present non-economic value transfers as deviants (e.g., environmental gains, educational attainment, social organizing), thus normalizing deviant praxis as an acceptable form of entrepreneurial action. Second, this proposition further advanced new understandings of entrepreneurial practices in ways not previously contemplated as new discourses of value; in terms of value related to culture, environment, health, and civic change are considered appropriate, thus normalized into the local discourse.

Social Dimension

This dimension presents entrepreneurship as a societal process. As such, the social dimension moves the entrepreneurial narratives from the image of the entrepreneur as an extraordinary individual undertaking extraordinary economic actions towards a focus on the mundane actions of individuals within the society to further all aspects of social and other forms of value creation. Thus, the social dimension frames entrepreneurship as an everyday (ordinary) development enacted by the multiple actors and stakeholders. This shift on focus towards regular individuals within society calls attention to dominant views that have been privileged taking part in entrepreneurial processes (e.g., heroic economic undertakings), while making visible, previously ignored, possibilities of entrepreneurial stories (Hjorth & Steyaert, 2003).

Giving voice to non-privileged entrepreneurial enactments, the social dimension brings an insight of society as a geopolitical space where community members can exchange ideas, goods, and services under their own rules, at their own times. Through this dimension, Steyaert and Katz (2004) make visible the ubiquity and everydayness of entrepreneurship. Thus, highlighting entrepreneurship as the type of action that can involve virtually anyone, can take place basically anywhere, and can occur at nearly anytime.

By recognizing the social ubiquity of entrepreneurship in everyday life of communities, the *third proposition* aims to remove elitist (heroic) views of entrepreneurship. Thus, this third proposition acknowledges entrepreneurship as the everyday (e.g., ordinary, mundane) spatial production of ordinary people doing ordinary actions within communities. Part of this shift moves away from the conceptualization of the entrepreneur as an economic superhero. This complex understanding allows for capturing previously ignored entrepreneurial processes and outcomes taking place anywhere (and everywhere) in the community, including the community's social, geographical, and political fringes.

The Geopolitics of Everyday Entrepreneurship: Reclaiming the Role of Entrepreneurship in Society

The term geopolitics comes from the Greek Geo (γῆ) meaning "earth, land" and Politikḗ (Πολιτική)/politiká (Πολιτικά), meaning "affairs of the cities." Combining both terms, Geopolitics refers to the study of the effects of the land's geography (human and physical) on the matters of the cities or communities. It is in this context that Steyaert and Katz (2004) article poses its core question; *Can we understand entrepreneurship beyond narrow economic views of wealth transfer?*

The geographical proposition serves to anchor entrepreneurship as a geopolitical phenomenon. It does so by presenting entrepreneurship as taking place at the intersection of sites (i.e., locations) and spaces (i.e., geographies). As such, the geographical proposition invites to reflect how entrepreneurial dynamics, beyond economics, may merge with spaces and geographies to create sites and locations related to value formation. This understanding of the phenomena leads to a natural gateway to conversations on environmental and social sustainability where the posing of economic gains above the preservation of the environment and creation of socially sustainable communities is made explicit and questioned.

Building from the geographical dimension, the discursive proposition enriches the dialogue as it helps to ask what is valuable and worthy of entrepreneurial efforts. Putting forward the idea of social construction of reality, the discursive proposition brings to light the role of entrepreneurship as political action in the (re)creating society and the collective recognition of value. Entrepreneurial actions aim to capture the value and/or make valuable resources accessible. As part of this entrepreneurial (and entrepreneuring) process, entrepreneurs assess the worth of their actions against the worth of the outcome of their entrepreneurial endeavor. If the outcome is not worth their effort, then their entrepreneurial process is not enacted. Thus emerging (political) discourses serve to (re)assess the value of the entrepreneurial actions based on the diverse value creation outcomes beyond merely economic gains.

The social proposition suggests looking at politics as everyday actions (discourses) of individuals moving throughout spaces (geographies) and making of the spaces into sites (places). This idea acknowledges that entrepreneurship is an everyday social production of ordinary people as they move on through their life within a community. This broader understanding of entrepreneurs and their entrepreneurial actions serves to bring a voice to non-privileged entrepreneurial enactments where the goal of the process is not to attain economic gains, or where the attainment of economic gains might be bound by other social discourses of value (e.g., quality of life, environment). The expansion of the concept of entrepreneurship to include social and geographic dimensions provides a framework to better understand the value created beyond merely the economic impact of entrepreneurial activities.

A Jewel in Entrepreneurship: Impact and Highlights by the Numbers

Steyaert and Katz (2004) work moves the entrepreneurship research spotlight outside of the economic domain to call attention to everyday entrepreneurial actions, including entrepreneurial aims beyond the economic wealth transfer and/or accumulation. Because of their contributions, Steyaert and Katz (2004) work has become a seminal article in entrepreneurship, as noted by its 99.764 prominence percentile in Scopus. Looking at the citation tree of Steyaert and Katz (2004) work as a proxy for the impact of its ideas, Web of Science identifies 7134 articles referring to works citing this article, through early 2020. A closer look at these reports shows 348 direct citations in Web of Science core collection and 881 direct citations in Google Scholar. This citation record was collected in the same time period ending in early 2020. Other markers highlighting the importance of this work are the research fields where these ideas have found root (Fig. 8.1) and the nature of the outlets where these ideas have been advanced (Fig. 8.2).

Looking at the fields where Steyaert and Katz (2004) work has found traction, the domain of Business Economics with 249 publications is the field with the highest impact (Fig. 8.1). The widespread interest in Steyaert and Katz (2004) work by Business and Economics scholars seems, at first, counter-intuitive as Steyaert and Katz (2004) work aims to move the entrepreneurship research agenda outside of the field of economics. Yet, a closer look highlights why Steyaert and Katz (2004) work has earned the distinction to be called a seminal work. Of the 249 articles in Business Economics, all of them include an aim to discuss the

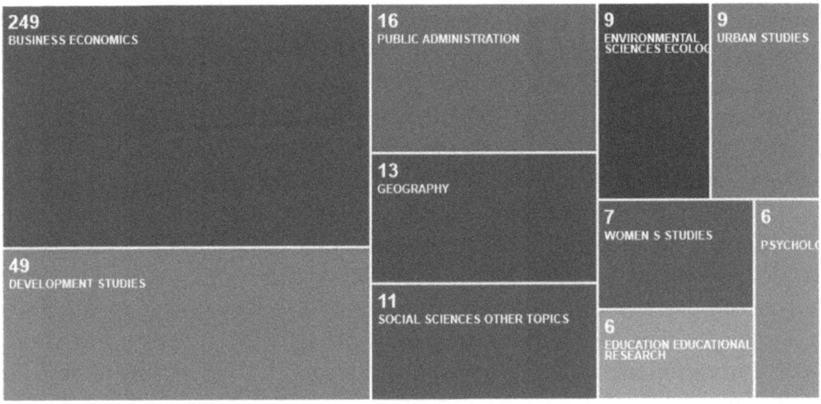

Fig. 8.1 Research fields with a dominant presence of Steyaert and Katz (2004) work as reported by Web of Science

Fig. 8.2 Type of outlets with a dominant presence of Steyaert and Katz (2004) work as reported by Web of Science

non-economic value of entrepreneurship. Further, five of these 249 articles are ranked as highly cited papers by Web of Science. For an article to merit the highly cited distinction in the index service Web of Science as of January/February 2020, a paper must have received enough citations to place it in the top 1% of its academic field based on the highly cited threshold for the field and publication year.

One hallmark of quality and the relevance of particular work is where new research citing that work is published. The Web of Science analytics indicates the largest presence of Steyaert and Katz (2004) has been in academic articles (247) and book chapters (58), proceedings (17), and other outlets (Fig. 8.2). A closer look into these outlets shows a strong presence of Steyaert and Katz (2004) work in its home journal: *Entrepreneurship & Regional Development* (40-direct citations), but also a wide reach in other outlets across many local geographies (e.g., Africa, Europe, Latin America) and topics of interest intersecting with entrepreneurship (e.g., Arts, entrepreneurial Government actions, environmental concerns).

While the standalone value of the article by Steyaert and Katz (2004) is enough to deem it a jewel, solely focusing on the face value of this work does not allow to get the full picture of its impact. As the introduction to a special issue, this article connects the other three articles within the special issue to advance its full argument. Thus, to get a better understanding of the merits of Steyaert and Katz (2004) work, it is advisable to also look at the impact of its three companion works; Conklin Frederking (2004), Rehn and Taalas (2004), and Johnstone and Lionais (2004).

The first of the three companion papers, the work of Conklin Frederking (2004) brings the reader on a journey from London, UK to Chicago, USA, to explore cultural determinism and entrepreneurship. Taking a closer look at the entrepreneurial actions within two culturally distinct groups at three culturally different neighborhoods (Punjabis in Southall in London, England; Gujaratis in Wembley in London, England; and both Punjabis and Gujaratis in the same neighborhood in Chicago, USA), Conklin Frederking (2004) illustrates the idea that local culture on itself does not determine entrepreneurial actions. Conklin Frederking (2004) work, illustrating the ideas of the Geographical, Discursive, and Social dimensions, further advances a wider view where the cultural, economic, spatial, relational, and institutional become understood through an integrative effect.

Web of Science identifies 1467 articles referring to works citing Conklin Frederking (2004), through early 2020 with about one-fourth of those citations in 2019. A closer look at these reports shows 43 direct citations in Web of Science core collection numbers during the same period ending in early 2020.

The second paper in this special issue, the work of Rehn and Taalas (2004), further questions the view of economics as the exclusive basis of entrepreneurial processes. Visiting some households of Russian families and citizens, Rehn and Taalas (2004) explore as to whether entrepreneurship is about the creation of organizations rather than the creation of organizing through a variety of spatial networks. Thus, they advance three points. First, entrepreneurship does not necessarily need to be an undertaking of exceptional individuals. Second, entrepreneurship may happen by necessity and not by choice. Finally, "[e]ntrepreneurship can be subversive and anti-systemic" (p. 247). These three ideas further advance the Geographical, Discursive, and Social dimensions, by presenting entrepreneurship as the non-economic actions born from the everyday necessity of individuals trading outside of the local market system.

The Web of Science identifies 2567 articles referring to works citing this article, through early 2020. A closer look at these reports shows 107 direct citations in the Web of Science Core Collection during the same period ending in early 2020.

The last paper in the special issue, the work of Johnstone and Lionais (2004), explores how entrepreneurship (and entrepreneurs) can adapt to places (geographies) with low economic values by leveraging (local) high social meaning. These places of low economic value are best understood as depleted communities. A depleted community is an area where the strength of capitalistic relationships has diminished; these locations (sites) are the result of uneven development, which is itself an innate trait of capitalism (Smith, 1990). These communities are characterized by being "depleted" of growth mechanisms (and resources) while residents still hold strong social ties to the community itself, thus providing them with a powerful resistance of leaving the location (Johnstone & Lionais, 2004). Depleted communities are core to illustrate the need for a critical lens to explore novel forms of entrepreneurship (value creation) that are crucial for the future and the wellbeing of geospatially located (anchored) social groups. Thus, advancing the Geographical, Discursive, and Social dimensions, by presenting entrepreneurship as a tool for non-economic community gains, rather than individual profiting.

The citation history of this article indicates the impact of this paper can be expressed by the number of times the work has been cited. Web of Science identifies 2347 articles referring to works citing this article, through early 2020. A closer look at these reports shows 122 direct citations in Web of Science during the same period ending in early 2020.

The impact analysis on Steyaert and Katz (2004) work suggests a strong impact on the research agenda in the area of entrepreneurship. A number of citations that increases every year indicate a growing interest in the ideas of their work. Yet, how this research interest has evolved and has grown roots in the field is a conversation about the nature of the impact rather than the magnitude of it. In the next section, we will explore the areas where the interest in this work has become prominent.

Current Work Based on Steyaert and Katz (2004)

Notions of entrepreneurship beyond narrow economic views have served to craft new businesses models and to address emerging community interests (Daskalaki et al., 2015; Korsgaard & Anderson, 2011; Mauksch & Rowe, 2016; McKeever et al., 2015; Parkinson et al., 2017). These emerging views present entrepreneurship as a tool for innovative thinking capable of reorganizing the established value hierarchy and crafting new organizing structures (Calás et al., 2009; Daskalaki et al., 2015). Because of their alternative focus, these understandings have gained visibility among government officials, policymakers, activists, NGOs, and others (Angelidou & Mora, 2019; Down, 2012; Steyaert & Katz, 2004). The resulting entrepreneurial actions come from a broad range of settings and spaces aiming to a diverse array of goals beyond those of simple commerce and economic drive. These emerging areas are informed by the three dimensions identified by Steyaert and Katz (2004) original work and further discussed in their special issue: geographical, discursive, and social.

Geographic Dimension: Current Work

Informed by the geographic dimension's ideas of reterritorializing spaces (geographies) to create (co-create and recreate) sites (locations), current work explores the relationships between entrepreneuring and geospaces (e.g., Martynovich, 2017). Thus, extant work in this stream has explored regions and urban locations as dynamic spaces that shape, and are shaped by the actions of the resident (embedded) entrepreneur.

Regions. In the context of the geographical dimension, a region can be understood as an extensive, continuous part of a geography delimited by spatial markers (landmarks and/or geopolitical boundaries). Highlighted by the intersection of spatial geographies and political boundaries, work on entrepreneurial regions has increasingly gained importance as regions are developed and collaborated. An example of the research in regions can be found in the work of Huggins et al. (2015). In their work, Huggins et al. (2015) explore how regional entrepreneurship first emerges, and later how this emergent entrepreneurship may change the regional enterprise policies and associated governance mechanisms. Another example is Hong et al. (2015) work where they integrate three perspectives to explain regional variations in startups. Presenting regions as socioeconomic ecosystems, Walsh and Winsor (2019) explore the sociocultural barriers inhibiting the development of a regional entrepreneurial ecosystem.

Taking a closer look at the nature of entrepreneurial ecosystems, Spigel (2017) is another example of the work in entrepreneurial regions. In his work, Spigel (2017) presents a model to characterize and explore regions as an entrepreneurial ecosystem, thus providing a framework to understand the regional emergence of different types of entrepreneurial endeavors as a response to local conditions. Moving the conversation on entrepreneurial regions from local conditions into entrepreneurial individuals, Smith et al. (2005) provide a different example of the work on entrepreneurial regions. In their work, they highlight the value of the agency of the individual when developing entrepreneurial regions, thus bringing back the focus on agents of regional change. Hence, highlighting the value of entrepreneuring as a tool of regional transformation rather than an economic extraction mechanism.

Urban Spaces. Urban spaces are built-up areas explained as a human settlement with a high population density (above average number of individuals per square mile) and endowed with an infrastructure of the built environment (e.g., roads, water systems, utilities). Urban spaces are usually synonymous with cities and may be controlled by a single local government system. A metropolitan area is a collection of geospatially contiguous urban spaces sharing industry, infrastructure, and housing possessing an urban core surrounded by a less-populated area. These metropolitan areas may include one or more cities. With the world population becoming dominantly urban, research at the intersection of entrepreneurship and urban spaces has moved front in many research agendas (Osorio, 2018).

These urban works explore both: how entrepreneurship may happen within urban contexts, and how, in return, entrepreneuring may shape the hosting urban space. For instance, Stabrowski (2017) looks at how the internet "home-sharing" platform Airbnb has commoditized housing in urban spaces. Similarly, others have explored the efficacy of social entrepreneurs to (purposefully) influence urban planning (e.g., Angelidou & Mora, 2019; Houtbeckers, 2016). Focusing on the urban space as a context, research has explored the urban emergence and impact of creativity, culture, arts. For example, Lange et al. (2008) discuss issues of governing creativity, presenting it as the self-organization and self-governance of urban creativity and creative industries in urban spaces. Similarly, Lange (2011) explores the dynamics of a creative milieu formation by the so-called "culturepreneurs" (i.e., cultural entrepreneurs).

Other research exploring the re-invention of urban spaces has focused on the role of arts and culture in the (re)creation of value in urban spaces (e.g., Kang, 2017). Considering the intersection of urban space and entrepreneuring, research has focused on the making of the urban landscape, as it is the case of Angrisano et al. (2016), who critically analyze the process to implement the UNESCO recommendation on historic urban landscapes. Paying attention to the "why" entrepreneurship happens in urban spaces; research has explored smart cities (Calisto & Goncalves, 2017), neighborhoods (Williams & Williams, 2012), enterprising communities (Lado-Sestayo et al., 2017), ecopreneurship (Houtbeckers, 2016), and Placemaking (Dodd et al., 2018). All this work is extending the understanding of entrepreneurship as a value-extracting tool where the geolocated extracted value is not economic in nature.

Discursive Dimension: Current Work

With a focus on entrepreneurship as a multidimensional phenomenon, extant works on this stream have helped further illuminate current (and emerging) non-economic societal understandings of value. Taking its cue from the core idea of entrepreneurial processes as complex political dynamics, current work on this stream has focused on entrepreneurship as an event of resistance, resilience, emancipation, and the phenomenon of arts, culture, and creativity.

Resistance. Resistance is the ability of not to be affected by something, especially adversely. Resistance may also be understood as a refusal to accept or comply with something and/or the attempt to prevent something from happening either by action or argument. Egan-Wyer et al. (2018) present a paradox where the discourse of resistance against corporative conformity becomes a productive part of entrepreneurial culture. In a similar manner, Courpasson et al. (2016) see resistance to managerial control as the tool to create spaces of creativity, solidarity, and alternative modalities of work in an organizational context.

Focusing on barefoot entrepreneur[ing] (i.e., the entrepreneurial practices and narratives of individuals primarily living in marginal, deprived, and excluded places and context), Imas et al. (2012) present entrepreneurship as a process of overcoming and contestation. Building on the processual notion of entrepreneuring-as-emancipation, Goss et al. (2011) advance a balanced conception of agency and active constraint embedded in the notion of power rituals. Along the lines of conceptualizing entrepreneurship as a tool to change power dynamics, Dashtipour and Rumens (2018) view entrepreneurship as the means to disrupt and disturb the social order. Taking the conversation one step further, Daskalaki et al. (2015) see entrepreneurship as an act of resistance but rather the new organizing of local social realities. Presenting entrepreneurial endeavors in a context of resistance and local tensions, Luthy and Steyaert (2019) argue entrepreneurship is a process of social experimentation that reconfigures and challenges the local dominant sociomaterial order. Recognizing the everyday resistance inherent in mundane entrepreneurial practices, Sabella and El-Far (2019) extend entrepreneuring arguments for the complex and dynamic nature of the phenomenon and exposing the intrinsic political nature of entrepreneurial action.

Resilience. Resilience can be best described as the capacity to recover quickly from difficulties. Thus resilience in this context is the ability to use entrepreneurship to build up capabilities to recover or using entrepreneurship as a process of recovering. Exploring what may constitute social and sustainable entrepreneurship (entrepreneurship that builds up capabilities of recovery), Larsson et al. (2016) discuss the determinants of organizational resilience and their relationship to enhanced sustainability in general. Their work suggests that in some instances, companies will undergo re-organization (transformation) and novel market innovations (adaptations) to enhance sustainability in general, and not to pursue profiting. Taking a larger view on resilience, Vlasov et al. (2018) examine how embeddedness, in place and in trans-local grassroots networks, may influence proactive entrepreneurship for local resilience.

Redefining understandings of value and purpose for entrepreneurial ventures, Korsgaard et al. (2016) offer an economic geography approach to understand local entrepreneurship. Thus, they highlight the importance of addressing non-economic concerns in our way of thinking about entrepreneurship to ensure local resilience under environmental and social duress. Exploring entrepreneurship as space (social) creation process, Heilbrunn (2019) looks into a refugee camp to examine how people may act entrepreneurially under extreme circumstances to improve their quality of life. Thus, using entrepreneurship as a recovery process. Similarly to Heilbrunn (2019) work, Garcia-Lorenzo et al. (2018) study how individuals may transition from un(der)employment to entrepreneurship to overcome their condition of necessity.

Emancipation. To be emancipated means to be free from restraint and/or the control or power of another. As an entrepreneurial endeavor, emancipation can be explained as any deliberate effort to secure equality or obtain economic, social, and/or political rights for a specifically disenfranchised (marginalized, excluded, alienated) group of individuals or social category (e.g., women, minorities, people of different abilities, immigrants). Presenting entrepreneurship as an emancipatory process with broad change potential, Tedmanson et al. (2015) explore the contradictions and potentialities of locally based communal entrepreneurship as expressions of dynamic tension, simultaneously transformative and exploitative in orientation. Focusing on the links between entrepreneurship, emancipation, and gender, Al-Dajani et al. (2015) explore how contractual conditions, supposedly set to protect women's interests, actually constrain the emancipatory potential of the women's entrepreneurial activities. Yet, they also identified how those very same conditions generate collaborative networks enabling women to challenge the constraints in efforts to assert control over their own entrepreneurial activities. Further, Goss et al. (2011) build on the processual notion of entrepreneuring-as-emancipation to discuss the notion of power rituals as a balanced conception of agency and active constraint. Their work seeks to inform debates in organization studies where the notions of agency and constraint are connected to concerns of power and resistance.

Considering how social visibility and spatial factors may hinder or help entrepreneurial actions, thus promoting emancipation and resilience, Jimenez and Escribano (2019) explore how geographical context may influence and condition the possibility of entrepreneurship for people with disabilities when the interpersonal and social plane makes them visible and recognizable. Thus, showcasing entrepreneurship as an emancipatory tool capable of releasing people from social conceptions of inability (disability).

Culture, arts, and creativity. Culture is the collective manifestation of human intellectual achievement, including creativity outcomes (i.e., shared knowledge, language, religion, cuisine, social habits, music, and arts) by a particular group of people. Exploring how individuals (co)create culture, as their desired value, Lange (2011) follows the actions of young "culturepreneurs" as their networking activities form a creative milieu as the social scaffold of a local cultural industry. Similarly, Sardana (2018) presents cultural entrepreneurship as a form of entrepreneurship where culture is a valuable resource to be created, co-created, extracted, and bartered. Thus, Sardana (2018) characterizes cultural entrepreneurship as its own kind of entrepreneurship with its own internal definitions of value creation.

Taking a closer look at how value might be ascribed to culture, Bango et al. (2018) explore the dissemination of culture and heritage (including arts and crafts) as a business model. Assessing the entrepreneurial value of the arts, Marins and Davel (2019) study the music scene within a region to explore how entrepreneurship may also be conceptualized as a local practice among artists. Paying attention to an art enterprise as an example of entrepreneurial experimentation (act of creativity), Luthy and Steyaert (2019) argue there is a need to "theorize the relationship between entrepreneurship and the political beyond the currently dominant neo-liberal and emancipatory narrative by turning to an onto-political conception of entrepreneurship based on the processes of entrepreneurial experimentation" (p. 582). Bringing the conversation from an individualistic lens into a collective effort, Emin and Guibert (2017) built an argument for a better understanding of the complexity and creativity inherent in entrepreneurship by posing it as a collective endeavor.

Social Dimension: Current Work

Looking at entrepreneurship as a social process, extant work informed by this dimension has focused on giving voice to non-privileged entrepreneurial enactments by highlighting entrepreneuring as the actions of regular individuals performed in their everyday lives within their communities. This work has focused on three broad areas: everyday context to entrepreneurial actions (embeddedness), entrepreneurial ecosystems (ecosystems), and the identity of entrepreneurs performing non-privileged entrepreneurial enactments (identity).

Embeddedness. Embeddedness refers to the degree in which (economic) activities are immersed, and shaped by the social context where they take place (Granovetter, 1985). Taking the idea of embeddedness at its core, de Beer (2018) explores if the geopolitical space where entrepreneurship takes place matters to the nature of the entrepreneuring. de Beer's (2018) findings suggest that the location of embeddedness matters. Her work identifies neighborhood-based (neighborhood-embedded) entrepreneurship as a source of local social value.

Expanding on this concept of embeddedness, yet still focusing on the core idea of being immersed in a well-defined space, researchers have looked at the impact of embeddedness into entrepreneurial actions. Murnieks et al. (2020) examine the identity-related social forces that may fuel entrepreneurial passion. In this work, Murnieks et al. (2020) found that gender moderates both; harmonious and obsessive entrepreneurial passion. Looking at geopolitical-occupational-cultural embeddedness, Velvin et al. (2016) explore embeddedness as a value-change-continuum. Their findings, working with a sample of farmers in rural Norway, show that when taken to extremes, the social value of self-reliance can hinder the growth of deeper commercial cooperation. Focusing on how serial-embeddedness (personal history of multiple relocation events) may affect outcomes of future entrepreneurial decisions, Martynovich (2017) suggests that entrepreneurial actions informed by multiple prior embeddedness may be expected to survive longer. This work brings an interesting point suggesting that acquired knowledge will travel with the individual into the next network, thus giving an advantage to the individual. Assessing the impact of religious (Christian) embeddedness in the actions of female entrepreneurs, Quagrainie et al. (2018) found that this type of embeddedness is positive for growth but not for startups. Further, they found this to be true when there is an ethical alignment in the ideology of the entrepreneuring and the religious beliefs of the church.

Shifting views, researchers have studied boundaries as the space of embeddedness rather than the areas inside the boundaries. In an introductory article to a special issue on international opportunities, Mainela et al. (2015) explore the value of being at the nexus of places rather than inside a place. In this argument, Mainela et al. (2015) make of the boundaries a place of embeddedness and connectivity rather than a line to mark the in-between spaces. Looking at variations across different geographies, Smith and Stevens (2010) create a typology of entrepreneuring hence highlighting the relationship between place and entrepreneurship.

Acknowledging that entrepreneurial actions are embedded in ideology, Jarrodi et al. (2019) explore how political views may inform the entrepreneurial activities of individuals. Their work explores a different type of embeddedness. Their work shows how political embeddedness relates to types of entrepreneurship and the goals of the entrepreneur.

Ecosystems. An ecosystem is a collection of living organisms in aggregation with the non-living elements of their local environment, interacting all as a system. An entrepreneurial ecosystem, in contrast, has been traditionally understood as the social and economic environment affecting the embedded entrepreneurship at the local or regional level (e.g., Malecki, 2018; Spigel, 2017; Stam & van de Ven, 2019; Walsh & Winsor, 2019). Work on entrepreneurial ecosystems has suggested that embeddedness in small communities results in types of entrepreneurship that are different from embeddedness in large ones (Roundy, 2019). Furthermore, work in entrepreneurial ecosystems also suggests that not all ecosystems are equally open to women entrepreneurs (e.g., Cukier & Chavoushi, 2020). Informed by these conversations on entrepreneurial ecosystems as socioeconomic environments, researchers have explored how to influence local ecosystem conditions by developing governing policies for a target area (e.g., Audhoe et al., 2018).

Identity. Identity is the physical attributes (e.g., height, sex, color, age), expressions, beliefs (e.g., religious, political), personality, and/or personal qualities that make an individual. A person's identity is defined as the totality of one's self-construal as it relates to self-image (one's mental model of oneself) (Weinreich, 1986). People can be regarded to share an identity (e.g., same age range, same cultural background, same gender) or to have a collective identity (i.e., belonging to a group, having the same religious beliefs). In entrepreneurship research, certain identities are considered to be privileged, thus provided voice; while others are seemed as deviant or not relevant or worthy, thus ignored (Hjorth & Steyaert, 2003). Steyaert and Katz (2004) work aims to provide a voice to these non-privileged entrepreneurial identities.

Using an intersectionality approach on female identity, work has explored the meaning of performing as a female entrepreneur. Some examples of work informed by this view include Ekinsmyth (2011) research exploring female entrepreneurs who operate at the interface between paid work and motherhood. This work carves out an identity for these individuals, calling them mumpreneurs. Taking a closer look at women at home, performing as homemakers (women positioned as mothers, wives, or careers), Meliou and Edwards (2018) explore how these women navigate changing household dynamics, related to the care and reproductive resources, and become entrepreneurial. In this project, Meliou and Edwards (2018) offer evidence of this female entrepreneurial agency within the context of their households. Presenting the role of women at the household as a homemaker, Gherardi (2015) discusses women's entrepreneurial choices as a matter of lifework balance (between career and duty). Recognizing that extant work on STEM and entrepreneurship presents STEM scientists as gender-neutral, Birkner (2020) acknowledges the existence of gender in scientists and the disparate treatment (and absence) of females in STEM. Thus this work aims to make visible this issue and recognize its implications when talking about STEM female entrepreneurs.

Further, work on the intersectionality of female identity has explored understandings of female entrepreneurs in contrast to male counterparts. Observing how female entrepreneurs may need to perform as social males while acknowledging their female identities yet avoiding the realm of female emotion, Martin et al. (2020) study how the female entrepreneurs' social performing puts emphasis on (emotionless) maternal roles. Highlighting gender inequality in Turkish society, Ozkazanc-Pan (2015) explores how secular and Islamic ideologies compete and produce different solutions to ongoing economic, sociocultural, and political issues. This work raises questions around the popular notion of "entrepreneurship as women's empowerment" in a Muslim majority nation. Bringing place of origin (birth) to the conversation, research on identities has also explored issues of immigration. Using the intersectionality approach, Kacar and Essers (2019) explore the relationship between the (local) identity construction processes of migrant women entrepreneurs and the (local) opportunity structures.

Looking at place of origin as an issue of identity, work has explored how different backgrounds offer different entrepreneurial outcomes. For example. Looking at the strength of cultural and national identity, acculturation, and perceived discrimination, Robertson and Grant (2016) explore how immigrants make entrepreneurial decisions in their new home country. Exploring immigration as a community-embedded process, Munkejord (2017) acknowledges the reciprocity between the immigrant entrepreneur and the host community. In particular, Munkejord (2017) "reveals how immigrants, when being supported by the rural community, may be able to successfully create and exploit entrepreneurial opportunities in rural communities, and, through entrepreneurship processes, may even contribute to (re) build the rural areas" (p. 111). Connecting immigrants and entrepreneurship in the informal economy, Afreh et al. (2019) explore the actions of young immigrants. This work focuses on the embeddedness of these entrepreneurs in their new country to explain entrepreneurial actions driven by interests other than economic.

In all, current research influenced by Steyaert and Katz (2004) seminal work focuses on alternative entrepreneurial endeavors emerging from three core areas: geographical dimensions, discursive dimensions, and social dimensions. Current work based on the geographical dimension looks at how entrepreneurship might be embedded in regions and urban spaces, both conceptualized as the intersection of physical place and social dynamic. The extant discursive approach brings into light entrepreneurship as a tool of resistance, resilience, emancipation, and creativity. Thus exploring how entrepreneurial actions may pursue other values besides economic gains and act as a social motor to contest the status quo. Looking into the social dimension, the present work inspired by Steyaert and Katz (2004) looks into the shadows to bring back to light what might be considered the actions by deviant agents. This work on the social dimension looks at how entrepreneurial actions might be embedded in the everyday actions by non-privileged social agents and how identities not considered to be entrepreneurial might navigate their social context to contest their entrepreneurial exclusion.

Future Work

By recognizing entrepreneurship as a social phenomenon embedded in social and spatial dimensions rather than just an economic praxis, the work of Steyaert and Katz (2004) can be said to be watershed publication. This work asked scholars to think of entrepreneurship not as an abstract business endeavor but rather as an everyday sociocultural exercise taking place at geopolitical spaces undertaken by embodied people. By doing so, Steyaert and Katz (2004) suggest that exploring entrepreneurship outside of the economic framework could serve to make visible entrepreneurs and their entrepreneurial practices (and outcomes) that have been previously overlooked.

Contrasting the dominant economic paradigm, Steyaert and Katz (2004) posed entrepreneurship as a socially embedded transformative process that creates and captures value in a broader sense. With this perspective, Steyaert and Katz (2004) aimed to reclaim the space in which entrepreneurship is seen "at work" as well as to challenge the extant understandings of entrepreneurial purpose. Thus, they offered the opportunity to (question) recognize other outcomes of entrepreneurial processes beyond economic gains, and also make visible the entrepreneurial actions of non-privileged individuals.

The ideas advanced by the work of Steyaert and Katz (2004) have served to frame ongoing and future conversations about identity and entrepreneurship, non-economic purposes of entrepreneurship, community-based entrepreneurship, family entrepreneurship, and public sector entrepreneurship among others. There is a wide range of possibilities for the continuation of the development of their framework. A closer look at their work at the intersection of the geographical, discursive, and social dimensions can further help to open the door to a new understanding of entrepreneurship for theory and praxis. These new perspectives may help inform views of entrepreneurial processes as pathways controlling the local flow of resources both inside a community and also in-and-out of it. Within these views, entrepreneurs might be best presented as agents managing the processes providing local access to products and services. As controllers of access, entrepreneurial actions may also be explored as processes (de)regulating local sustainability. This work can be, on its own, a turning point on understandings on social movements and urban equity as well as community resilience.

Considering the intersection of entrepreneurial ecosystems and environmental sustainability, future research could extend understandings of entrepreneurial ecosystems to go beyond socioeconomic spaces to also include the living and non-living organisms in the area as part of the local system where the entrepreneuring takes place. Adding social discourse to extended view of entrepreneurial ecosystems, new research can inform policy and help to develop inclusive strategies to address millennium development goals, including issues of climate change and food security. Thus ensuring that social progress comes on hand with environmental preservation.

New research looking at the intersectionality of the entrepreneurial identity can bring light to unconventional solutions to the inclusiveness that allows for social resilience and resistance as geospatial praxis of emancipation. The framework provides a means to incorporate the intersectionality of issues related to race, nationality, gender, and economic standing in the community. Taking advantage of the discursive tool on itself, new research may explore how entrepreneurship actions may construct new understandings of socially acceptable gender practices. Further, moving away from the economic-driven white, male, technological, heroic model of acceptable entrepreneurial behavior provides for a wealth of possibilities to better understand fully the role that the phenomena of entrepreneurship plays in society. Finally, this extended view brings light to all actors and enactors of entrepreneurship voicing the reasons and outcomes, even if at first considered as deviants to dominant paradigms.

Also, changes in the understandings of entrepreneurship itself will lead to new forms to teach entrepreneurship. This will open a new research space where entrepreneurship may not be presented as a tool for economic extraction but as a means of social transformation. Thus bringing entrepreneurship outside of the business school into other spaces like sociology, anthropology, urban education, environmental science, social work, public policy where its role will be to help the implementation of ideas rather than the economic exploitation of them.

References

Afreh, B., Rodgers, P., Vershinina, N., & Williams, C. C. (2019). Varieties of context and informal entrepreneurship entrepreneurial activities of migrant youths in rural Ghana. *International Journal of Entrepreneurial Behavior & Research, 25*(5), 996–1013.

Al-Dajani, H., Carter, S., Shaw, E., & Marlow, S. (2015). Entrepreneurship among the displaced and dispossessed: Exploring the limits of emancipatory entrepreneuring. *British Journal of Management, 26*(4), 713–730.

Angelidou, M., & Mora, L. (2019). Developing synergies between social entrepreneurship and urban planning evidence from six European cities. *Disp, 55*(4), 28–45.

Angrisano, M., Biancamano, P. F., Bosone, M., Carone, P., Daldanise, G., De Rosa, F., Franciosa, A., Gravagnuolo, A., Iodice, S., Nocca, F., Onesti, A., Panaro, S., Ragozino, S., Sannicandro, V., & Girard, L. F. (2016). Towards operationalizing UNESCO recommendations on "historic urban landscape": A position paper. *Aestimum, 69*, 165–210.

Audhoe, R., Thompson, N., & Verduijn, K. (2018). Expanding entrepreneurial, innovative and sustainable (EIS) ecosystems: A cultural-historical activity theory perspective. In J. Leitao, H. Alves, N. Krueger, & J. Park (Eds.), *Entrepreneurial, innovative and sustainable ecosystems: Best practices and implications for quality of life* (pp. 67–89).

Bango, S. P., Ndiweni, E., Galloway, L., & Verhoeven, H. (2018). Survivalism, collectivism and proud heritage: A study of informal arts and crafts entrepreneurship in rural Zimbabwe. *South African Journal of Business Management, 49*(1).

Berger, P. L., & Luckman, T. (1967). *The social construction of reality: A treatise in the sociology of knowledge*. Doubleday-Anchor Books.

Birkner, S. (2020). To belong or not to belong, that is the question?! Explorative insights on liminal gender states within women's STEMpreneurship. *International Entrepreneurship and Management Journal, 16*(1), 115–136.

Bonacich, E., & Modell, J. (1980). *The economic basis of ethnic solidarity: Small business in the Japanese-American community*. University of California Press.

Calás, M. B., Smircich, L., & Bourne, K. A. (2009). Extending the boundaries: Reframing "entrepreneurship as social change" through feminist perspectives. *Academy of Management Review, 34*(3), 552–569.

Calisto, M. D., & Goncalves, A. (2017). Smart citizens, wise decisions: Sustainability-driven tourism entrepreneurs. In *Handbook of research on entrepreneurial development and innovation within smart cities* (pp. 20–43). IGI Global.

Caplin, L. (1983). *The business of art*. Prentice Hall Trade.

Conklin Frederking, L. (2004). A cross-national study of culture, organization and entrepreneurship in three neighbourhoods. *Entrepreneurship & Regional Development, 16*(3), 197–215.

Courpasson, D., Dany, F., & Marti, I. (2016). Organizational entrepreneurship as active resistance: A struggle against outsourcing. *Entrepreneurship Theory and Practice, 40*(1), 131–160.

Cukier, W., & Chavoushi, Z. H. (2020). Facilitating women entrepreneurship in Canada: The case of WEKH. *Gender in Management, 35*(3), 303–318.

Dashtipour, P., & Rumens, N. (2018). Entrepreneurship, incongruence and affect: Drawing insights from a Swedish anti-racist organisation. *Organization, 25*(2), 223–241.

Daskalaki, M., Hjorth, D., & Mair, J. (2015). Are entrepreneurship, communities, and social transformation related? *Journal of Management Inquiry, 24*(4), 419–423.

de Beer, M. (2018). Local social value creation by neighborhood-based entrepreneurs: Local embeddedness and the role of social networks. *Social Enterprise Journal, 14*(4), 450–469.

Dobers, P. (2003). Image of Stockholm as an IT-city: Emerging urban entrepreneurship. In C. Steyaert & D. Hjorth (Eds.), *New movements in entrepreneurship* (pp. 200–217). Edward Elgar.

Dodd, S. D., Wilson, J., Bhaird, C. M., & Bisignano, A. P. (2018). Habitus emerging: The development of hybrid logics and collaborative business models in the Irish craft beer sector. *International Small Business Journal-Researching Entrepreneurship, 36*(6), 637–661.

Down, S. (2012). Evaluating the impacts of government policy through the long view of life history. *Entrepreneurship and Regional Development, 24*(7–8), 619–639.

Egan-Wyer, C., Muhr, S. L., & Rehn, A. (2018). On startups and doublethink—Resistance and conformity in negotiating the meaning of entrepreneurship. *Entrepreneurship and Regional Development, 30*(1–2), 58–80.

Ekinsmyth, C. (2011). Challenging the boundaries of entrepreneurship: The spatialities and practices of UK "Mumpreneurs." *Geoforum, 42*(1), 104–114.

Emin, S., & Guibert, G. (2017). Complexity and self-organization within collective entrepreneurship: An analysis of a local music scene. *Revue Internationale PME, 30*(2), 87–113.

Garcia-Lorenzo, L., Donnelly, P., Sell-Trujillo, L., & Imas, J. M. (2018). Liminal entrepreneuring: The creative practices of nascent necessity entrepreneurs. *Organization Studies, 39*(2–3), 373–395.

Gherardi, S. (2015). Authoring the female entrepreneur while talking the discourse of work-family life balance. *International Small Business Journal, 33*(6), 649–666.

Goss, D., Jones, R., Betta, M., & Latham, J. (2011). Power as practice: A micro-sociological analysis of the dynamics of emancipatory entrepreneurship. *Organization Studies, 32*(2), 211–229.

Granovetter, M. (1985). Economic action and social structure: The problem of embeddedness. *American Journal of Sociology, 91*(3), 481–510.

Halprin, L. (1970). *The RSVP cycles: Creative processes in the human environment*. George Braziller.

Heilbrunn, S. (2019). Against all odds: Refugees bricoleuring in the void. *International Journal of Entrepreneurial Behavior & Research, 25*(5), 1045–1064.

Hitt, M. A., & Bartkus, B. R. (1997). International entrepreneurship. In J. A. Katz (Ed.), *Advances in the study of entrepreneurship, firm emergence and growth* (Vol. 3, pp. 7–30). JAI Press.

Hjorth, D. (2003). *Rewriting entrepreneurship—For a new perspective on organisational creativity*. Liber/CBS Press/Abstrakt.

Hjorth, D., & Steyaert, C. (2003). Entrepreneurship beyond (a new) economy: Creative swarms and pathological zones. In C. Steyaert & D. Hjorth (Eds.), *New movements in entrepreneurship* (pp. 286–303). Edward Elgar.

Hong, E., Lee, I. H., Sun, L. X., & Harrison, R. (2015). Entrepreneurship across time and space: Empirical evidence from Korea. *Small Business Economics, 44*(3), 705–719.

Houtbeckers, E. (2016). The tactics of ecopreneurs aiming to influence existing practices. *Small Enterprise Research, 23*(1), 22–38.

Huggins, R., Morgan, B., & Williams, N. (2015). Regional entrepreneurship and the evolution of public policy and governance Evidence from three regions. *Journal of Small Business and Enterprise Development, 22*(3): 473–511.

Imas, J. M., Wilson, N., & Weston, A. (2012). Barefoot entrepreneurs. *Organization, 19*(5), 563–585.

Jarrodi, H., Byrne, J., & Bureau, S. (2019). A political ideology lens on social entrepreneurship motivations. *Entrepreneurship and Regional Development, 31*(7–8), 583–604.

Jimenez, A. M., & Escribano, J. J. G. (2019). Entrepreneurship in people with disabilities: Cultural and social aspects. *Suma De Negocios, 10*(22): 27–34.

Johnstone, H., & Lionais, D. (2004). Depleted communities and community business entrepreneurship: Revaluing space through place. *Entrepreneurship & Regional Development, 16*(3), 217–233.

Kacar, S. O., & Essers, C. (2019). The interplay between identity construction and opportunity structures: Narratives of Turkish migrant women entrepreneurs in the Netherlands. *International Small Business Journal-Researching Entrepreneurship, 37*(7), 713–731.

Kang, T. Y. (2017). Bricolage in the urban cultural sector: The case of Bradford city of film. *Entrepreneurship and Regional Development, 29*(3–4), 340–356.

Korsgaard, S., Anderson, A., & Gaddefors, J. (2016). Entrepreneurship as re-sourcing towards a new image of entrepreneurship in a time of financial, economic and socio-spatial crisis. *Journal of Enterprising Communities-People and Places in the Global Economy, 10*(2), 178–202.

Korsgaard, S., & Anderson, A. R. (2011). Enacting entrepreneurship as social value creation. *International Small Business Journal, 29*(2), 135–151.

Lado-Sestayo, R., Neira-Gomez, I., & Chasco-Yrigoyen, C. (2017). Entrepreneurship at regional level: Temporary and neighborhood effects. *Entrepreneurship Research Journal, 7*(4).

Landström, H. (1999). The roots of entrepreneurial research. *New England Journal of Entrepreneurship, 2*(2), 9–20.

Lange, B. (2011). Professionalization in space: Social-spatial strategies of culturepreneurs in Berlin. *Entrepreneurship and Regional Development, 23*(3–4), 259–279.

Lange, B., Kalandides, A., Stober, B., & Mieg, H. A. (2008). Berlin's creative industries: Governing creativity? *Industry and Innovation, 15*(5), 531–548.

Larsson, M., Milestad, R., Hahn, T., & von Oelreich, J. (2016). The resilience of a sustainability entrepreneur in the Swedish food system. *Sustainability, 8*(6), 550.

Laurent, A. (2000). *Entrepreneurial government: Bureaucrats as businesspeople* (pp. 1–36). Washington, DC. http://www.businessofgovernment.org/sites/default/files/LaurentReport.pdf.

Luthy, C., & Steyaert, C. (2019). The onto-politics of entrepreneurial experimentation: Re-reading Hans-Jorg Rheinberger's understanding of "experimental systems." *Entrepreneurship and Regional Development, 31*(7–8), 652–668.

Mainela, T., Puhakka, V., & Servais, P. (2015). Boundary crossing for international opportunities. *Journal of International Entrepreneurship, 13*(3), 173–185.

Malecki, E. J. (2018). Entrepreneurship and entrepreneurial ecosystems. *Geography Compass, 12*(3), 21.

Marins, S. R., & Davel, E. P. B. (2019). Entrepreneurship as practice: Cultural entrepreneurship in the festive practice of Bahia's Pagode. *Teoria E Pratica Em Administracao-Tpa, 9*(2), 14–34.

Martin, L., Jerrard, B., & Wright, L. (2020). Identity work in female-led creative businesses. *Gender Work and Organization, 27*(3), 310–326.

Martynovich, M. (2017). The role of local embeddedness and non-local knowledge in entrepreneurial activity. *Small Business Economics, 49*(4), 741–762.

Mauksch, S., & Rowe, M. (2016). Austerity and social entrepreneurship in the United Kingdom: A community perspective. In J. Liddle (Ed.), *New perspectives on research, policy and practice in public entrepreneurship* (Vol. 6, pp. 173–193). Emerald.

McKeever, E., Jack, S., & Anderson, A. (2015). Embedded entrepreneurship in the creative re-construction of place. *Journal of Business Venturing, 30*(1), 50–65.

Meliou, E., & Edwards, T. (2018). Relational practices and reflexivity: Exploring the responses of women entrepreneurs to changing household dynamics. *International Small Business Journal-Researching Entrepreneurship, 36*(2), 149–168.

Munkejord, M. C. (2017). Becoming spatially embedded: Findings from a study on rural immigrant entrepreneurship in Norway. *Entrepreneurial Business and Economics Review, 5*(1), 111–130.

Murnieks, C. Y., Cardon, M. S., & Haynie, J. M. (2020). Fueling the fire: Examining identity centrality, affective interpersonal commitment and gender as drivers of entrepreneurial passion. *Journal of Business Venturing, 35*(1).

Osorio, A. E. (2018). The urban quality of life and entrepreneurship: Past, present, and future. In G. Javadian, V. K. Gupta, D. D. Dutt, G. C. Guo, A. E. Osorio, & B. Ozkazanc-Pan (Eds.), *Foundational research in entrepreneurship studies*. Palgrave Macmillan.

Ozkazanc-Pan, B. (2015). Secular and Islamic feminist entrepreneurship in Turkey. *International Journal of Gender and Entrepreneurship, 7*(1), 45–65.

Parkinson, C., Howorth, C., & Southern, A. (2017). The crafting of an (un)enterprising community: Context and the social practice of talk. *International Small Business Journal-Researching Entrepreneurship, 35*(4), 385–404.

Perlmutter, F. D., & Cnaan, R. A. (1995). Entrepreneurship in the public sector: The horns of a dilemma. *Public Administration Review, 55*(1), 29–36.

Quagrainie, F. A., Opoku Mensah, A., & Adom, A. Y. (2018). Christian entrepreneurial activities and micro women entrepreneurship development:

Church embeddedness in action. *Journal of Enterprising Communities-People and Places in the Global Economy, 12*(5), 657–676.
Rehn, A., & Taalas, S. (2004). 'Znakomstva I Svyazi' (Acquaintances and connections)—Blat, the Soviet Union, and mundane entrepreneurship. *Entrepreneurship & Regional Development, 16*(3), 235–250.
Robertson, D. W., & Grant, P. R. (2016). Immigrant entrepreneurship from a social psychological perspective. *Journal of Applied Social Psychology, 46*(7), 394–409.
Roundy, P. T. (2019). "It takes a village" to support entrepreneurship: Intersecting economic and community dynamics in small town entrepreneurial ecosystems. *International Entrepreneurship and Management Journal, 15*(4), 1443–1475.
Sabella, A. R., & El-Far, M. T. (2019). Entrepreneuring as an everyday form of resistance An exploration of the experiences of Palestinian women street vendors in the occupied Old City of Jerusalem. *International Journal of Entrepreneurial Behavior & Research, 25*(6), 1212–1235.
Sarason, S. B. (1972). *The creation of settings and the future societies*. Jossey-Bass.
Sardana, D. (2018). What facilitates cultural entrepreneurship?—A study of Indian cultural entrepreneurs. *Journal of Creative Behavior, 52*(1), 35–51.
Smith, B. R., & Stevens, C. E. (2010). Different types of social entrepreneurship: The role of geography and embeddedness on the measurement and scaling of social value. *Entrepreneurship and Regional Development, 22*(6), 575–598.
Smith, H. L., Glasson, J., & Chadwick, A. (2005). The geography of talent: Entrepreneurship and local economic development in Oxfordshire. *Entrepreneurship and Regional Development, 17*(6), 449–478.
Smith, N. (1990). *Uneven development: Nature, capital and the production of space*. Blackwell.
Spigel, B. (2017). The relational organization of entrepreneurial ecosystems. *Entrepreneurship Theory and Practice, 41*(1), 49–72.
Stabrowski, F. (2017). 'People as businesses': Airbnb and urban micro-entrepreneurialism in New York City. *Cambridge Journal of Regions Economy and Society, 10*(2), 327–347.
Stam, E., & van de Ven, A. (2019). Entrepreneurial ecosystem elements. *Small Business Economics*.
Steyaert, C., & Katz, J. (2004). Reclaiming the space of entrepreneurship in society: Geographical, discursive and social dimensions. *Entrepreneurship & Regional Development, 16*(3), 179–196.
Tedmanson, D., Essers, C., Dey, P., & Verduyn, K. (2015). An uncommon wealth ... Transforming the commons with purpose, for people and not for profit! *Journal of Management Inquiry, 24*(4), 439–444.

Velvin, J., Bjornstad, K., & Krogh, E. (2016). Social value change, embeddedness and social entrepreneurship. *Journal of Enterprising Communities-People and Places of Global Economy, 10*(3), 262–280.

Vlasov, M., Bonnedahl, K. J., & Vincze, Z. (2018). Entrepreneurship for resilience: Embeddedness in place and in trans-local grassroots networks. *Journal of Enterprising Communities-People and Places in the Global Economy, 12*(3), 374–394.

Waldinger, R. D., & Aldrich, H. (1990). *Ethnic entrepreneurs: Immigrant business in industrial societies*. Sage.

Walsh, J., & Winsor, B. (2019). Socio-cultural barriers to developing a regional entrepreneurial ecosystem. *Journal of Enterprising Communities-People and Places in the Global Economy, 13*(3), 263–282.

Weinreich, P. (1986). The operationalisation of identity theory in racial and ethnic relations. In J. Rex, & D. Mason (Eds.), *Theories of race and ethnic relations: Comparative ethnic and race relations* (p. 299). Cambridge University Press.

Williams, N., & Williams, C. C. (2012). Evaluating the socio-spatial contingency of entrepreneurial motivations: A case study of English deprived urban neighbourhoods. *Entrepreneurship and Regional Development, 24*(7–8), 661–684.

CHAPTER 9

Causation and Effectuation

Ba Anh Khoa Dao

Introduction

In her 2001 article "Causation and effectuation: toward a theoretical shift from economic inevitability to entrepreneurial contingency," Sarasvathy brings forward an idea that would change the landscape of the entrepreneurship domain. That seminal work suggests that, contrary to the logic predominant in the field, entrepreneurs trying to start a new venture within an uncertain context might not be able to plan all their steps as well as predict its future. Sarasvathy not only introduces the concept of effectuation but she also puts forth the suggestion of naming causation as the dominant logic in entrepreneurship. She opposes the two ideas with a simple argument. She indicates that, in a causation logic, entrepreneurs know what their end goal is and gather the necessary means to reach those means. On the other hand, in an effectual logic, entrepreneurs do not have a clear and distinct end goal in mind but have a set of means at hand. As such, she argues that, in the dominant paradigm, entrepreneurs "proceed inward to specifics from a larger,

B. A. K. Dao (✉)
Université du Québec à Montréal, Montreal, QC, Canada
e-mail: dao.ba_anh_khoa@uqam.ca

A. E. Osorio et al. (eds.), *Modern Classics in Entrepreneurship Studies*,
https://doi.org/10.1007/978-3-030-61029-6_9

general universe—that is, to an optimal target segment from a predetermined market" (Sarasvathy, 2001, p. 246) while, in an effectuation paradigm, entrepreneurs would "begin by examining the particular set of means or causes available [with] extremely limited monetary, [they] should think creatively to bring the idea to market with as close to zero resources as possible" (Sarasvathy, 2001, p. 246). In this instance, she clearly demonstrates that an entrepreneur with a definite idea in mind would try to reach that objective by acquiring the resources that are (presumably) required in order to reach that objective. This is contrasted to the effectuation logic in which entrepreneurs do not have a clear idea but rather rely on the resources they possess on hand. This affords them the flexibility to adjust toward an idea that would be the best fit for them. An effectual logic allows entrepreneur to face uncertainty and have multiple options of end goals.

The article has garnered significant interest since 2001, with more than 4500 citations up to September 2019. From 2001 to 2006, in the effectuation infancy, it was not cited more than a hundred time per year. However, from 2007 onward, its growth was phenomenal, being cited more than 500 times every year from 2015 (with 360 citations halfway through 2019). It illustrates the massive interest toward effectuation and its unique place within the entrepreneurship literature. It also shows that it has successfully outgrown its infancy phase and reached a level of maturity that would require a diversification of research and methods. Figure 9.1 depicts the evolution of the number of citations throughout the years.

The relevance of this paper resides in how it has effectively changed the field of entrepreneurship. Sarasvathy questioned the dominant logic in the field and introduced effectuation as an alternative to causation. In doing so, she brought forth a discussion about how entrepreneurs can act in the face of uncertainty. She asserts that choosing a goal, planning a venture, and selecting assets might not always be possible for the nascent entrepreneur when knowledge of the environment and the context are not clearly defined from the beginning.

The present chapter is organized as follows: first, we will present a summary of the article. Second, we will discuss how the concept of effectuation (Sarasvathy, 2001) evolved in its early days. We will look at the two topics of research in effectuation that was most interesting and prompted the most enquiries: uncertainty and expertise. Third, we will explore how the concept of effectuation has evolved 18 years after

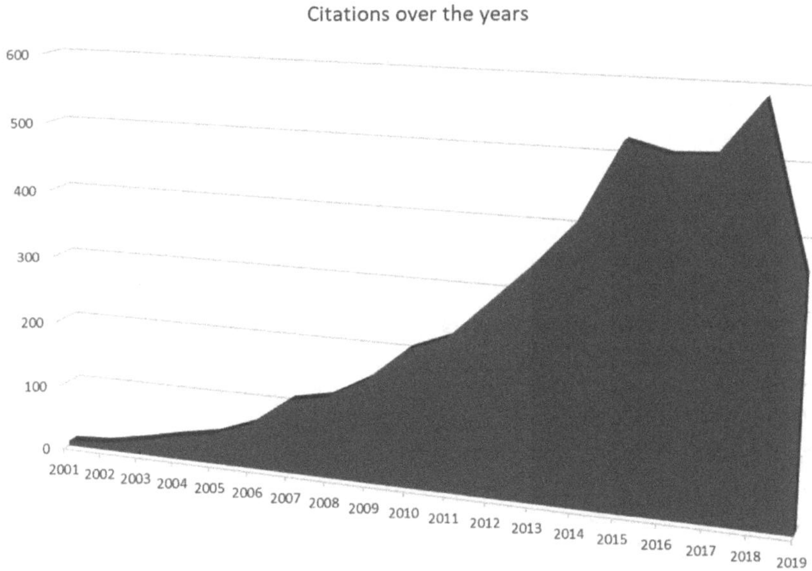

Fig. 9.1 Citations over the years

its introduction. An overview of the research field provides three topics related to effectuation that show potential: decision-making, uncertainty, and internationalization. Each of these topics extends the concept of effectuation. Finally, we will conclude with a synthesis of how the Sarasvathy article has helped the field of entrepreneurial and what effectively makes it a foundational article.

The Chef in the Kitchen

Sarasvathy (2001) describes the difference between causation and effectuation with the example of a chef in the kitchen:

> *Imagine a chef assigned the task of cooking dinner. There are two ways the task can be organized. In the first, the host or client picks out a menu in advance. All the chef needs to do is list the ingredients needed, shop for them, and then actually cook the meal. This is a process of causation. It begins with a given menu and focuses on selecting between effective ways to prepare the meal.*

> *In the second case, the host asks the chef to look through the cupboards in the kitchen for possible ingredients and utensils and then cook a meal. Here, the chef has to imagine possible menus based on the given ingredients and utensils, select the menu, and then prepare the meal. This is a process of effectuation. It begins with given ingredients and utensils and focuses on preparing one of many possible desirable meals with them.* (p. 245)

As shown, the distinction is clear between the two processes. In the first case, the entrepreneur pursues a venture chosen from the onset and gathers the assets that (he thinks) he needs to reach the objectives. In the second case, the entrepreneur looks at his assets first and cooks something up based on the current context.

She bases some of her arguments on the classic work from Kolter (1991). She explains how the segmentation, targeting, and positioning process for bringing a product or service to market follows a causation logic. Alternatively, with an effectual logic, the entrepreneur, with limited means, would try to find a way to enter ***a*** market, not necessarily ***the*** market. As such, he would take any opportunity presented instead of planning ahead and researching the various markets to find the right one. The entrepreneur, in this instance, is "continually listening to the customer and building an ever-increasing network of customers and strategic partners, the entrepreneur can then identify a workable segment profile" (Sarasvathy, 2001, p. 247). The end goal would thus evolve as the entrepreneur co-creates the venture with his stakeholders. Therefore, a causation logic is based on prediction and planning while an effectuation logic is based on control and creation. So, in the event of a measurable or predictable future (in the mind of the entrepreneur), a causation logic could be preferable. On the other end, a fairly unpredictable future could be better served by an effectuation logic.

Sarasvathy (2001) proposes four principles of effectuation. In a book published in 2009, Sarasvathy refines those principles and adds a fifth principle. Those principles dictate the behaviors that would be inherent to an effectual entrepreneur. The first principle, **affordable loss**, indicates that the entrepreneur would not try to maximize the potential returns but rather minimize losses. The entrepreneur, in this instance, would try to protect his assets and set a limit to what he is ready to lose if the venture fails. The second principle, strategic alliances, preaches precommitments from stakeholders in order to generate traction for the venture and reduce the uncertainty. These partners and commitments provide the entrepreneur with resources that would help along the way. The effectual entrepreneur would try to "rapidly engage in conversations with a variety of people they already know or come into contact with, some of whom end up making actual commitments to the new venture [and to] put 'skin in the game' because they see opportunity in cocreating the venture with the entrepreneur" (Sarasvathy et al., 2014, p. 74). This principle is subsequently called **Crazy Quilt** because of the effectual entrepreneur's propensity to find partners whenever possible and it might look like a mish mash that could not make sense to outside onlookers. The third principle, exploitation of contingencies, implies that an uncertain context can bring unpredictable results and consequences. An effectual entrepreneur would leverage those contingencies to create opportunities to build the venture. This principle is also called **Lemonade** because the entrepreneur would profit from embracing surprises and be flexible enough to adjust the direction of the venture. The fourth principle, controlling an unpredictable future, dictates that since an unpredictable future cannot be predicted, it is better for the entrepreneur to control it. Later named **Bird-in-Hand**, this principle states that entrepreneurs possesses three types of assets: identity, knowledge, and networks. As such, they can ask themselves the following questions: "Who I am?," "What I know?," and "Whom I know?" The combination of these questions ultimately leads to the important question of "What can I do?" instead of the question "What should I do" that would follow a causation logic. The final principle, added in 2009, Pilot-in-the-Plane is a compound of the previous principles. It puts the emphasis on the entrepreneur in shaping the venture. In an effectual logic, entrepreneurs play an active part in transforming and reshaping their environment, particularly if it is an uncertain one.

Early Influence of Effectuation

Expertise and Effectuation

The early focus of effectuation researchers has been on linking expertise to entrepreneurship. Read and Sarasvathy (2005) thoroughly explain the concept of expertise and its influence on entrepreneurship. They view expertise as a number of complex factors "revolving around how players store information, perceive problems, and generate solutions" (p. 46) providing the experts with extensive practice and experience. They define the four theoretical approaches of expertise: individual differences, knowledge structures, experience, and deliberate practice. In summary, they found that individual differences would not make a major difference in building expertise and that "superior knowledge storage and retrieval abilities of experts with quicker and more accurate problem solving in a domain" (Read & Sarasvathy, 2005, p. 47). Furthermore, they distinguish between experience and deliberate practice by expressing that experience might not enhance performance while deliberate practice, an articulation of experience, might. Deliberate practice might require five different requirements in order to build up expertise. Individuals would require objectives to **motivate** themselves as well as being able to **understand** the patterns of complex tasks. Additionally, they require proper **feedback** in order to adjust their methods and that they need to **repeat** those performances. Finally, a **fit** between the tasks and the characteristics of individuals would be required to acquire expertise. They argue that this acquired expertise depends on the context. As such, entrepreneurship expertise would have its own set of complex tasks:

> *The entrepreneurial process is conceived as a collection of decision tasks such as selecting an idea or opportunity to begin with, creating a legal entity, garnering resources, bringing stakeholders on board, managing growth and exit strategies, and so on. Becoming an expert entrepreneur involves mastering these staged elements of the entrepreneurial process, particularly the recurring decisions and actions that constitute those elements. [...] Studying entrepreneurship as a form of expertise encourages us to match the general elements of expertise with heuristics specific to the new venture domain.* (p. 48)

It is important to note that entrepreneurial expertise puts the emphasis on the entrepreneur's success and separates it from the firm's success. They argue that the level of commitment required of entrepreneurs provide them with the settings required to gain expertise. From there, they come to four observations taken from the expertise literature that would be pertinent to effectuation and the entrepreneurship literature. First, effectual (and expert) entrepreneurs would filter external sources of information based on their own experience. In doing so, they are less likely to use tools such as market studies to try to predict an uncertain future. Second, effectual entrepreneurs based their actions on past experience. As such, their stored patterns would allow them to know what they **can** do when confronted with a particular situation. Third, experts possess a vast pool of knowledge than novice as well as a better understanding of how to integrate and synthesize them. This, in turn, allows them to acquire flexibility in how they set their venture goals. Finally, experts use their vast knowledge and experience, along with their propensity for flexibility, to choose paths that contain multiple outcomes. This is represented by effectual entrepreneurs selecting strategies with a multitude of possible results as well as being able to turn surprising, and even negative, outcomes toward a path to success. Going back to the argument that expertise is dependent on context, they propose that an effectual entrepreneur with a highly entrepreneurial expertise could be locked into the particular context of start-ups within an uncertain environment.

Wiltbank et al. (2006) further the idea of entrepreneurial expertise by comparing expert entrepreneurs with novice. They suggest experts and novices possess "a different logical frame in their decision-making and a different set of heuristics" (p. 291). Furthermore, novices are overloaded by information when confronted with complex tasks. Because of their lack of knowledge and previous experience, they might not possess the required capacity to make proper decisions based on very little information. Additionally, novices would look at a situation and perceive the immediate tasks at hand. On the other hand, experts would have a holistic view of the situation and possess the cognitive ability to perceive the flow of things. They also are not as easily affected by the information they receive from a particular context. In this instance, their judgment would be led by their previous experience and knowledge. Without such, novices have to rely solely on information from the environment. From their study, they come to a few findings. First, they find that experts put more emphasis on how much they can afford to lose rather than how much they stand to gain. Second, they observe that novices are more inclined to follow textbooks because of their limited comparative cognitive abilities while experts frame problems differently based on their prior experience. Third, they notice that decision-making is different for experts and novices. It is cognitive-based for experts and logic-based for novices. Based on the previous findings, this difference is related to pattern recognition. Since novices do not possess a large bank of pattern points, their judgment could not be cognitive-based. Finally, they found that entrepreneurial expertise is achieved through the repetitions of some critical tasks such as "pitching their venture idea to potential stakeholders and negotiating details of means and ends shaping the new venture, business plan writing, evaluating commercialization opportunities, and the continual seeking, parsing, accepting and rejecting of feedback and advice from a variety of sources" (p. 302)

Dew et al. (2009) also discuss the differences between experts and novices. They found that, on top of possessing "a larger mental database of actual experiences to draw from, they also have better access to it than novices do" (p. 291). The previous discussion on heuristics is related to this point. Since it is harder for novices to access their experience and knowledge, they would have difficulties in using them to help make decisions when faced with problem situations. Read, Song, et al. (2009) also discuss those differences and show that, because novices rely on textbooks and market studies, they would have a tendency to follow a single path while experts have more examples from prior experience and would seek multiple paths to making a situation work. Additionally, not only, do they possess more knowledge from their experience but the way it is organized based on outcomes help them have a better understanding of what strategies to use and when to use them. They show some of the main differences in the process of decision-making:

> *Experts are more likely to frame problems comprehensively, using a top-down framework or schema, within which they contextualize specific decisions and link them to other decisions. In contrast, novices tend not to frame problems within a conceptual scheme but rather approach them from the bottom-up and according to surface characteristics rather than their underlying structures. Experts' ability to group problems into fundamental categories and relate them to other decisions results in knowledge architectures that link multiple occasions of connected decisions in the task domain over time, with feedback and interpretation.* (p. 7)

The focus on expertise has helped the effectuation literature by highlighting how and why entrepreneurs act in the face of uncertainty.

Uncertainty and Effectuation

The concept of uncertainty is directly linked to effectuation. Sarasvathy, S. D. (2001) differentiates how uncertainty is perceived in within a causation logic and an effectual logic. Read, Dew, et al. (2009) build on that and develop how effectual entrepreneurs react in an uncertain context.

They use the work of Knight (2012) to illustrate that unknowable uncertainties cannot be tackled with a causation logic. Because causation preaches modelization and prediction, it would not be effective in an uncertain situation while an effectual logic would be better suited. This applies particularly to new ventures because they face "substantial uncertainty surrounding technology, organizational design, target customers, customer preferences, marketing channels, competitive strategies, and employee recruitment" (Wiltbank et al., 2009, p. 120).

McKelvie et al. (2011) argue that entrepreneurial uncertainty is subjective and its interpretation by entrepreneurs would be critical to the entrepreneurial venture. As such:

> *Entrepreneurs make different decisions with regard to exploitation depending on the type of uncertainty that they experience. In addition, depending on how uncertainty it is manifested in the environment (e.g., through technology or customer demand) and on the expertise of the entrepreneur, [...] decision-makers [...] made different and sometimes counter-intuitive decisions with regard to their willingness to engage in entrepreneurial action.* (p. 274)

They use the work of Milliken (1987) and distinguish between three different types of uncertainty. First, **state** uncertainty is related to the environment of the firm and the difficulty to assess how it can change. Second, **effect** uncertainty is related to how the changes in the environment can affect the firm. Finally, **response** uncertainty is related to how the firm or the entrepreneur reacts to the changes in the environment and what are the consequences that response could have. In linking uncertainty and expertise, they posit that "domain expertise contributes to the ability to construct complex cognitive representations of uncertain and dynamic decision tasks, which in turn begets improved decision performance" (p. 279). They find that the different types of uncertainty are interpreted differently and also evaluated differently by entrepreneurs. This brings forth two implications to the entrepreneurship literature. First, the assessment of uncertainty would be cognitive-based and its evaluation could be dependent on the entrepreneur's knowledge and prior experience. As such, expert entrepreneurs and novice entrepreneurs would perceive uncertainty differently. Second, expert entrepreneurs would concentrate on what they have control over. In this instance, their emphasis would be on response uncertainty since they have no control over state and effect uncertainty, "they accept that a more fruitful approach is to attempt to create a future instead [and that] expertise leads decision-makers to focus less on prediction" (p. 288).

The work on uncertainty has highlighted its importance in the effectuation literature. The most important element would be how effectual entrepreneurs react in the face of uncertainty. By emphasizing the fact that different types of uncertainty can be interpreted differently by entrepreneurs, they show the difficulties of plans and predictions within an uncertain context.

Contemporary Research on Effectuation

Research on effectuation not only has not slowed down but instead has picked up steam more than 15 years after its introduction. Scholars working on effectuation have been more detailed and have started to diversify the type and methods of research. Furthermore, the advancement of the effectuation literature has helped the understanding of other streams of literature. For that reason, Sarasvathy (2001) has been cited more than 500 times each year from 2015 with a peak of 587 in 2018.

The topics that are of particular interest and that are linked to effectuation are decision-making, uncertainty, and internationalization.

Effectual Decision-Making

A focus of the research in entrepreneurial decision-making has been how it can be achieved in uncertainty. Shepherd et al. (2015) highlight the interest in "how, when, where, and by whom opportunities to bring future goods and services into existence are discovered, evaluated, and exploited under uncertainty." Figure 9.2 taken from Shepherd et al. (2015) shows the status of research in entrepreneurial decision-making.

As can be seen, there is a parallel with topics of interest in effectuation research, most particularly in regard to heuristics and biases. They also suggest how an opportunity is perceived and exploited on the basis of the entrepreneur's knowledge and resources. As such, with an evolution of the venture and changes of those knowledge and resources, the way the opportunity and the decision-making related to it would also change. This would be similar to the leveraging of contingencies in effectuation. In their assessment of an individual's decision to become an entrepreneur, they argue that it is related to their attitude toward loss as it is an entirely

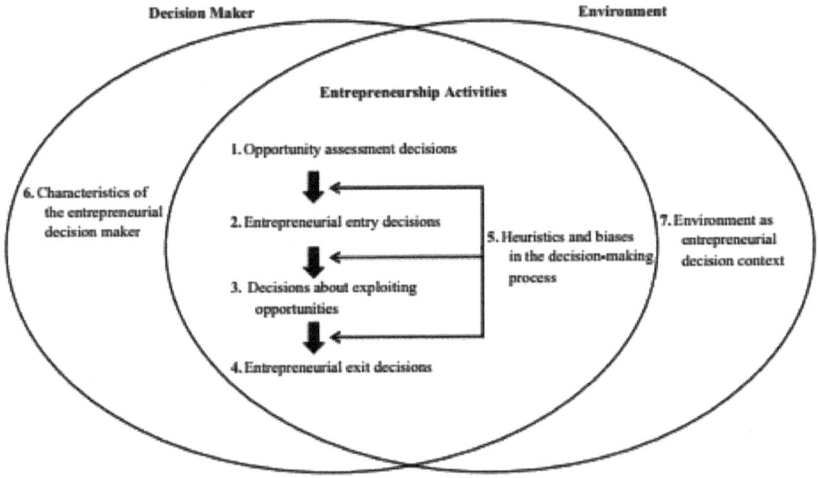

Fig. 9.2 Map of entrepreneurial decision-making research taken from Shepherd et al. (2015)

uncertain proposition. This would be in relation to the effectuation principle of affordable loss. They also suggest that the decision to create a new venture is dependent on the entrepreneur's prior experience and connections which are related to the principles of Bird-in-Hand and Crazy Quilt. In evaluation how entrepreneurial decisions are taken, they determine that entrepreneurs rely on heuristics and biases. Entrepreneurs would not look for the best solution but rather the first one that would seem adequate to them. Since they operate in an uncertain environment with little information available, they are better off making quick decisions than trying to gather all the data and facts in order to predict the future and plan for the best possible results. They also state that experienced entrepreneurs rely on their prior experience in order to filter the market's signals and information. As such, they do not rely as much on market studies and trying to predict the future based on these data.

In a study of decision-making in technology ventures, Reymen et al. (2017) state that decision-making logics shift over time depending on the context of the firm. They argue that new ventures, particularly in technology, are faced with technological and market uncertainty. This makes their venture exceptionally unpredictable. As such, "the viability of a venture's business model is thus hard to predict in advance. New ventures will find it difficult to define the most appropriate model with their first attempt" (p. 596). They also add that ventures that were able to adapt their business model had better chances of success. They found that decision-making logics would follow the uncertainty surrounding the firm. An effectual logic would be predominant at the start of the venture with a high level of uncertainty. As the venture grows and more is known of their context, uncertainty would diminish over time and the decision-making logic would shift toward causation.

Zhang and Cueto (2017) study the effect of bias in entrepreneurship, most notably how it affects decision-making. They posit that "biases permeate decisions in entrepreneurship, and entrepreneurs display higher levels of bias [...]. This can be due to various factors including [...] high uncertainty, information overload and velocity, a lack of historical information and organizational routines, and time pressure" (p. 420). Biased entrepreneurs (and arguably effectual ones) are better suited to make decisions under ambiguous, uncertain, and complex situations.

While discussing uncertainty and entrepreneurial action, Townsend et al. (2018) discuss how entrepreneurs, without predicting the future, are "compelled to make a series of 'stepping stone' decisions along the twisting river bends of irreducible uncertainty" (p. 2). As such, entrepreneurs, when confronted with uncertainty and a lack of information, have to make quick decisions based on their own heuristics in order to evolve their venture. To achieve this process of incremental decisions and actions, the simplification of the decision environment would play a role. This could be linked to the expert entrepreneur who uses heuristics and filters the information from the environment to make decisions. This removes some ambiguity from the decision-making process and allows the entrepreneur to avoid hesitations while making decisions.

Decision-making is a relevant research domain in entrepreneurship as it relates to how entrepreneurs pursue their venture and how they grow it. It is a topic in particular for effectuation scholars because the effectual decision-making logic plays a major role in new ventures.

Uncertainty

As discussed previously in this chapter, uncertainty plays a critical role in the effectuation literature. Just as the work that relates to uncertainty in the early day of effectuation helped its development, the later work further builds on it.

In an attempt to better understand the dynamic process of entrepreneurial networking under uncertainty, Engel et al. (2017) suggest that uncertainty might serve as both a constraint and a facilitator of different forms of networking. They argue that "networking processes are embedded in venturing processes, they are bound to involve unpredictability, goal ambiguity, and an interactive environment that keeps changing with every action" (p. 36). This could reflect how difficult it is for entrepreneurs to predict who can help them and express how important the principle of Crazy Quilt is within effectuation. They argue that since entrepreneurs might not have a clear idea of the venture at the start, networking might be the first step for the entrepreneur to reduce uncertainty and grow the venture. Figure 9.3 illustrates the interplay between networking and uncertainty as presented by Engel et al. (2017).

They define an effectual networking as trying to combine social and business relations. What this entails is that networking should not be done with a specific goal in mind. However, it also means that effectual entrepreneurs should be "out there" to socialize and create ties as much as they can. Since the goal of effectual networker is to build relationships regardless of the utilities of those links, entrepreneur would profit from a reduction of uncertainty just by putting themselves in the right position to connect with others. In doing so, they allow themselves to be exposed to "diverse social resources [that] provides a 'requisite variety' for idea generation, creativity, and growth" (p. 43). The authors argue that intelligent altruism might provide a means to reduce uncertainty while networking. They define this concept as:

> *[A] behavior that is neither extremely selfless nor completely opportunistic but recognizes that individuals may have evolved to sense when to emphasize which. Interestingly, under uncertainty, altruism and opportunism are often intertwined, as entrepreneurs understand that helping others may also help themselves.* (p. 44)

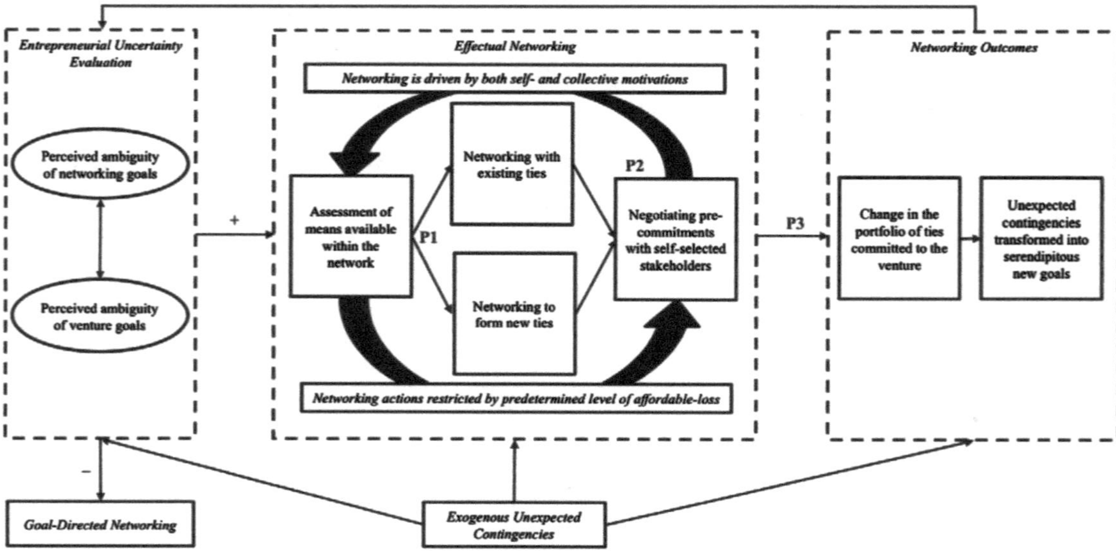

Fig. 9.3 A dynamic process model of entrepreneurial networking under uncertainty taken from Engel et al. (2017)

It entails that helping others might help themselves in the long run since entrepreneurs don't know yet which ties can be useful or not. They also state that creating random relationships could serve to generate contingencies for future goals. As such, entrepreneurs have to be open to suggestions and feedbacks from their contacts. This serves to reduce uncertainty as new goals emerge.

In a paper about the uncertainty surrounding the creation of new entrepreneurial ecosystem, Dattée et al. (2018) show that in a setting of double uncertainty (of both venture and ecosystem), successful ecosystem creators were not "trying to tackle this uncertainty head on by betting on one specific application, they distributed the explorative generation of alternatives" (p. 490). Coherent with the effectuation literature, those firms discovered the ecosystem instead of trying to predict its outcomes. It allowed to learn what mattered to their environment. With so much uncertainty, it is not always possible to not only plan ahead but also decide which options to start with. In this instance, it could not even be possible to design multiple hypothesis to test. They might have to test one hypothesis at a time and adjust based on the contingencies, or pivot in the entrepreneurship literature.

Townsend et al. (2018) discuss uncertainty and try to define boundary conditions with other concepts related to unknowingness. They argue that uncertainty is not a negative concept as such because entrepreneurship would not exist without it. Entrepreneurs are able to be successful with their ability to bear and navigate through uncertainty. Successful entrepreneurs would therefore extract value from opportunities borne out of uncertainty.

In the same stream of literature, Welter and Kim (2018) discuss the opposition between uncertainty and risk. Most particularly, they argue that entrepreneurs within an uncertain context are better off with a control-based logic while those within a risky context would be better off with a prediction-based logic. This is differentiated by how much information is available to the entrepreneurs. It is possible to plan and predict in a risky environment because data is accessible and comparables can be used. However, they find that entrepreneurs only profit from causation when their predictions are effective at guessing the future at least 75% of the time. They thus argue that not only for uncertain contexts but also most risky ones, an effectual logic might be more successful.

They conclude that entrepreneur's confidence level might dictate which logic they would follow. The repercussion of this is an overconfident entrepreneur who might choose to try to predict the future while not possessing all the required information. They therefore recommend that an effectual logic might be the safer bet.

Internationalization

An emergent topic of research related to effectuation has been the internationalization of firms. Most particularly, new ventures that aim to either internationalize immediately or quickly might be better served to follow an effectual logic.

Fletcher et al. (2011) discuss this topic of internalization through the lenses of effectuation. They differentiate the classic view of internalization with other models. In this classic view, firms would choose one market to enter, usually based on closeness to their current market known as psychic distance, and master that new market before moving on. The authors suggest that other models might differ greatly, particularly the model of born global. The authors argue that rapid internationalization require a strong personal network. However, the level of uncertainty would be quite high since they are entering markets without much prior information. This is why, they suggest, effectuation might be the proper logic for those firms wishing to be born global. As such, the born global entrepreneur would not plan their venture but rather exploit opportunities from stakeholders in their network. With the affordable loss principle, the entrepreneur uses "resource lean entry modes [and] can enter many markets in a short time with a low risk" (p. 638). With this perspective, the effectual entrepreneur might be the best suited to exploit international opportunities quickly.

Harms and Schiele (2012) also discuss internationalization within an effectuation logic but go further in highlighting its characteristics. They present the psychic distance as "an information gap that [entrepreneurs] can try to close with formal planning [rather] than as a fundamental uncertainty" (p. 111). They suggest that this might be the reason why the traditional view of internationalization is to conquer markets that have low psychic distance first since they can use their prior knowledge of their current market in order to plan their next internationalization steps. They also argue that it could be the reason why causation-based logics might dictate exporting as the internalization mode. On the other hand, effectuation-based logics would provide entrepreneurs with different entry modes since opportunities would open to them based on the feedbacks from their network.

Sarasvathy, S. et al. (2014) review the work on internationalization entrepreneurship and discuss how it could be supported by Effectuation. They argue that three characteristics of cross-border business might require a perspective such as effectuation. First, **Cross-border uncertainty** indicates that, no matter the psychic distance, some uncertainty remains. Second, new ventures would possess **limited resources** to dedicate to internalization. Finally, **networks dynamics** make it difficult for entrepreneurs to seek out contacts once they've decided on a market. The authors explain how an effectuation logic might be pertinent within the international entrepreneurship literature:

> *Technology, competition, and opportunity may be modeled not only as antecedents, but also as artifacts of the entrepreneurial (or more precisely in this model, the entrepreneurial internationalization) process. Not only does it matter who the entrepreneurs are (bird-in-hand), but also the environment they are in gets transformed due their acting on it (pilot-in-the-plane). This implies that as entrepreneurs internationalize, not only their perceptions of technology, competition, and opportunity may change, but also the actual technologies, competitive landscapes, and opportunities themselves may change and be reshaped through the actions, reactions, and interactions of entrepreneurs and their stakeholders.* (p. 77)

The principle of affordable loss might explain why some firms are able to internationalize quickly as opposed to others. It could be the difference between entrepreneurs setting expectations of what they can afford to lose in order to move quickly into a new market versus others who have to take their time to gather necessary resources. As a matter of fact, all the principles of effectuation would play a role into the facilitation of international entrepreneurship. The interplay of Crazy Quilt and Lemonade would give entrepreneurs the incentive to seek out markets based on feedbacks from stakeholders. In the same manner, Pilot-in-the-Plane, Bird-in-hand, and affordable loss provide entrepreneurs with a context in which they can afford to quickly move into the previously found new market without delays associated with finding more information or resources. However, they also argue that, once the first steps of market penetration have been achieved, it might be better for entrepreneurs to switch toward a causal logic. After gaining knowledge and resources within the new market, they might be able to use a predictive-based perspective to plan for the next steps of growing in the market.

The Impact of Effectuation on the Entrepreneurship Domain

It has been 18 years since the Sarasvathy (2001) paper brought up the concept of effectuation. Since then, it has outgrown its infancy period and reached a theoretical maturity. Within that time frame, it has effectively changed the field of entrepreneurship. Its major impact has been to offer a different paradigm. By suggesting that entrepreneurs do not plan out their venture and cannot predict an unpredictable future in an uncertain context, Sarasvathy provided scholars the opportunity to look at the creation of a new venture from a different lens. The work on effectuation since then has been spreading quickly and broach a wide variety of topics. And although, it has received its fair share of critics about whether or not it can be considered a theory (Arend et al., 2015, 2016), there is no denying that entrepreneurship scholars embrace it. Much more work is still to be done within the effectuation literature and the potential for impactful research is great. However, after reaching a certain level of maturity, it might be time to have a convergence and a definite definition of what it is and how it is enacted. As Grégoire and Cherchem (2019) has shown, effectuation is perceived differently by different scholars creating a confusion on what it is. Some describe it as a theory, an approach, a logic, or a process. The authors suggest using mode of action as its denomination. Whether that would be an accepted term or not, there needs to be one field-approved term in order to advance the concept further. Furthermore, they argue that “the methodological strategies leveraged to capture effectuation in different studies do not necessarily align with the particular conceptions of effectuation these studies advance” (pp. 13–14). It be might because scholars do not possess a deep understanding of the concept of effectuation. Therefore, there should be a concerted effort to improve the methodology required to study it properly. Once the field can cross those hurdles, research would be able to reach a whole new level, potentially making effectuation a major domain of research within the entrepreneurship field.

References

Arend, R. J., Sarooghi, H., & Burkemper, A. (2015). Effectuation as ineffectual? Applying the 3E theory-assessment framework to a proposed new theory of entrepreneurship. *Academy of Management Review, 40*(4), 630–651.

Arend, R. J., Sarooghi, H., & Burkemper, A. C. (2016). Effectuation, not being pragmatic or process theorizing, remains ineffectual: Responding to the commentaries. *Academy of Management Review, 41*(3), 549–556.

Dattée, B., Alexy, O., & Autio, E. (2018). Maneuvering in poor visibility: How firms play the ecosystem game when uncertainty is high. *Academy of Management Journal, 61*(2), 466–498.

Dew, N., Read, S., Sarasvathy, S. D., & Wiltbank, R. (2009). Effectual versus predictive logics in entrepreneurial decision-making: Differences between experts and novices. *Journal of Business Venturing, 24*(4), 287–309.

Engel, Y., Kaandorp, M., & Elfring, T. (2017). Toward a dynamic process model of entrepreneurial networking under uncertainty. *Journal of Business Venturing, 32*(1), 35–51.

Fletcher, M., Loane, S., & Andersson, S. (2011). International entrepreneurship, born globals and the theory of effectuation. *Journal of Small Business and Enterprise Development*, *18*(3), 627–643.

Grégoire, D. A., & Cherchem, N. (2019). A structured literature review and suggestions for future effectuation research. *Small Business Economics*, 1–19.

Harms, R., & Schiele, H. (2012). Antecedents and consequences of effectuation and causation in the international new venture creation process. *Journal of International Entrepreneurship, 10*(2), 95–116.

Knight, F. H. (2012). *Risk, uncertainty and profit*. Courier Corporation.

Kolter, P. (1991). *Marketing management: Analysis, planning implementation and control*. Prentice Hall.

McKelvie, A., Haynie, J. M., & Gustavsson, V. (2011). Unpacking the uncertainty construct: Implications for entrepreneurial action. *Journal of Business Venturing, 26*(3), 273–292.

Milliken, F. J. (1987). Three types of perceived uncertainty about the environment: State, effect, and response uncertainty. *Academy of Management Review, 12*(1), 133–143.

Read, S., Dew, N., Sarasvathy, S. D., Song, M., & Wiltbank, R. (2009). Marketing under uncertainty: The logic of an effectual approach. *Journal of Marketing, 73*(3), 1–18.

Read, S., & Sarasvathy, S. D. (2005). Knowing what to do and doing what you know: Effectuation as a form of entrepreneurial expertise. *The Journal of Private Equity, 9*(1), 45–62.

Read, S., Song, M., & Smit, W. (2009). A meta-analytic review of effectuation and venture performance. *Journal of Business Venturing, 24*(6), 573–587.

Reymen, I., Berends, H., Oudehand, R., & Stultiëns, R. (2017). Decision making for business model development: A process study of effectuation and causation in new technology-based ventures. *R&D Management, 47*(4), 595–606.
Sarasvathy, S., Kumar, K., York, J. G., & Bhagavatula, S. (2014). An effectual approach to international entrepreneurship: Overlaps, challenges, and provocative possibilities. *Entrepreneurship Theory and Practice, 38*(1), 71–93.
Sarasvathy, S. D. (2001). Causation and effectuation: Toward a theoretical shift from economic inevitability to entrepreneurial contingency. *Academy of Management Review, 26*(2), 243–263.
Sarasvathy, S. D. (2009). *Effectuation: Elements of entrepreneurial expertise.* Edward Elgar.
Shepherd, D. A., Williams, T. A., & Patzelt, H. (2015). Thinking about entrepreneurial decision making: Review and research agenda. *Journal of Management, 41*(1), 11–46.
Townsend, D. M., Hunt, R. A., McMullen, J. S., & Sarasvathy, S. D. (2018). Uncertainty, knowledge problems, and entrepreneurial action. *Academy of Management Annals, 12*(2), 659–687.
Welter, C., & Kim, S. (2018). Effectuation under risk and uncertainty: A simulation model. *Journal of Business Venturing, 33*(1), 100–116.
Wiltbank, R., Dew, N., Read, S., & Sarasvathy, S. D. (2006). What to do next? The case for non-predictive strategy. *Strategic Management Journal, 27*(10), 981–998.
Wiltbank, R., Read, S., Dew, N., & Sarasvathy, S. D. (2009). Prediction and control under uncertainty: Outcomes in angel investing. *Journal of Business Venturing, 24*(2), 116–133.
Zhang, S. X., & Cueto, J. (2017). The study of bias in entrepreneurship. *Entrepreneurship Theory and Practice, 41*(3), 419–454.

CHAPTER 10

Conclusion

Arturo E. Osorio, Banu Ozkazanc-Pan, Dev K. Dutta, and Vishal K. Gupta

Taking a reflective moment at the conclusion of this project, we as editors are pleased with its results. This edited book, covering the first decade

A. E. Osorio (✉)
Rutgers Business School, Rutgers, The State University of New Jersey, Newark, NJ, USA
e-mail: osorio@business.rutgers.edu

B. Ozkazanc-Pan
School of Engineering, Brown University, Providence, RI, USA
e-mail: banu_ozkazanc-pan@brown.edu

D. K. Dutta
Peter T Paul College of Business and Economics, Univerity of New Hampshire, Durham, NH, USA
e-mail: dev.dutta@unh.edu

V. K. Gupta
Culverhouse College of Business, The University of Alabama, Tuscaloosa, AL, USA
e-mail: vkgupta@cba.ua.edu

A. E. Osorio et al. (eds.), *Modern Classics in Entrepreneurship Studies*,
https://doi.org/10.1007/978-3-030-61029-6_10

of the 2000s, adds to our ongoing efforts to explore entrepreneurship as a scholarly field of study by mapping its history while pointing out some directions for its future. Before this edited book, as the first step in this journey, we had analyzed the early stages of the evolution of entrepreneurship research by looking into articles published during the 1980s and 1990s. During that initial effort, we identified the foundational articles—seminal research papers—that provided the early impetus for entrepreneurship studies transforming the field from a small group of enthusiasts into a vibrant academic discipline (see Javadian et al., 2018). This first part of our journey covering the 1980s and 1990s was received favorably by other scholars (e.g., Shankar, 2019). In this second step of the journey, we go beyond the initial foundational period of the 1980s and 1990s as we look into the first decade of the twenty-first century. During this subsequent era, entrepreneurship research has seen the publication of the "modern classics." These "modern classics" have helped to make entrepreneurship one of the most dynamic and relevant disciplines in social sciences. It is because of the impact of these works that this first decade of the twenty-first century has been described as a "golden era" for entrepreneurship research (Wiklund et al., 2010, p. 1). A period that deserves its own space of reflection, as we do in the book you are now reading.

Exploring the scholarly works that took place during this golden era, this edited book presents several notable academic works that have merited the term "modern classics." As such, we aimed to provide novel insights for further scholarship in entrepreneurship as well as a solid basis for building a robust teaching infrastructure. When one looks at the impressive evolution of entrepreneurship research over the years, it is tempting to see it as "destiny," a sort of natural outcome for a field centered on one of the oldest human activities (buying and selling goods with a profit motive). Yet, it is worth remembering that new scientific quests can evolve in many ways, such as quick demise, marginalized existence, occupation by other more-established field(s), and growth and success. Thus, in this book, we sought to provide a compass to help guide progress in the field of entrepreneurship. We understand our efforts are limited to this book's length and constrained by the urgency of finishing the project while the field keeps moving forward. We realize there very likely are other works that could have been included yet were not. That is both the peril of hindsight and the opportunity of the future in this very vibrant field of research. Why and how entrepreneurship survives and thrives as an independent scientific field is a complex question beyond the scope of the present endeavor (but see Gupta, 2020; Landstrom, 2020). Yet, it is difficult not to attribute the legitimacy of entrepreneurship as an academic field, at least in some part, to the quality of scientific research that took place in the first decade of the twenty-first century. It is our aim here to present some of these modern classics pushing the field forward.

When we reflect on our efforts in this edited book to showcase the "modern classics" in entrepreneurship, we are very pleased with the substantial ground that has been covered here. The contributing authors responded to our mandate to highlight the contributions of key articles published during the 2001–2010 time period and layout how the ideas and insights will continue to inform future inquiry in a productive fashion. Our hope is that reading these chapters will help the reader to consider some of the defining issues that engaged the field in the first decade of the new millennium and laid out directions for future research. Of course, as entrepreneurship scholars, we are well aware that the true worth of an idea can only be assessed in the market. As such, we look forward to seeing how the community of scholars responds to the insights presented in the chapters of this book born from the seminal articles highlighted here. We are also cognizant that it is virtually impossible to arrive at a definitive list of high-impact articles, and nor was such a list our goal. When people are asked what they see as important, their responses are likely to be shaped by their own values and research interests. Consequently, different readers will tend to reach different conclusions regarding which articles belong on a list of modern classics in entrepreneurship. We hope the present endeavor will advance this discussion. We welcome additional efforts to highlight other works that researchers see as playing an important role in the development and future trajectory of entrepreneurship research.

In this edited book, the contributors come from around the world, including the United States, United Kingdom, India, and Canada. The contributing authors also represent different stages of academic life, including senior scholars with years of entrepreneurship research experience as well as doctoral students. We were inspired by the deep level of understanding of the participants in this project and their efforts to map the field and discuss its future.

Finally, we would like to recognize the contributions of a number of people who made it possible to bring this book into its present form, even in the midst of the global pandemic that made it difficult for many of the participants in this project to attend to deadlines. The contributing authors diligently worked with us to deliver the chapters in a way that we believed would add value to the reader and the field. Academia runs on the selfless efforts of voluntary reviewers, and this book is no exception as we relied heavily on our networks to request peer reviews of the submitted chapters. We doubt that our ideas for a book showcasing the "modern classics" in entrepreneurship would have seen the light of day had it not been for Marcus Bellenger of Palgrave (now a division of Springer), who was more patient with our shifting deadlines than we could have asked for. We also want to thank Ashwini Elango, who understood the complexity that the pandemic brought into this project and worked with us to ensure the book was completed. The Palgrave team is a joy to work with, and we are tremendously grateful for all they did to help bring this book to fruition.

References

Gupta, V. K. (2020). *Great minds in entrepreneurship research: Contributions, critiques, and conversations*. Palgrave Macmillan.

Javadian, G., Gupta, V. K., Dutta, D. K., Guo, G. C., Osorio, A. E., & Ozkazanc-Pan, B. (2018). *Foundational research in entrepreneurship studies: Insightful contributions and future pathways*. Palgrave Macmillan. https://doi.org/10.1007/978-3-319-73528-3.

Landstrom, H. (2020). The evolution of entrepreneurship as a scholarly field. *Foundations and Trends in Entrepreneurship, 16*(2), 65–243.

Shankar, R. (2019). Book review: Foundational research in entrepreneurship studies. *International Small Business Journal, 37*(4), 419–420.

Wiklund, J., Davidsson, P., Audretsch, D. B., & Karlsson, C. (2011). The future of entrepreneurship research. *Entrepreneurship Theory and Practice, 35*(1), 1–9. https://doi.org/10.1111/j.1540-6520.2010.00420.x.

Index

A. E. Osorio et al. (eds.), *Modern Classics in Entrepreneurship Studies*, https://doi.org/10.1007/978-3-030-61029-6

FSC
www.fsc.org
MIX
Papier | Fördert gute Waldnutzung
FSC® C083411

Kolibri 360 GmbH
Ferdinand-Jühlke-Straße 7
99095 Erfurt, Deutschland
produktsicherheit@kolibri360.de